READ IN THE NAME
OF YOUR LORD

PUBLIC CULTURES OF THE MIDDLE EAST AND NORTH AFRICA
Paul A. Silverstein, Susan Slyomovics, and
Ted Swedenburg, editors

READ IN THE NAME OF YOUR LORD

~

ISLAMIC LITERACY DEVELOPMENT IN REVOLUTIONARY EGYPT

NERMEEN MOUFTAH

INDIANA UNIVERSITY PRESS

This book is a publication of

Indiana University Press
Office of Scholarly Publishing
Herman B Wells Library 350
1320 East 10th Street
Bloomington, Indiana 47405 USA

iupress.org

First printing 2024

Cataloging information is available from the Library of Congress.
978-0-253-07103-3 (hdbk)
978-0-253-07104-0 (pbk)
978-0-253-07105-7 (web PDF)

For my parents,
Hussein Talaat and Ebtisam Mouftah,
and the people of Batn al-Baqara,
a place that was and is no more.

CONTENTS

ACKNOWLEDGMENTS

Over the course of researching and writing this book, my feelings of gratitude have been, at times, overwhelming. Sometimes during fieldwork, on a long commute or while waiting for an interview, I would remind myself of all the people whose kindness and generosity I needed to acknowledge. I hope that I have expressed my appreciation to these special individuals in person. In Egypt, my interlocutors were exceedingly patient with me. I was always warmly hosted for a drink or meal with friends in Batn al-Baqara. I am particularly grateful to the woman I call Umm Hazim and her family, who helped weave me into neighborhood life. I am grateful to all the students who allowed me to become a part of their attempts, frustration, and boredom in learning to read and write. I hope this work conveys the dignity of their efforts and lives. Life Makers' interest in my project facilitated access to classrooms throughout the city and was essential for my entry into the shipyard. I am grateful to the volunteers for their endurance with my presence and questions. I am particularly grateful to Saleh Muhammad; not only was he interested in my project and generous with his time, but his nickname for me, the Joker, became crucial to my understanding of myself and my fieldwork. He facilitated introductions throughout various levels of the organization as well as within the literacy development world in Cairo.

The friendships I made between 2006 and 2008 while working for the International Labour Organization in Cairo helped to lure me back to Egypt for fieldwork. Omnia Ahmed and Amal Saleh are dear friends who have been a big part of what makes Egypt feel like home. Our discussions about my research and life in Cairo inform this book. Visits with my extended family in Alexandria were a welcome break from work and were always filled with a new kind of learning. I am especially grateful for the time I spent with my late grandmother, Teta Butta, whose strength and humor nourished me. I miss her.

This project began as a dissertation that was guided by formidable forces in the anthropology of religion. I was tremendously fortunate to work with Amira Mittermaier, a model in her commitment to her students and craft. She offered support from the early days of a fledgling interest in reading and religion. Michael Lambek's prodding questions turned over my assumptions and often set me off in new and fertile directions. As my project transformed into one with literacy at its center, Francis Cody's guidance opened me up to thinking about literacy's social consequences in new ways.

I am grateful to friends and classmates at the University of Toronto in the Department of Near and Middle Eastern Civilizations, Anthropology, and the Department for the Study of Religion. I enjoyed a warm community of colleagues at Butler University as I wrote the manuscript. I am especially grateful to wonderful friends in Butler's Religious Studies and Race, Gender, and Sexuality Studies programs. At the University of Illinois, I am indebted to the students, faculty, and staff whose support during my first year was invaluable to finishing this project. I am fortunate to have such inspiring colleagues and friends in the Departments of Anthropology and History, and the programs in Religion and Global Middle East Studies.

My homes in Doha, Indianapolis, and Chicago brought with them supportive colleagues and dear friends who have discussed the ideas in these pages and many who have read and commented on several drafts. Emmanuelle Stefanidis and Alexandre Caiero were close friends to turn to for unending conversations in Egypt and beyond. Emmanuelle's guidance in Quran studies and her incisive comments improved this manuscript. Erin Moore, Sarah Dees, and a wonderful cohort of postdocs at Northwestern University were careful readers and partners in writing. I am always grateful to the formidable Jessica Winegar, who so often urged me to consider the big picture; Robert Launay taught me to have patience with ideas I may have otherwise thrown away.

I am grateful for critical comments from Aun Hasan Ali, Roshan Iqbal, Shabana Mir, Maliha Chishti, Maryam Kashani, and others who forged important writing communities that helped me through the writing process. Indiana University Press was a true pleasure to work with. I benefited from the incisive comments of the anonymous reviewers. My deep thanks to Yunus Doğan Telliel, Basit Iqbal, Katherine Hallemeier, and Timothy Gutmann, who all offered comments on later drafts. Mark Freeman assisted with digital images in the eleventh hour. I am greatly indebted to dear friends who held me up over the last years, especially Katherine Hallemeier, Chad Bauman, Terri Carny, Laura Nussbaum-Barberena, Edward Curtis, and Sarah Millermaier.

My family has patiently endured my comings and goings for several years. I hope that I will somehow be able to return their understanding, love, and encouragement. Samina and Syed S. M. Quadri and Sumaira Shah, Omair Quadri, and their children, Inayah and Ismail, always pamper us and yet try to ensure that I have time to write. My older sisters, Maye and Nadine Mouftah, continue to be my first teachers and along with their husbands, Moataz Kamel and Mohammed Abdallah, and their children, Adam and Leena Kamel, and Zayn and Layla Abdallah, show me the art of living. My parents, Ebtisam and Hussein Mouftah, encouraged me to pursue my interests, even when they did not always seem practical. Fieldwork accidentally became a way to excavate their stories and learn about the place and people anew, including my own mom and dad.

Junaid Quadri knows how grateful I am for his support and discerning eye, but he prefers that I not say it aloud, and especially not in front of others, so I will leave it at that. My life with him and Aziza brought me the joy I needed to complete this project.

In 2011, I decided to conduct fieldwork in Egypt after it became clear that my original plan to go to Damascus would be impossible. In the more than a decade that this project has been in the making, Egypt and the countries around it have been remade through resistance, repression, elections, loans, earthquakes, floods, and countless social interventions like the ones I describe here. While this book is in some ways a story of (the limits of) hope, I am moved by the ones who most believe that what started in late 2010 and spread across the region is an unfinished project. My deepest respect and gratitude are to those who have labored and sacrificed in their struggle.

NOTE ON TRANSLITERATION
AND TRANSLATION

As a book about literacy, it is also about language. I have tried to capture the varieties of spoken interactions and written texts for English readers as simply as possible. I have generally adopted a simplified transliteration of the *International Journal of Middle East Studies* (*IJMES*), except for passages from the Quran and students' incipient writing, where I use *IJMES*. My aim in using the full diacritical markings for written passages is to allow those who read Arabic transliteration to have an accurate representation of those texts. For all other cases, simplified *IJMES* facilitates a more approachable text for non-Arabic specialists. I do not employ diacritics in places or names. In the simplified version, I mark long vowels and use ʿayn (ʿ) or hamza (ʾ) (except when they appear at the beginning of a name); I omit diacritic dots that distinguish between Arabic letters. For frequently used terms like *tafsir*, I do not employ diacritics. The exceptions to *IJMES* include Quran(ic) instead of Qurʾan(ic) and sharia instead of shariʿa. I have used the English spelling of names for those who have them as well as the spelling conventions of those frequently written about in English.

Most of my conversations were in Egyptian dialect, except when noted on infrequent occasions when conversations with pedagogues were in Modern Standard Arabic. To convey the sounds and meanings of my informants, I render Egyptian colloquial phrasing according to the spellings of el-Said Badawi and Martin Hinds's *Dictionary of Egyptian Arabic* (1986). This includes changing the letter *jīm* (*j*) to *gīm* (*g*) and rendering the letter *qāf* (*q*) as hamza (ʾ), as it is pronounced among my Cairene interlocutors. Plurals typically use the Arabic singular form with an *s*, such as *tafsirs*.

xiv   NOTE ON TRANSLITERATION AND TRANSLATION

Translations of the meaning of the Quran are those of M. A. S. Abdel Haleem. All other translations are my own.

Many of my interlocutors requested that I preserve their names in my writing. In keeping with their wishes, I have done so, while using pseudonyms for all others.

ACRONYMS

Bible Society of Egypt (BSE)
Corporate Social Responsibility (CSR)
Central Agency for Public Mobilization and Statistics (CAPMAS)
Egyptian Authority for Adult Education (EAAE)
Egyptian Federation of Independent Trade Unions (EFITU)
Egyptian Trade Union Federation (ETUF)
Fund for the Development of Slum Neighborhoods (FDSN)
Independent Teachers Association (ITA)
Modern Standard Arabic (MSA)
New Literacy Studies (NLS)
Supreme Council of the Armed Forces (SCAF)

Literacy Campaigns and Curriculum Titles

Read in the Name of Your Lord (RITNOYL)
The Baghdadi Primer (TBP)
Knowledge Is Power (KIP)

READ IN THE NAME OF YOUR LORD

Prologue

Girl in a School Uniform

We made our way past concrete block apartment buildings, over buckling roads. Sheep gathered in dense alleys as we arrived in the green of Kom al-Ahmar. Before disembarking the minibus, Marwa kneeled on a seat facing the back of the bus. Hands held in front of her face, eyes closed, she led the group of a dozen volunteers in supplication (*duʿāʾ*). She asked God to bless and reward their effort. Those around her punctuated each of her requests to God with an "*Āmīn*" (Amen). They asked that their work benefit the lives of the people they were about to meet. *Āmīn*. They intended to please God in what they were about to do. *Āmīn*. And be granted paradise in the hereafter. *Āmīn*. This moment was essential to how they performed their work. Through supplication, they sought to purify their intentions, to dedicate their work to God.

The day's goal was to recruit students for new literacy classes that would soon open in their local mosque. The *Knowledge Is Power* literacy campaign volunteers gathered there, praying short prayers of greetings to the mosque and then breaking into groups of three or four for their day's work. Most came from the nearby neighborhood of Imbaba; for them, this trip, less than a thirty-minute drive, was a trip to the wilds of the Egyptian countryside.

The group I joined made their way down a row of half-finished apartment blocks. The women who answered their front doors were generous, unbothered by the disruption as they prepared lunch for their families. Some laughed at the keen eagerness of the volunteers and offered their names. Sure, they would come to a class, if time allowed.

After a morning of door knocking, people in the streets began to refer to the group as "the people for the eradication of illiteracy." It was September 2011 and young people with their revolutionary projects were still well received and often celebrated. Local shopkeepers handed volunteers bottles of soda.

Down the street, a school bus dropped off eight girls in neat blue uniforms. I turned my attention to the woman in front of the door. When asked if she wanted to join a literacy class, she responded that she was educated. The volunteer pressed on: "Then could you lead a class? Be a part of the campaign to eradicate illiteracy." As the woman at the door began to ask questions, I felt a hand on my arm.

One of the girls from the bus was at my side. She looked as though she were about twelve years old. "Excuse me, excuse me. I want to join a class. I want to learn to read."

Marwa heard the girl's request and came over to respond: "You are too young. You have school. Our classes are for adults." The girl remained still. Marwa coaxed her: "Now go home so you can do your studies."

PART I

~

FAITH IN READING

Introduction

God's First Command

"What was God's first command?" The preacher spoke into a lectern microphone in an air-conditioned hotel ballroom on a hot September morning in 2011. The Supreme Council of the Armed Forces (SCAF) had been governing the country since Hosni Mubarak's ouster in February. One of the world's most recognizable Muslim preachers, Amr Khaled, addressed a conference at the Nile Hilton in Cairo's Tahrir Square. Khaled opened the event for the United Nations' World Literacy Day, posing a question: "What was God's first command?" The audience gathered teachers and pedagogues from civil society and government ministries. He continued: "It wasn't to pray, or to fast. No, it was to read. 'Read in the name of your Lord.'"

Khaled invoked the verse Muslims believe was the first to be revealed, "Read in the name of your Lord" (*iqra' bi-smi rabbika alladhī khalaq*) (96:1), to teach literacy as a religious duty and the foundation for continuing Egypt's revolution. The uprising spurred millions to action with a cacophony of demands. Away from the international media spotlight, literacy became a major project for Egyptians to realize aspirations for change. While Khaled is widely known for his television programs that teach Islam to Egyptian and global audiences, as the keynote for World Literacy Day, he spoke as the founder and chair of Life Makers (*Sunā' al-Hayāt*). This nongovernmental organization (NGO) led Egypt's most visible literacy campaign, Knowledge Is Power (KIP, *Al-'Ilm Quwwa*), mostly through youth volunteers. Launched days after Mubarak's ouster, the campaign enlisted seventy thousand volunteers within days. Khaled had been focused on mobilizing youth since the launch of his television series *Life Makers* in 2004. The series kicked off grassroots projects across the country, from building rooftop gardens to distributing food bags. With the uprising, the organization prioritized literacy (literally, "the eradication of illiteracy," *mahw al-ummiyya*). Indeed, Khaled promoted reading as the basis of his vision of Islam. Through literacy, he continued a long tradition of Muslim reformers' focus on education, but he did so in a novel way: by making the very act of reading a Muslim duty.

As Khaled addressed the conference at the hotel, Tahrir Square filled with forty thousand teachers from across the country. The crowd was the first teacher-organized strike in Egyptian history. Dressed in burial shrouds, protesters staged a mock funeral carrying an effigy of a teacher. One placard read: "The teacher is dead." Following Mubarak's ouster, a newly formed Independent Teachers Association (ITA) replaced the state-organized Teachers Union. The demands of teachers in the new ITA ranged from the removal of the minister of education to an increase in money earmarked for education. They described deplorable conditions in the country's public schools, stories Egyptians are familiar with either through their own experiences or those of friends or through frequent news coverage. As one teacher that day said to me: "We have secondary school graduates who cannot read, and teachers who cannot feed their families."

The UN World Literacy Day and the teachers' protest, both taking place in the iconic Tahrir Square, unfolded at a moment of potential and confusion, when Egyptians sought to define how to make the 2011 uprising a breaking point in Egyptian history. Both scenes captured one of the uprising's major demands—the need to redress what was commonly referred to as Egypt's education crisis (*azmat al-taʿlim*). The government, the UN, and NGO representatives who chatted over cake in the Hilton lobby, and the teachers who donned protest garb in Cairo's September heat, shared the same goal: to build Egypt through basic education. They had been spurred by the revolution and saw their work as realizing the demands of protesters. Their plan was a response to the possibilities of the moment and the staggering statistics: twenty-eight percent of adult Egyptians—some seventeen million—were not literate, making Egypt's nonliterate population one of the largest in the world (Huebler and Lu 2012). The country is part of a special high-priority group within the UN referred to as the E9.[1]

The two scenes crystallized crucial questions that haunted the January 25 uprising after the climax of eighteen days of protest that led to Mubarak's resignation: What is the best way to continue the revolution? What role should education play? That September morning revealed various contending agendas for how to manage illiteracy in the context of Egypt's intensified economic neoliberalization and competing forms of Islamic outreach (daʿwa). The campaign tried to hold together two goals: to make literacy a technique to discipline a modern Muslim civic life *and* to use literacy as a program for carrying out the revolution.

Khaled's call for volunteers—while teachers demanded better conditions in public education—amplified the ongoing dispute over whether education was a right that should be afforded to all or whether it was beyond the scope of state responsibility. Articulating the latter view in 2017, the minister of education, Tariq Shawqi, asserted that education was a "commodity" (silʿa).[2] By prioritizing literacy and mobilizing volunteer teachers, Khaled did not simply represent an Islamic reformist response to a crisis in Egyptian education (while teachers represented a revolutionary one). Instead, Khaled's call attempted to bring together an Islamic reformist emphasis on modern education while simultaneously carrying out the revolution. He promoted literacy as a platform where Muslim reformers and revolutionaries converged, and yet he went about revolutionary educational reform in ways that departed from the protesters in the square that day. So when college students and recent graduates volunteered in the tens of thousands as teachers, they were inspired by revolution and convinced by Khaled's call that made reading—and literacy—an Islamic duty.

Knowledge Is Power, like the organization that led the campaign, is indicative of an Islamically inflected developmentalism—one that draws on the Islamic tradition to articulate the moral and civic responsibility "to develop—both oneself, and the nation." KIP volunteers spoke of the need to share their time and knowledge as a Muslim duty in carrying out the aims of the revolution. In this way, they mobilized a rights discourse distinct from the protesting teachers. The volunteers were part of a major trend in Muslim development, charitable, and humanitarian organizations, seen in Egypt and elsewhere, characterized by their emphasis on meritocracy and professionalism, the calculation of spiritual reward, and often the provisioning of services once imagined to be the domain of the state, such as medical care and education. Life Makers specifically refer to their work as inspired by faith development (tanmiyya bi-l-īmān). The mobilization of volunteer teachers captured youths' abandonment of former president Gamal Abdel Nasser's promise that all university graduates would be guaranteed a government job.[3]

This book tells the story of why and how Egyptians made literacy essential to accomplish the goals of the revolution. While literacy is only a part of what is broadly discussed within the country as Egypt's education crisis, adult literacy is the culmination of the problems that beleaguer the public and private education systems at all levels. The young girl described in the prologue who complained that she did not learn how to read at school is a young version of my adult interlocutors who, when recalling their education, scoffed at the idea of learning during their school days. While I focus on literacy, the questions I ask connect it to debates about education and development and how to carry out the revolution. Intimately entwined with revolutionary literacy are enduring questions about what (religious) education is for and how it is best instructed.

Read in the Name of Your Lord examines the political impetus and ramifications of literacy as well as its epistemic stakes. I explore how various Islamic reformers adopted literacy as a set of techniques to promote modern Muslim civic practice and connect the neoliterate to God. I delineate their contending visions over how literacy should be taught and what kind of subjects it should mold. Literacy, as an Islamic reformist project, was carried out by government employees, revolutionary activists, and volunteer teachers who made *iqra'*—a term with multiple meanings that I discuss in the following pages—central to their project for pious and national improvement. Their campaigns and programs mobilized distinct text practices, uses of language, and pedagogies that refined and redefined conceptions of education, including what constitutes "Islamic education." Through literacy, I probe the contradictions that arise from its propagation as a revolutionary action.

What can a movement for literacy—through its propagation, pedagogies, and practices—reveal about shifting values and virtues of education? To trace the literacy movement that emerged from this moment, I pay close attention to who underwrites the push for literacy, delineating distinct actors and their initiatives, what Deborah Brand calls literacy sponsors, "any agents, local or distant, concrete or abstract, who enable, support, teach, model, as well as recruit, regulate, suppress, or withhold literacy—and gain advantage by it in some way" (1998, 166). Paying attention to literacy sponsorship through individuals (teachers, family members), institutions (schooling, NGO-based programs, mosque lessons), and broader social forces (political uprising, gendered expectations of literacy, shifts in the labor market) allows us to better understand the significant role that religion plays in the push for literacy.

Islamic literacy development demonstrates the reach of what I refer to as Egypt's late Islamic revival—an evolution of Egypt's Islamic revival marked by the January 25 uprising.[4] It reveals the changing sites of *da'wa* beyond the "explicitly religious" to shape the demands of the uprising and how Egyptians responded to those demands. As a concept that draws attention to the major role religion plays in articulating the urgent need for literacy, Islamic literacy development draws attention to how Islamic and developmentalist logics came together to plan, advocate for, and implement literacy.

As contested categories, I do not take revolution or Islamic reform as self-evident but, rather, as terms deployed and made meaningful on the ground.[5] I use various terms to refer to and evoke this period, alternating between *uprising, revolution (thawra)*, and *counterrevolution (thawra mudādda)*. What I refer to as "a moment" includes what many Egyptians refer to as the eighteen days of mass protests (from January 25 to February 11, 2011) that precipitated Mubarak's resignation. *Moment* also means the transitional period presided over by the SCAF during parliamentary and presidential elections (February 12, 2011, to June 30, 2013) and even the election and first year of the Muslim Brotherhood in power (June 30, 2012) up until the military coup that removed President Mohamed Morsi in July 2013.

Literacy was a major focus of organized actions that emerged as a response to revolutionary demands. At times, I refer to these heterogeneous activities as activism. The activism of Egypt's January 25 uprising has been most recognizably located in Tahrir Square (Armbrust 2019; Bayat 2021; Said 2023). Of course, revolutionaries are many, including those who are more widely recognized as such, from the secular leftist Kifaya movement to the youth mobilizations of the April 6 Youth Movement. Volunteer teachers were not typically among those referred to as revolutionaries *(thuwwār)*, although many saw their work as continuing the revolution. Some volunteer teachers saw themselves as activists, or revolutionaries, while others did not. Friends with whom I shared my research at times expressed skepticism or explicitly mocked Life Makers, whom they saw as politically naive. The language of activism situates Egypt's push for literacy alongside other revolutions that made literacy a priority. One of the tragedies of the push for literacy that I show is how thoroughly the lines of activism and development blurred in twenty-first-century Egypt, often to devastating effect.

Islamic literacy development is constrained by the same blurred boundaries between state support and state critique that have marked Egypt's civil society since the 1980s. Egypt, like India and other developing economies with massive neoliberal development, has an active civil society that, in many ways, supports state projects. Egyptian civil society is vast and includes those who oppose the state, such as the charitable services of the Muslim Brotherhood and other Islamist and Islamically motivated groups. As an alternative to state service provisions (such as education or medical care), these organizations advance a development agenda promoted by a state that often surveils and threatens to limit their work. The NGOs I examined with major literacy programs ultimately assisted the state project of mass literacy (even when their programs did so in ways that subverted it, like the Salafi and Christian ones based on scripture that I explore in chap. 2).

Moving across the various sites of literacy propagation reveals how literacy was "made Islamic" in various initiatives spearheaded by state programs and major NGOs. My approach to understanding religion in literacy propagation is informed by Islamic studies debates on the contours and boundaries of defining Islam (Ahmed 2015; Asad 1986, 1993). The differences among the education programs illustrate distinct activist and textualist moves within Egypt's late Islamic revival. What emerges across the various efforts is a common thread with reformers of earlier generations, namely, that education is the key to becoming a good Muslim (Hourani 1962; Adams 1968). In her study of modern Muslim reformism, Samira Haj explains: "The notion of an educated, rational Muslim subject who was responsible for his or her actions became, by the turn of the century, a constitutive feature defining a 'good' Muslim. A proper Muslim was now expected to participate responsibly and effectively toward the cultural and material advancement (*ruqqy*) of his or her society" (2009, 11).

Through literacy programmers' efforts, we can glance at how reading is taken as a practice with the potential to cultivate a particular kind of modern pious subject. As Michael Allan observes in his illuminating examination of Arabic reading in world literature, British colonial administrators saw reading as the ability not only to "decipher words, sounds, and meanings" but also to cultivate the "sensibilities necessary to the supposedly virtuous ends of liberal government" (2016, 15). As Allan delineates through the construction of the category of world literature, reading is a cultivated practice, associated with particular institutions and given value.

While significant interventions in the anthropology of Islam elaborate embodied pedagogical practices that seek to cultivate particular virtues (Asad 1993, 2003; Mahmood 2004; Hirschkind 2006; Ware 2014), reaching back to classical ideals of education leaves out the significant role of how ideals and norms of modern education shape not only Islamic education but also notions of virtue associated with education more broadly. It is in fact the role of autonomous reading—a skill associated with cognition as central to understanding—rather than the embodiment of virtues from classical modes of Islamic learning that has enabled contemporary modes of autodi-dacticism so distinct in contemporary *daʿwa*. Through the seemingly mundane activity of reading, I reorient what practices are considered to cultivate virtue by paying attention to the various senses and discursive habits called upon in distinct reading practices.

Discussions about (il)literacy are never about only reading or writing or even education. They involve heated debates over morality and religion, notions of civilization and progress, and anxieties around social class. Presidential candidates, talk show hosts, and everyday Egyptians describe illiteracy as a primary obstacle to the country's flourishing and a social illness to be eradicated. I track these discourses, attentive to their contestations, which I refer to as Egyptian literacy politics. Egyptian literacy politics includes what we might think of as the explicitly political: the negotiation of social hierarchies and questions about who has access to what kind of education. At the same time, it is forged by the hermeneutical stakes of promoting and instructing basic literacy. It includes distinct ideas about Arabic-language literacy and how to teach it. Egyptian literacy politics is shaped by discussions about what kind of subjectivities education should cultivate. I trace this discursive terrain through media, textbooks, and teachers' moral lessons as they were incorporated into literacy classes. I underline the disjunctures between literacy's ideals with what literacy activism looked like on the ground, including how students participated in classes and lived their lives beyond them.

The reformers I turn to in these pages took literacy as a central program for their revitalization projects. As I show, they did so in different ways (sometimes centering the Quran, and at other times, the national identity card) and to different effect (sometimes promoting literacy for cognitive understandings of the Quran, and at other times, instructing literacy to cultivate civic sensibilities). As I sketch the contours of distinct reformist interventions, I ask: In what ways did reformist idioms marshaled by religiously sponsored literacy initiatives speak to and against each other? How has basic literacy been connected to the Quran? How did literacy classes seek to forge reading communities? How did students negotiate teachers' aims? What literacy and

language ideologies undergirded literacy as a method of religious propagation? What does the phenomenon of religiously sponsored literacy tell us
about contemporary scripturalism? What are the political implications of
reformist literacy activism?

By examining twenty-first-century religiously sponsored literacy, I track
unrecognized elisions: how methods of secular education become indispens-
able to religious knowledge and education, just as how secular knowledge
and education are made Islamic. Through the push for literacy, I uncover the
secularizing of religious education and an Islamizing of modern education.
Literacy propagation crystallizes these elisions from two crucial angles—
among literacy programs that use scripture as curriculum (part 2) and those
that instruct literacy to cultivate civic-religious virtues (part 3). To do so, I
identify how notions of Islamic education are transformed through practices
and epistemologies formed through modern education. The literacy initiatives I depict unite in promoting literacy as a technique to influence how
people understand and interact with God's Word and, more broadly, how it
ought to form modern Muslim life.

Egyptian Literacy Politics Yesterday and Today

The meanings of literacy—along with what it means to be educated—have
shifted dramatically in Egypt over the last 150 years. Historically, literacy
was associated with Quranic knowledge and practices (Hanna 2007; Launay
and Ware 2016; Mitchell 1988). In the premodern period, to be literate for
Muslims—just as it was for Christians and Jews—meant a fluency predicated on, steeped in, and demonstrated through scripture (Boyarin 1993;
Gilmont 2003; Wollenberg 2023). Quranic literacy meant not only a facility
with the text but also a training of the body, senses, and character.[6] Through
the transformations in education that I describe, modern literacy emerged
in the twentieth century as a sign of a country's development. In the modern
period, literacy has been one of the country's largest and most enduring development projects (Cochran 1986; Heyworth-Dunne 1968). Indeed, reading
has long been an integral part of state projects to forge a modern Middle East
(Fortna 2002, 2011; Yousef 2016). The effort to seize Mubarak's ouster as a moment to push for literacy is part of a long history of hope in progress—hope
that has been continually dashed (Schielke 2015).

The 2011 push for literacy must be situated historically within the modernization of Egyptian education. Under British colonial rule in the 1860s and,

later, under the modernizer Muhammad Ali Pasha (d. 1849), basic literacy was a primary technique to usher in modernity in Egypt. Europeans radically transformed Egyptian education and values of knowledge, including conceptions of literacy (Allan 2016; Sedra 2011; Mitchell 1988; Yousef 2016). In Egypt, as elsewhere, British colonizers endeavored to remold their subjects through modern methods of education that sought to create order. They did not appreciate the epistemological distance between the systems of knowledge and the corollary practices of classical Islamic education and new modes of colonial modern education. Paul Sedra describes the educational reforms of nineteenth-century Egypt as "epistemological warfare" in which two forms of knowledge were at odds, the written and the spoken (2011, 10).

Protestant missionaries proffered literacy as the exclusive path to enlightenment, leading to the destruction of forms of knowledge and authority based on oral instruction shared by Muslims and Copts. The British were not alone in their diagnosis that Quran education in the *kuttāb* (the institution of primary learning) needed major reform.[7] Islamic reformers proposed book reading to modernize education. The period gave rise to a textualizing impulse among Egyptian Muslim and Christian thinkers and their prescriptions for education. Sedra describes the shift away from oral culture to the emergence of the "hegemony of the text" through the figure of Islamic reformer Muhammad Abduh (d. 1905) and his Coptic contemporaries, such as Orthodox patriarch Cyril Kirolus IV (d. 1861), who played a similar role within the Coptic Awakening. A hallmark of the emphasis on textual authority was the foregrounding of the Quran and the need to read and understand its meaning.

In the early days of Egyptian independence, Gamal Abdel Nasser championed modern education as essential to the state's progress. He articulated education as essential to chart an Egypt independent of colonial rule. Under Nasser, universal literacy was part of making mass education crucial for national development. The country had already established the right to free education in the 1940s when education was declared to be a human right. This idea was reinforced in the 1971 Constitution that enshrined education as a right provided by the state. At the same time, the high rate of illiteracy became a pressing concern in the country. Egypt became something of a paradox in the region—the country was at once the capital of Arabic letters, attracting students to its universities and exporting teachers throughout the Arabic-speaking world. At the same time, it was home to the highest population of nonliterate people.

The growing social divisions spurred by the economic liberalization of the 1980s were reflected in disparities in access to education. Intellectuals, from the writer and minister of education Taha Hussein (d. 1973) to feminist supporter of Egyptian independence Hoda Sha'rawi (d. 1947), promoted education as a means of liberation. Through the participation of international development sponsorships like the United Nations Educational, Scientific and Cultural Organization (UNESCO), much of Egyptian literacy programming stressed literacy skills as an essential practice for market expansion and democratic governance.

In the 1990s, first lady Suzanne Mubarak became the patron of literacy. Programs in her name mobilized literacy as a way to modernize women and families. She created a host of institutions and high-profile public initiatives, including the establishment of the Mubarak Public Libraries, government-subsidized publications, the Egyptian Authority for Adult Education (EAAE), and the National Council for Childhood and Motherhood (with literacy programs of its own). In addition, the government actively encouraged NGOs to offer literacy classes and specifically called on religious organizations, both Muslim and Coptic, to play a leading role in adult education. Under a law passed in 1991, civil society organizations were required to develop adult education programs to support a national action plan.[8] Literacy programs multiplied throughout the country with modest impact on the national literacy rate. With the fall of Mubarak, activists turned, once again, to literacy. Undeterred by previous basic literacy failures among Egypt's urban and rural populations—especially its women—the uprising motivated the state and activists alike to continue to put their faith in literacy.

Today, the Egyptian state subscribes to what UNESCO describes as literacy's "multiplying effects."[9] In this view, the skills of reading and writing have cascading effects to empower and enable people, particularly women. By questioning this commonsense framework, I argue that Islamic literacy development does not address the long-standing social conditions and political structures that lead to high rates of illiteracy in the first place. I do not ask whether literacy is "good" or "bad" but, instead, uncover the often unanticipated consequences of the push for universal literacy, to understand its animating ideologies, the impacts of campaigning on people's lives, and the ramifications of skills partially learned, sometimes exercised, and often forgotten. My aim is not to delineate failures or offer policy solutions. I understand the failure to make substantial progress in improving literacy rates not as an end point; rather, I look at failure as a point of departure. In this way, the book explores how the fractured project of mass literacy—through its very incompleteness—functions as a powerful mobilizing aspiration. At the same time, I uncover the epistemological blind spots—the erasures of multiple ways of knowing and being—that can be seen in the endeavor for universal literacy.

Education for Revolution, Education for Islamic Reform

Campaigning for literacy was set against a backdrop of revolution and counterrevolution, the rise and fall of the Muslim Brotherhood, and the strengthening powers of Egypt's military elite. This was a period of intense contestation over what role Islam should play in charting the future of the country and indeed the region. It was also a period of figuring out *who* was responsible for providing social services. Government programs and Egypt's vast NGO network competed and collaborated on initiatives ranging from the provision of medical services to infrastructural projects in the cities' growing slums ('ashwā'iyyat).[10] While the uprising set many projects in motion, disputes arose over which projects were vestiges of corruption and which offered legitimate paths to address Egyptians' demands, including the common complaint that education was inaccessible and ineffective.

Mass literacy has been both the engine of Islamic revival and one of its goals. Egypt's Islamic revival is marked by an increase in religious discussion and practice in the public sphere, with calls for reform variously articulated as *tajdīd* (renewal), *ihyā'* (revival or revitalization), and *nahda* (renaissance).[11] The revival gave rise to new religious publications, radio and television programs, women's public participation and emphasis on dress, and a proliferation of religious education opportunities for everyday people, both men and women (Mahmood 2004; Hefner and Zaman 2007; Kalmbach and Bano 2011). In this landscape, Islamic reformist thinking was diverse and dynamic, often manifesting in competing visions, including the emergence of new Islamist political parties, television programs produced by a spectrum of voices, and rivalries among renowned institutions like the Dar al-Ifta and al-Azhar. Notably, the state was heavily involved in this competition, not only weighing in by favoring some and persecuting others but also promoting its own articulation of Islam (Bano 2018; Bayat 2007; Rock-Singer 2019). Underlining the varieties of Islam that could be observed at that moment, Amira

Figure 0.1. Life Makers volunteer recruiting teachers and students for Knowledge Is Power literacy campaign. Cairo, September 2011. Photo: Author.

Mittermaier describes how "Islam is not one fixed thing but is continuously made and remade, in conversation not only with the secular but also with its own many iterations" (2019, 9).

The revolution marked a new chapter of the revival. While the ouster of Mo-hamed Morsi and the Muslim Brotherhood led many to believe that Islamism in Egypt was a bust, it did not mark the end of reformist influence on politics and the public sphere. Rather, the spark of 2011 created a moment of rupture that galvanized an activism that promoted Islamic reformist ideas—variously contended—as the appropriate response to bring about the goals of the revolu-tion. Individuals and groups previously taken as apolitical—such as Khaled and Salafis—entered the political fray, experimenting with new projects, forming and dissolving political parties, and creating a new public religion.

Those who seized upon the 2011 uprising to make a major push for lit-eracy cited a long history of literacy breakthroughs that have accompanied national revolutions. Some teachers I spoke with invoked the revolution-ary literacy breakthroughs of Cuba and Nicaragua. They championed leftist educationist-philosopher Paulo Freire, best known as a proponent of critical pedagogy. Teachers and educationists often evoked his name to elicit a leftist revolutionary call for critical consciousness (conscientization, from the Portuguese *conscientização*), a pedagogical style grounded in dialogic exchange that engages learners as actors in their world. As I show, Freire was a rhetorical touchstone for many teachers mobilized by the uprising. Yet, while he was mentioned often, only a few long-term educationists engaged his ideas. More often, particularly among novice teachers, Freire was a symbol of revolution, a Che Guevara of education.[12]

Education historians Robert Arnove and Harvey Graff demonstrate the role of literacy movements amid large-scale moral and political consensus-building projects in the twentieth century (e.g., USSR, 1919–1939; Vietnam, 1945–1977; Brazil, 1967–1980; and China 1950–1980): "Historically, the initiation of a literacy campaign has been associated with major transformations in social structures and belief systems. Typically, such campaigns have been preceded and accompanied by more gradual changes, such as the spread of religious doctrine, the growth of market economies, the rise of bureaucratic and legal organizations, and the emergence of national political communities. But usually there is a profound, if not cataclysmic, triggering event: a religious reformation or a political revolution, the gaining of political independence and nationhood" (1987, 4).

Yet while the critical pedagogy techniques of revolutionary contexts spurred literacy breakthroughs, Egypt experienced a small increase in formally documented literacy between 2011 and 2013 before returning to literacy rates similar to the Mubarak years.[13]

As much as literacy has been associated with liberation and emancipation, it is also regarded by authorities as dangerous. While revolutions of the twentieth century have brought about literacy breakthroughs, they have also brought about backlash against literacy, attempting to control what is read through the arrest of journalists and literati, increased censorship, and even book burnings. Notably, in 2015, under Abdel Fattah el-Sisi, Egypt saw a major increase in the imprisonment of journalists, second in the world behind China. Revolutionary literacy presents a paradox: there is a simultaneous effort to promote literacy, while controlling what is read. Literacy classes, with their didactic civic lessons and talk of the Quran, not only deployed benign pedagogical instruments that yoked reading with morality. Literacy lessons also directed reading away from danger.

Although none of my interlocutors spoke of it as a model, Egypt's Islamic literacy activism had a notable predecessor in the region. Ayatollah Khomeini promoted Iran's massive, centrally organized Literacy Movement of Iran (*Nehzat-e Savad Amuzi-ye Iran*), which emerged from the 1979 revolution. Critics of Islamism in Egypt held up the Islamic Republic of Iran as a cautionary tale. And yet the Iranian push for literacy is a success story. Before the revolution, UNESCO estimated the nonliterate population of the country to be 63.5 percent, a group mainly composed of women and people living in rural communities. Iran's literacy movement is believed to have significantly reduced the nonliterate population to 38.3 percent (Mehran 1992, 194). In this way, the Iranian experience could have been taken as a model of sorts, not only of a revolutionary literacy activism but also of Islamic literacy activism. Just as Egyptian literacy activists understood their work to be reaching the poor and forgotten, the Iranian program spoke of reaching the oppressed (*mostaz'afin*). In both cases, illiteracy was frequently described in the media as a national shame. Mehran describes Iran's literacy breakthrough as being defined by Islamizing and politicizing aims, the goal of which was to educate pious Muslims inculcated with "the ruling elite's ideology" (Mehran 1992). Like the Iranian case, in Egypt literacy was a revolutionary program that simultaneously promoted stability.

While activists mobilized in the context of the uprising, their pedagogies and techniques were not novel. Indeed, teachers generally taught using the same teaching methods they themselves were brought up with in Egyptian schools. When a student did not advance to the stage of taking the state exam or if they failed the test, this failure was largely taken by teachers as the fault of the student or, on occasion, of a neglected class. The ethnography here points to different reasons.

First, and most generally, many nonliterate Egyptians do not see literacy as essential to their daily lives. I consider the social world in which literacy campaigning unfolds, paying attention to how nonliterate people work, learn, and live without basic literacy skills. Second, there is a lack of recognition for multiple and underappreciated modes of experiencing texts—including the Quran—that do not require basic literacy. So while illiteracy is widely regarded as a religious and moral failing, I illustrate examples of nonliterate engagements with the Quran. The third reason is the pedagogical challenges of teaching Arabic-language literacy, a diglossic language that poses challenges in determining which form of the language should be taught in basic literacy classrooms. In more quiet moments, interlocutors spoke about the cost of books and sending children to public schools. In Egypt, just as among my colleagues and students in the United States, there is always the crunch on time, which, in the case of developing literacy later in life, makes maintaining literacy a challenge. Without time to read, neoliterates are unable to consolidate their learning through practice and frequently forget their newly developed skills.

While activists and literacy programmers promoted reading and writing as techniques of equality, the intensification of literacy talk spurred by the uprising contributed to the yoking of education and morality and the exacerbation of social hierarchies premised on education. It is not simply that Islamic reformers committed to the project got it wrong or put forward an ideological vision of literacy that obscured its liberatory effects. Rather, the project, in toto, is rife with the potential to disappoint and humiliate the students it aims to uplift. It risks the authoritarian demand to control reading and its ends. As Asad points out, the pursuit of equality, whether religious or secular, "can, paradoxically, produce inequality—and, hence, a sense of injustice" (2018, 38). The Knowledge Is Power campaign and the broader push for revolutionary literacy crystallize the paradox of literacy as a democratizing and equalizing force.

One of the unplanned consequences of campaigns that reinscribed strong class categories premised on education was viewing the "educated person" (*muta'allim*) and "cultured person" (*muthaqqaf*) as enlightened and the association of the nonliterate (*ummī*) with general ignorance (*jāhiliyya*). Drawing on insights from Bourdieu and Passeron (1977), I detail how, in the slums and factories in which literacy campaigning was afoot, social categories premised on education were reinscribed. It is for this reason that I describe the impact of revolutionary efforts for mass literacy as ultimately counterrevolutionary. The momentum for literacy born out of and revitalized through the uprising is a microcosm of Egypt's revolution—its hopes, its obstacles, and its apparent failures to date. It is an illustration of how Egyptians grappled with ideas about and demands for "social justice" (*'adāla igtimā'iyya*). We can glimpse the uprising's challenges through the fissures that literacy activism exposes.

The Virtues of Autonomous Reading

In literacy promoters' common refrain to "read in the name of your Lord," they quoted verses of the Quran that Muslims believe to be the first revealed to Prophet Muhammad: "*Iqra'*! In the name of your Lord who created: He created man from a clinging form. *Iqra'*! Your Lord is the Most Bountiful One / who taught by [means of] the pen, who taught man what he did not know" (Quran 96: 1–5).[14] The term *iqra'* (here in the imperative form) has multiple meanings—to read, to recite, to recite from memory, and to proclaim.[15] The concept of *qirā'a* is so significant that historian George Makdisi calls the verb from which it is derived "the most basic technical term of Muslim education and the most versatile" (1981, 141). It is the verb's versatility that, I argue, has been lost over the years.

The polysemy of the term *qirā'a* underscores distinct epistemologies that relate readers to texts and audiences in different ways. And yet literacy programmers and thousands of volunteer teachers took the word *iqra'* to promote a particular *type* of reading, what I call *autonomous reading*. I use autonomous reading to specify a particular type of text processing associated with basic literacy, which is only one of several meanings for *qirā'a*.[16]

When Egyptian educationists spoke generally of *qirā'a* without any modifiers, they pruned the multiple meanings of *iqra'* to make the concept exclusively the individual skill of deciphering text from a page. The activity of reading as the individual deciphering a word on the page is now usually taken to be the universal and immutable understanding of how people encounter texts. But, as historians of reading have pointed out, this is not the case. Understanding *qirā'a* as silent reading removes the term's association with oral and auditory experiences of texts (that remain fundamental to encounters with the Quran as well as daily life functions, such as ordering food, navigating public transportation, and the daily work of laborers at a shipyard). To take *iqra'* as autonomous reading is to presume norms of modern education that devalue multiple modes of text processing.

I use the terms *autonomous* or *independent reading*, while other adjectives that describe the reading taught in literacy, such as *silent* or *private*, emphasize a different aspect of this reading that captures my interest. The autonomous reading of basic literacy is a practice with internal implications, not because it is "private" but because of—as many involved in literacy campaigns have explained—the cognitive consequences and psychological benefits literacy promises to "culture" and "liberate" the neoliterate subject. In this way, autonomous reading is not a lone practice but an individuated skill that can be done with others. In his history of reading in the Mamluk period, Hirschler notes distinctions in types of reading. He points out the emergence of the term *qara'a bi-nafsihi* to indicate that a person reads on their own, in this sense, meaning "silent and individual reading" (2011, 15). Similarly, Makdisi elaborates on the concept of reading to oneself, drawing attention to how the individual was described in relation to the practice: "To emphasize the fact of independent reading, the addition of *li-nafsih*, to himself, was added to the verb: *qara'a li-nafsih*. More interesting in this regard was the addition of *nafsih* to the equivocal verb plus preposition: *qara'a 'ala nafsih*, he read aloud, or recited, to himself, or under his own direction, to emphasize the fact that the person in question had not had the benefit of studying under a master, but did so under himself" (1981, 242–243).

In yet another context, Brinkley Messick's discussion of Yemeni classical education (*darasa*) distinguishes the kind of reading one does with a library book as *mutāla'a* (1993). The variety of terminology that has shifted across time and in relation to the educational practices and book cultures of particular locales alerts us to transformations in education, as well as shifting concepts of self and audience. The Arabic terminology underscores the idea of independence explicitly, marking the act as a particular kind of *qirā'a* that cannot be captured with the English word *reading*. Important to the story of literacy campaigning in post-Mubarak Egypt, literacy activists marshaled *qirā'a* to reach back to a Quranic reference, bypassing a history of terminology that would better capture the kind of reading more closely associated with basic literacy.

This book surfaces the modern misrecognitions among different modes of *qirā'a*. Autonomous reading is now the hegemonic way to encounter a text. Other modes are taken as backward and a hindrance to an individual's proper understanding and the country's progress. I emphasize the capaciousness of *qirā'a* as bringing together practices that Egypt's project of modern education has sought to pull apart. In this way, *qirā'a* is a battleground for understanding debates over modernity, education, and culture.

The multiple modes of text processing within *qirā'a* are suggestive of the critical move in literacy studies to go beyond the dichotomies of oral and literate societies (cf. Goody and Watt [1963] and Ong [1982]) to appreciate multiple *literacies*. New Literacy Studies scholars stress how historical and cultural contexts shape reading and writing practices. In this view, literacy must be understood not as a single concept but rather in its variety, with special attention paid to its uses and meanings.[17] As Collins explains, a view of literacies in the plural recognizes "relativist or situated literacies seen as diverse, historically and culturally variable practices with texts" (1995, 75–76). In her history of emergent reading and writing practices in Egypt in the late nineteenth and early twentieth centuries, Hoda Yousef explains how literacies "could be employed even by those who were technically 'illiterate'" (2016, 6).

She draws attention to the ways that nonliterate people engaged in the public sphere, from the use of scribes to oral readings of newspapers.

However, the cultural relativism of "multiple" or "alternative" literacies is only a starting point (Cody 2013; Debenport and Webster 2019). An appreciation for multiple literacies contrasts the autonomous reading of citizenship-based and Enlightenment-inspired literacy programs against methods and practices of classical Islamic education that underwent major changes since the nineteenth century. While recitation and proclamation are the basis of classical Islamic education, the emphasis on these skills is widely criticized by modernists as mere "rote learning," not amenable to proper understanding. While it is important to distinguish between the very real differences of autonomous reading with classical religious forms of text processing, taking classical Quran practices as the putative other of universal literacy or critical reading misses the ways in which "religious reading" (a concept I explore in the following chapter) has adapted autonomous methods. Just as important is how autonomous reading has been made sacred by various religious reformers and secular state institutions.[18]

The relatively recent vintage of literacy as autonomous reading is reflected in how it is discussed in Arabic. There is no single Egyptian colloquial term for literacy; official reports employ the MSA term *al-qirā'iyya*. Notably, the colloquial Arabic term for literacy classes is *mahw al-ummiyya*, which literally means the "eradication of illiteracy." One further reason to demarcate *autonomous* is to signal the liberal ideal of the rational, self-governing individual that undergirds the developmentalist project of basic literacy. As a central feature of modernity, the liberal autonomous subject is presumed to be capable of self-care and independence. Literacy is widely promoted by activists and pedagogues as the key to this independence. While trumpeted as the free and self-sufficient agent of liberal philosophers, others, including political theorists, feminist scholarship, and bioethicists, have critiqued autonomy as an obsession, illusory, and reflective of masculine ideals that leave no room for the social. The contradiction at the heart of literacy campaigning, for religious reformers and secular developmentalists alike, is the aim of cultivating the autonomous reader as essential to forming the self-governing subject of secular modernity.

While many literacy advocates understand this individual subject as a politically awakened agent of resistance, the autonomous reading of basic literacy similarly supports the kinds of autonomy encouraged in neoliberal models, where individuals are ideally self-dependent for their own well-being.

In this sense, autonomy supports the market ambitions of developmental-ist literacy as well as the philosophical premise that the acts of reading and writing are what produce the self-reflective modern subject.

Notably, Islamic literacy development aims to cultivate a gendered au-tonomous subject, which I explore through the emphasis on reading among mothers and writing among male workers. Wendy Brown describes gen-dered autonomy where male autonomy "refers to the absence of immedi-ate constraints on one's entry into and movement within civil society" that "contrasts directly with women's encumbrance by familial responsibilities that limit her movement into and within civil society" (1995, 156). Through women's and men's differentiated participation in literacy programs, I show how male workers were instructed to deploy literacy to improve efficiency, while women's literacy emphasized reading to perform the role of the mother. I also consider how the goal of autonomy cuts against the stated aims of revolutionary activists who turned to literacy as a way to unite Egyptians and bring dignity to neoliterates. In this way, autonomy is a contradiction at the heart of literacy activism. I trace at what moments literacy programs invest in the values of liberal democracy, through their endeavor to create legible and participating citizens, and in what ways they may simultaneously and distinctively forge reading communities around scripture.

While Benedict Anderson (2006) takes modern reading as a unifying act that builds a national imaginary, religiously sponsored literacy demonstrates how the role of reading in the modern state does not supersede scriptural strategies. Unlike Anderson's examples, the Arabic-speaking Middle East did not replace classical or modern standard forms of Arabic with dialect. So-called religious and autonomous modes of reading are not distinct but rather are brought together in a movement for literacy that draws on religio-nationalist idioms. Today's literacy programming promotes modern autono-mous reading as the ultimate arbiter of the literate and, more broadly, *know-ing* subject. Reformist literacy initiatives make secular education religious, while scripturally based literacy programs deploy skills associated (at least historically) with secular education as an essential practice for religious life, including how the Quran ought to be *read* or, more accurately, experienced.

Quran, Language, Scripturalism

The Quran is the backdrop for literacy. And yet its place in religiously sponsored literacy is defined by its relative absence. Literacy promoters emphasized the Quran as *the* reason for learning to read autonomously, yet the vast majority of Egyptian literacy classrooms did not actually work with the Quran. As literacy activists went door-to-door and mosque-to-mosque from Kom al-Ahmar to Bulaq al-Dakrur to recruit students, they enticed potential students with the refrain: *Learn to read, read the Quran.* Similarly, students explained that they joined literacy classes so they could read the Quran. When student-recruits asked if they would learn how to read the Quran in literacy classes, they indicated a modern scriptural practice that forms a particular relationship between the reader and the text, one based on autonomous reading. While rhetorically significant to articulating the need for literacy, in practice, the Quran's use in classes created pedagogical obstacles. Its centrality in literacy campaigning is indicative of how Quran practices that do not depend on autonomous reading are increasingly illegible to modern notions of how scripture should be encountered.

In KIP, like most other literacy programs, the Quran was ever present in *talk* of literacy but disappeared in its instruction. In fact, the mosques where recruiters visited to locate students were often the very places where Quran lessons taught recitation and memorization to nonliterate people. But literacy volunteers and the people they recruited spoke of a different kind of Quranic encounter, one where reading the Quran meant deciphering the letters of words on the page. Significantly, this method of encountering the Quran emphasized a focus on its meaning rather than on Quran practices such as memorization (*hifz*) and training in proper elocution (*tajwīd*), which instructed learners to embody the Quran.

One reason for the rhetorical centrality of the Quran and its relative absence from the curriculum was the pedagogical challenge of managing Arabic's diglossic divide between Quranic Arabic and the everyday spoken dialect.[19] As many educationists explained to me, Arabic literacy poses challenges: What form of the language should be taught? To this day, Arabic-language literacy programmers struggle to manage the significant chasm between the classical Arabic (*fushā*) and the Egyptian dialect (*ʿāmmiyya*).[20] Dialect is used in oral exchanges between people of all social classes and education levels and admits national and regional variances. *Fushā* is typically the written form of the language (consistent across the Arabic-speaking world).

Arabic's diglossia leaves Arabic literacy in limbo: Is literacy supposed to support reading the Quran? Or is literacy supposed to be to facilitate daily life? In terms of language form, it cannot be both. In the Arabic-speaking world, since dialect is rarely written, basic literacy typically teaches a "modernized" or "simplified" version of classical Arabic (Haeri 2009). This view of literacy as a technique grounded in everyday language by extension recommends that Arabic literacy ideally be instructed in vernacular language. However, since the Arabic dialect is rarely written, this is not the case.[21] In other words, the language form of literacy classes is not familiar, nor does it support the many people who enroll in it to read the Quran.

While definitions of literacy have evolved to encompass the ability to navigate media and technology, fundamental discrepancies in language form continue to stymie Arabic-language literacy efforts.[22] Most educationists locate the gulf between spoken and written Arabic as the primary reason literacy classes struggle to foster long-term literacy. The chapters that follow consider how pedagogues and teachers have managed the Arabic language and how language debates and conceptions of Arabic as a sacred language have played a role in Egyptian literacy politics. Only in more candid conversations with close interlocutors did we discuss the material realities that made Arabic literacy in Egypt challenging, from the cost of books to the pressures on time that make it difficult to make reading a habit. While some literacy planners wished that more money was invested in education, most conversations focused on the problem of language.

The significant differences between language forms demarcate sacred and secular tongues, where classical Arabic (not only Quranic) is the language for formal learning and literature and is regarded by some as sacred, in contrast with dialects (Egyptian and others) that are profane. Unlike the majority of pedagogues I spoke with, my Salafi interlocutors explained that Arabic is a miraculous language through which learning is facilitated through God's will. Part of their understanding of Arabic as sacred was that it was also miraculous in its ability to be quickly learned when properly instructed.[23] In maintaining the sacred language of Arabic—rather than distinguishing between the classical Arabic of the Quran, Modern Standard Arabic, or vernacular, they endowed literacy instruction with sacred powers. This was a move that distinguished them from other literacy specialists who saw the Arabic of the Quran as distinct from the Arabic of the vast majority of literacy instruction.

The Quran's place in literacy efforts highlights a major thrust of contemporary Islamic reformism: scripturalism. By scripturalism, I refer to what Nguyen describes as "a particular intellectual and cultural attitude toward

the formation of religious authenticity and authority; namely, that hermeneutic priority ought to be afforded to the text of the Quran. [. . .] Most
modern scripturalists simply understand the Quran as central and indis-
pensable to their respective frameworks of religious understanding and their
personal identity politics" (2016, 64). The Quran's place in Islamic revivalism
indicates a textualizing strand of reformism, which can be traced back to the
nineteenth century through intellectuals such as Abduh, who saw revelation
as the way for Muslims to understand and get close to God. In Abduh's and
other reformers' views, instead of an intermediary scholastic elite, the masses
should access God's Word directly (Hourani 1962; Haddad 1994). In his vision, it was not that everyday people should simplify Islamic scholasticism,
but rather, Abduh wanted everyday people to study and experience the rigors
and discipline of education.

Scripturalist trends of the twentieth century were accompanied by new
notions, namely, those of Arabic-speaking Salafis, that endow knowledge of
the Arabic language with the ability to directly comprehend an immediate
and accessible meaning of the Quran (Reinhart 2010). In *Islam Observed*,
Geertz identifies scripturalism as a response to colonialism (1971, 73).[24]
While in Geertz's view, scripturalism narrows religious life, I take it in the
opposite direction—by observing how a textual approach broadens our
understanding of what we might consider "religious reading." Religiously
sponsored literacy programming reveals how the elevation of text can be
projected onto texts writ large. Through Islamic literacy activism, we see
how a rhetorical focus on the Quran is used to invite potential new readers
into a world of other texts, texts that are not limited to scripture or scholasticism. Scripturalism facilitates a dynamic of making secular texts sacred.
In contemporary Egypt, scripturalism can be seen from the expansion of
various types of Quran education to broader trends in print and publishing.
Literacy activists—at times wittingly and at others unwittingly—became the
handmaidens of this scripturalism. Indeed, modern scripturalism underpins
literacy activism.

Contemporary scripturalism has been shaped by trends in print and other
visual and auditory technologies. On the one hand, the status of the book
has only gained traction amid the rise of other influential media. The result
has been that books often take on a symbolic status, significant even when
they go unused. A defining feature of Egypt's Islamic revival has been the
rise in self-learning through low-cost books and mass literacy (Eickelman

1992, 1995; Eickelman and Anderson 2003). I situate these trends as extensions of scripturalist modes of contemporary Islamic reform. A proliferation of new forms of Islamic publications such as low-cost books, booklets, and learning manuals are sold at street kiosks and outside of mosques. Booklets of supplications and religious advice are distributed at weddings and funerals. Book markets behind al-Azhar mosque and other parts of the city specialize in Islamic learning where students and laypeople alike purchase books ranging from multivolume tracts of Islamic jurisprudence to inexpensively produced contemporary works by well-known scholars, such as Yusuf al-Qaradawi.[25] Despite the influence of print, much scholarly attention on media in the Middle East is given to new media rather than traditional print forms, which, as I demonstrate, persist in shaping education and knowledge construction, even among the nonliterate.[26] I argue that while technological advancements in sound and television have become critical mediums of religious propagation, they have not replaced the (often symbolic) power of texts. In fact, the persistence of print and text practices demand our attention since they underline the endurance of what Brinkley Messick calls "textual domination" in Muslim milieus (1993). The story of Islamic literacy activism centers texts in *da'wa* alongside and in interaction with sonic and visual mediums, as I detail in the chapters that follow. By paying attention to (il)literacy in the late Islamic revival, I trace the enduring power of texts, even when they are not read autonomously.

Ethnography of a Moment

I arrived at Cairo's new airport, nearly empty and pristine, in the spring of 2011. My cousin and his friend came to pick me up. They both worked in tourism and had recently lost their jobs. They were upbeat and said what a blessing this was, how they could finally do something more important, especially now that there was so much to be done. I had been coming and going from Egypt most of my life. As a girl, arrival meant dozens of relatives waiting outside the Alexandria airport with uncles sucking on cigarettes, aunts dabbing at the sweat on their cheeks, children creating new games to pass the time.

In my twenties, I moved to Cairo to work for the International Labour Organization (ILO). It was my first time experiencing the country without my family's firm hand guiding me to where I should and certainly should *not* venture. It was an intense period of discovery of a place I thought I knew. For two years, I worked on a project devising policies to address the lack of youth employment opportunities in Egypt. Sponsored by the Canadian International Development Agency (CIDA) to work on Egypt's National Action Plan (NAP) on Youth Employment, I reported to a boss in Geneva and went to work daily at Egypt's Ministry of Manpower (*Wizārat al-Quwwa al-ʿĀmila*). At the ministry, a large, unremarkable government building in a part of Nasser City where Egypt's bureaucracy expands over several city blocks, I watched men wait nervously for the necessary signatures to procure a work visa to travel abroad. I had unexpectedly joined Egypt's infamously bloated and underpaid civil servants. My boss led the largest national comprehensive policy package for creating decent work opportunities for Egyptians, and as I made my way to her office, I passed an administrative body that authorized visas to find work abroad.

One of the key ideas behind NAP was that youth should have a voice in policy creation, to be articulated through a youth consultative group. In 2011, the importance of the group was underlined by voices of youth interviewed by television news networks saying they were sick of being ignored. The consultative group consisted of about twenty young people representing different youth NGOs. They were invited to "capacity building" training sessions run by the World Bank, the ILO, and other international agencies with funds earmarked for youth initiatives, particularly ones that encouraged youth participation as a strategy for democracy-building. Through my work with them, I discovered an NGO culture in Cairo where young people met to create grassroots projects. They came from all sorts of backgrounds—from the well-established Risala, a well-known Islamic *khayr* ("good works") organization, to a one-office NGO run by half a dozen volunteers who organized annual projects like building a free internet café for local residents or creating a green area for children next to a local market. A few of the young people held day jobs and worked for their organizations on evenings and weekends, while others worked full time for the organization, whether paid or unpaid. Years later, when I returned for my dissertation research, I did not expect that the volunteer teachers would so resemble the youths I worked with in my previous development work.

It was during this time that I first observed the predominance of Egyptian literacy campaigning. On a summer afternoon in 2007, while crossing the Qasr al-Nil Bridge, I noticed colorful banners hoisted atop lampposts that read: "Reading for All" (*Al-Qirā'a li-l-Jamī'*). The newly launched public campaign was the latest of the first lady's programs to make reading central to the development of children and healthy families. The banners advertised to the reading public that Egypt was continuing to invest in reading. The Reading for All campaign was announced on a prominent thoroughfare connecting the Opera House and the Arab League. The campaign, like other strategies in the push for Egyptian literacy, was a public spectacle. Those who could not make out the words saw bright colors and an abstract image of an open book resting on its spine, while readers were assured that their government was doing something to address the country's high rate of illiteracy. After Mubarak's downfall, the first lady's appeal for literacy endured, even as she all but vanished from the public eye.

One day, early after my return to Cairo in 2011, I sat on a bus stuck in traffic. I noticed a large Vodafone branch with floor-to-ceiling signage on the front glass. The font appeared like handwriting across the storefront window: *Our goal is that by the year 2017, every Egyptian will be able to read this sentence and write it too (hadafna inna qabla sanat 2017 kull maṣrī yaqdir yiqra' al-jumla dī wa yaktibhā kamān).* Below the sentence were the words *Knowledge Is Power (Al-'Ilm Quwwa).* When I returned home, I searched the internet and learned that Amr Khaled had pledged to eradicate illiteracy in Egypt. The campaign was financed by the British multinational telecommunications company, Vodafone, and drew together volunteers from various NGOs, including the lead organization at the time, Life Makers. While I tracked a dozen initiatives in the following months, Knowledge Is Power was my way into the world of Egyptian literacy planning and campaigning.

Most KIP literacy teachers mobilized by the uprising were unemployed youth looking to be productive rather than idling away their days with empty timewasters, like a hand of cards. Among these volunteer teachers, I was known as the Joker: a regular presence but not a true participant—a face in a deck of cards. Saleh, a KIP director, gave me my new name at a teacher training session where he explained my role to the volunteer teachers. Having earned a nickname, I felt a part of the campaign camaraderie, but I also knew that the ambiguities of the name Joker were part of their ambivalence toward me. After all, the implications of a Joker in a game depend on the game in question. I could move between roles, like the power of a trump card; I could both benefit and harm the cardholder; or I could be the Fool—a card best avoided. After receiving this name, I saw myself as the kind of Joker used as an excuse card, shifting identities based on the circumstances. As the excuse card, the Joker implies a sort of (empty) presence, similar to how I was part of door-to-door literacy campaigning and classroom life but never bore the responsibilities or consequences of a teacher.

Like the participant-observer, the Joker is both part of the game and outside of it. The nickname was a reminder that the anthropologist is not the only observer. I was closely observed by my interlocutors, many of whom encouraged my research as a way to improve educational methods in literacy training, and few of whom saw value in research on education that could not be directly applied to solving problems within Egyptian education. As the Joker, I could move easily between different social classes and genders; I was allowed to transgress the sorts of social class boundaries that structured the lives of my interlocutors. As I explain in chapter 1, education is a part of a person's identity and social status. People relate to each other and avoid others based on it.

During my fieldwork, I lived in Dokki, a central district that gave me access to public transportation networks and facilitated my ability to move through a city notorious for its dense traffic. The apartment I rented was on a main artery linking the Giza governorate (the western half of Cairo) to the Cairo governorate. A twenty-minute walk to Tahrir Square, I lived on a popular route that funneled protesters from the western districts of the city into the square for regular Friday demonstrations. I conducted the bulk of my fieldwork (between 2011 and 2012 and the springs of 2013 and 2015) in Cairo and its surrounding peri-urban and industrial areas tracing literacy campaigning, from door-to-door student and teacher recruitment days to long-term participant-observation among the country's major targets of literacy development: women in informal neighborhoods and men in factories. I followed a number of literacy programs, some long-standing, and others initiated in the welter of revolution. I attended literacy classes run by the state, NGOs, and religiously sponsored charitable organizations and institutes. These included classrooms set up by the Egyptian Authority for Adult Education (EAAE), the National Council for Childhood and Motherhood, a Salafi institute in Nasr City, and the Egyptian Bible Society. Of the campaigns and programs I tracked, my focus was on KIP from its launch days after the fall of Mubarak to its premature demise under the severe regulation of NGOs led by President Abdel Fattah el-Sisi.

With KIP, I volunteered as a classroom observer (*murā'iba*) in an informal neighborhood, Batn al-Baqara, where KIP launched its first class. I sat with women on the front steps of their homes in narrow alleys that brought their lives so closely together. There, among a dozen primary interlocutors, I began to situate how the effort for literacy fit into women's lives and their neighborhood. I joined them in their long-standing Quran lessons in the same small community center where literacy classes took place and joined them in their celebrations and their boredom. I also worked in the Arab Contractors Maʿsara shipyard with KIP, where I observed the men's lives at work, sneaking out with them for their cigarette break, or loitering after class to help them put off the inevitable return to work. I spent hours each day on long commutes with teachers who told me their stories, shared their frustrations, and planned for their futures.

The period between June 2011 and 2013, the two years during which I conducted the bulk of my fieldwork, felt like the ideal time to be conducting ethnographic research. People were eager to share their thoughts and willing to open their doors. I was able to move between meetings with high-level government officials and NGOs and to chat with people on the bus. It was a period of possibility and openness. The rapid change in mood—from ecstasy to despair—and the quick turnover of ruling regimes of the day were defined by some pivotal moments, typically associated with an event, a bout of violence, mostly the result of political protests and violent military and police crackdowns. There was also much discussion about a decline in security, from the sexual assault of women at protests to an escalation of attacks on Copts. The period is difficult to characterize—it changed by the day—which is why I often include the date of particular exchanges or events to give a sense of what was happening at that moment when it is pertinent to a particular conversation.

Following Mubarak's ouster in February 2011, the country was first ruled by a SCAF interim government. In June 2012, the Muslim Brotherhood presidential candidate (running for the Freedom and Justice Party), Mohamed Morsi, narrowly won the country's first democratic elections. Throughout the months of my research, election rounds for each of the Upper and Lower Houses of Parliament and the presidential elections were conducted over multiple days, followed by second-round runoffs. During elections, some journalists and public intellectuals (including judges and notable figures such as presidential candidate Mohamed ElBaradei and novelist Alaa Al Aswany) recommended that nonliterate people be denied the right to vote, arguing that they did not have the capacity to make informed decisions. However, the electoral process ensured accessibility for nonliterate individuals by incorporating symbols representing political parties and candidates, which were displayed alongside written names on election ballots and promotional materials.

After one year in power, on June 30, 2013, demonstrations against Morsi led to the fall of the Muslim Brotherhood. On July 3, the army publicly announced that Morsi and his government failed to meet the demands of the people and overthrew him. Adly Mansour was installed as the interim president, although the minister of defense, Abdel Fattah el-Sisi, enjoyed credit for the overthrow and was lauded by most Egyptian media. In June 2014, he was elected Egypt's sixth president. In December 2023, he was elected to a third six-year term in elections that independent and foreign media described as marred by political repression and election committee violations. Egyptian human rights activists and international human rights organizations have fiercely criticized el-Sisi's arrest of thousands of Muslim Brotherhood members, journalists, unionists, and leftists, describing his rule as more repressive than any other previous leader of the country.

Literacy campaigning was born out of this rapidly shifting political terrain that shaped the lives of those involved. At the same time, life was often quotidian. Friends shared a meal and discussed television shows and celebrity gossip. Families arranged holidays on the north shore or the Red Sea. Students worried about exam results, made plans to marry, and met each other in coffee shops. The moment was ordinary as much as it was extraordinary.

Overview

The book is in three parts. Part 1 (introduction and chap. 1) introduces the reader to the modern history of educational transformation in Egypt and explains how religious value was entwined with basic literacy. Part 2 (chaps. 2 and 3) explores how scripture shapes what it means to read and examines the Quran's place in both basic literacy and Quran education. I delineate contemporary trends in scripturalism that at once drive and stymie the effort for universal literacy. Part 3 (chaps. 4 and 5) follows KIP, not only because it was the largest single campaign born out of the revolution but because the campaign captured a religiously sponsored literacy that made reading and writing virtuous acts for the state. Volunteer teachers marshaled a secular curriculum to promote Islamic values aimed at teaching women to read in a slum of Old Cairo (chap. 4), and to emphasize writing among workers at a shipyard in an industrial zone of the city (chap. 5).

The first chapter explores historical and theological issues that shape notions of literacy and turns to public discourse and state programs that sought to manage *illiteracy*. By underlining the moral and religious valences of illiteracy, and the association of autonomous reading with the miraculous, the chapter probes how autonomous reading is made religious in national discourse and state-run literacy classrooms. Chapter 2 examines distinct literacy projects that deploy scripture as curriculum. Three religiously sponsored literacy programs based on conceptions of God's Word (*kalām Allāh*) depict the dense field of revivalist efforts to center scriptural reading practices that emphasize semantic meaning over the recitational arts of pronunciation and elocution: the unpopular state-sponsored program Read in the Name of Your Lord (*Iqra' bi-smi Rabbika alladhī Khalaq*); the internationally successful Quran-based curriculum The Baghdadi Primer (*Al-Qāʿidat al-Baghdādiyya*), as taught to children and adult women at a private school in a Salafi community; and, finally, the Bible Society of Egypt's Read Your Book (*Iqra' Kitābak*) for Coptic children and adults. A comparative look across distinct reformist voices allows us to grasp how twenty-first-century religious revivalism makes God's Word the aim and instrument of autonomous reading. Chapter 3 is the first of two chapters centered on local educational projects aimed at women in an informal neighborhood of Old Cairo. The chapter breaks with the focus on basic literacy to contemplate an alternative mode of text processing, one that is not dependent on autonomous reading and yet is deeply scripturalist. The Quran lesson depicts a kind of literacy that is illegible to secular notions of autonomous reading.

Chapter 4 picks up in the same neighborhood as the Quran lesson. Batn al-Baqara was where KIP opened its first classroom. While the KIP campaign functioned in nine governorates, early mass mobilizations took place in cities, where volunteer teachers directed their energies in slums. There, teachers grappled with women's ambivalence toward literacy, redirecting their focus to instruct women to *want* to read.[27] Lessons focused on deploying literacy as essential to modern Muslim motherhood. Since literacy development throughout the Global South primarily targets women to make up the "gender gap," work on gender and education has focused on women (Abu-Lughod 2005; Agnaou 2004; Cody 2013; Khamis 2004; Robinson-Pant 2004; Street 2001). Building on critical feminist insights, I show the limits of education as empowerment and extend the gendered analysis to literacy classes among male workers at the shipyard. The final chapter examines shipyard workers in Maʿsara, an industrial zone south of Cairo's city center. By tracking the moral lessons of the literacy campaign there, namely the emphasis on creating happy, cultured, and productive laborers, this chapter inquires into how literacy (dis)enabled workers' communicative strategies. By strategically shifting communicative practices, workers navigated not only campaign and shipyard authorities but also the powers of writing itself. The chapter examines workers' writing samples as a strategy to gain recognition and contrasts the content of their incipient writing with their spoken words to illustrate how they navigated claims to dignity through different modes of communication. They made face-to-face complaints while depicting themselves as worker-patriots in their writing . Together, the final two chapters illustrate the contradictions of Islamic literacy development as revolutionary action.

Notes

1. The education partnership was established in 1993 and includes Bangladesh, Brazil, China, Egypt, India, Indonesia, Mexico, Nigeria, and Pakistan.

2. The comment sparked widespread debate. See, for example, *Mada Masr*, "New Minister of Education: Education Is a "Commodity" and the State May Not Continue to Pay Its Bill," http://www.madamasr.com/ar/2017/02/16/news/سلعة-التعليم-الجديد-التعليم-وزير/سياسة.او. For a discussion of the neoliberalization of Egyptian education through private schools, and the exacerbation of social inequality in schools and the teaching profession, see Herrera (2022) and Herrera and Torres (2006).

3. Adly (2014) explains the political predicaments of the use of Nasserism as a political strategy in contemporary Egypt. He describes Nasserist policies such as free university education and guaranteed employment for graduates as central to cementing support among government workers and students.

4. Egypt's Islamic revival, also referred to as Islamic awakening (*al-sahwa al-islāmiyya*), began in the 1970s and was shaped by other religious revivalist movements, the failure of Arab nationalism, and the return of migrant workers from the Gulf. Egyptian intellectuals and media influenced Islamic movements across the world, while Egypt was simultaneously shaped by both regional and global revivalist trends from Indonesia to the United States.

5. In this way, I treat revolution as what Moll (2020) calls a "thick concept" (adapting Clifford Geertz's coining *thick description* as a central anthropological writing strategy). This approach does not seek to answer whether Egypt did or did not experience a revolution (as many have debated) but rather regards revolution as a contested concept in Egypt in the months and years following Mubarak's ouster.

6. Scholarly attention to the art of recitation has highlighted the centrality of the Quran's performance for both the listener and the reciter, particularly through

the embodiment of ethical capacities honed through performance and audition. These works emphasize how the Islamic tradition maintains that learning should not be undertaken to discover knowledge for its own sake but that it is rather to be embodied. See, for example, Gade (2004), Lambek (1993), and Nelson (1985).

7. The *kuttāb* was the earliest stage of schooling made up primarily of Quran study, including memorization, dictation, and writing. Other subjects included learning the basic beliefs of Islam. Primary schooling replaced the prominence of the *kuttāb* in early education; however, the state revived *kuttābs* in the 1980s as a way to encourage and control early Islamic education. On the Egyptian *kuttāb*, see Mitchell (1988), Sedra (2011), Starrett (1998), and Yousef (2016).

8. See the discussion of Law No. 8 of 1991 in Radwan (2008). See also Awad (2017) and Herrera and Torres (2006) on the role of NGOs in Egyptian education.

9. This language was used by UNESCO interlocutors and other literacy programmers during my fieldwork. See for example, Krystyna Chlebowska's *Literacy for Rural Women in the Third World* (1990), a source recommended to me by an EAAE employee from their library.

10. *'Ashwā'iyya*, which literally means "random," refers to a "slum" or "informal" neighborhood. While I alternate between slum and informal neighborhood, I find the term "informal" vague in Cairo's urban context in which much of the city's living quarters, not to mention its commerce, transportation, and employment, are "informal." Marked by their informality and impromptu infrastructure, a variety of settings are commonly referred to as *'ashwā'i*.

11. As Loimeier points out, the terms used to describe such projects reveal much about their associated values and aims (2016). In his explanation of the dense field of religious reformers, he explains that reform "stands for many different notions and ideas and may have conservative, modernising, liberal, progressive, egalitarian, activist or revolutionary connotations" (18).

12. The translation of Freire into Egypt's revolutionary context was typical of many Freirean-inspired literacy campaigns. Even during his lifetime, his ideas were already adapted and often unrecognizable to the methods and ethos of education that he counseled. See Kirkendall (2010) on the "diffuse" applications of Freire's literacy techniques and his impact on the literacy politics of Cold War Latin America.

13. National statistics are reported through CAPMAS. I briefly consider the state's statistical documentation of (il)literacy during this period in the postscript.

14. The M. A. S. Abdel Haleem translation renders *Iqra'* as "read" (2005). To insist on the multivalent meanings of the term, I have maintained the Arabic.

15. Lane's (1978) definition of *qirā'a* includes both reading and recitation, while Wehr's (1979) includes the third meaning, "to declaim." Notably, Makdisi observes that the verb *sami'a* (to hear) was used synonymously with the term (1981, 143). The Arabic *qirā'a* resembles the Hebrew q-r-'. In his contribution to

The Ethnography of Reading (1993), Daniel Boyarin examines biblical references to reading (q-r- ʾ), which are always used to indicate an oral act, whether there is a written text to speak aloud or none at all. He argues that the meaning therefore suggests the English "proclaim" as a possible rendering of the Hebrew. He shows how instances of "to read" suggest that an individual present in the audience of a text being read aloud could be considered the one "reading." Boyarin explains how "to read" meant to be of "public consequence," where reading requires a response from the audience since it is "a proclamation, a declaration, and a summons" (1993, 14).

16. My use of *autonomous* differs from New Literacy Studies (NLS) scholars' critique of classical treatments of literacy and orality by anthropologists such as Ong and Goody. See, for example, Brian Street's characterization of earlier anthropological accounts of literacy in establishing a new turn in literacy studies: "A major tenet of NLS has been that literacy is not an 'autonomous' thing, a skill that when learned has consequences that follow simply from the nature of the medium. Technological determinism has previously dominated the account of literacy, hence the term 'autonomous model' referring to the model of literacy that assumes the technology of literacy in itself had 'impact'" (2003).

17. For examples of formative works in NLS that underline approaching literacy practices in their plurality, see Street (1993), Collins and Blot (2003), and Bartlett (2010).

18. It is worth remarking on my use of *sacred* and *making sacred*. I describe my interlocutors' conception of Arabic as a sacred language (cf. Asad 2018) and autonomous reading as a sacred practice; I also briefly consider how secular texts are made sacred. Unlike the Durkheimian conception of the sacred and the profane, my use of the sacred is attuned to the ways in which people have endowed objects and practices with a particular power. I follow on Asad's warning that Durkheim's sacred and profane must be further troubled beyond criticisms that the categories cannot be held apart but rather a more thoroughgoing conception must "look to what makes certain practices conceptually possible, desired, mandatory—including the everyday practices by which the subject's experience is disciplined. Such an approach [. . .] would give us a better understanding of how the sacred (and therefore the profane) can become the object not only of religious thought, but of secular practice too" (2003, 36–37). This view helps uncover the ways that secular education comes to have moral and religious weight, just as classical religious education has been made and remade over the last two centuries to disembody classical educative practices and has come to rely on the practice of autonomous reading for modes of understanding previously reserved for a scholarly class.

19. On diglossia, see Ferguson's definition of the general concept (1959) and later elaboration in relation to Arabic (1996), as well as Bassiouney's assessment of it in light of linguistic changes (2014, 2020). See also Versteegh (2014) on the

history of the Arabic language and the division between a high standardized form and dialect.

20. Following on Niloofar Haeri, I include under classical Arabic (*al-lugha al-ʿarabiyya al-fushā*) what is widely referred to as Modern Standard Arabic (MSA). The written form, whether in the Quran or newspapers, is referred to in Arabic as *fushā*, with no Arabic term for MSA. See Haeri's important discussion on how the forms of Arabic are labeled in Arabic and English, respectively: "The term MSA was coined by a number of linguists at Harvard University in the 1960s, according to the renowned linguist Charles Ferguson. In addition, its use implies that we understand the 'modernity' of contemporary Classical Arabic and that the modernization of this language is now an accomplished fact. The term has allowed us to take the entire question of modernization for granted and hence has prevented inquiries into the many complex issues surrounding it" (2003, xi).

21. Increasingly new forms of writing in social media as well as in literature adapt vernacular language in the written form.

22. Today, definitions of literacy encompass skills beyond reading, writing, and arithmetic. According to UNESCO, "literacy is now understood as a means of identification, understanding, interpretation, creation, and communication in an increasingly digital, text-mediated, information-rich and fast-changing world" ("What You Need to Know," unesco.org/en/literacy/need-know).

23. In this way, these interlocutors maintained a view of Arabic distinct from what Asad describes when he explains the particularity of Arabic as sacred in the context of reciting the Quran: "It is not the Arabic language that is sacred but the enunciation of divine virtues in the presence of what is believed to be a transcendent, creative power" (2018, 60). I elaborate on this language ideology in chapter 2. On Arabic-language ideology, see Haeri's discussion of Classical Arabic as a sacred language (2003).

24. While Geertz falls into contrasting Arab-Moroccan scripturalism against a more vital Islam in Indonesia, he helpfully associates how scripturalism gives rise to nationalism (1971).

25. On the influence of mass print culture on the production of accessible Islamic publications, see Robinson (1993), Eickelman and Anderson (1997), and Starrett (1996).

26. For more on the impact of popular media, see Armbrust (1996) and Fahmy (2011). On cassette tapes, see Hirschkind (2006) and Simon (2022). On television, see Brinton (2015) and Moll (2018, 2020).

27. See Hosny (2017) on literacy development focused on rural women in post-Mubarak Egypt.

1

Religious Reading in an Unlettered Nation

We are an unlettered nation, we do not write and do not
calculate (*innā umma ummiyya, la naktubu wa la nahsubu*).

—The Prophet Muhammad, as narrated in the hadith
collection of Bukhari, chapter no: 31, Fasting no: 137

Cairo, mid-December 2011. Almost a year after Mubarak's ouster. After three
weeks of demonstrations in front of the cabinet building where protesters
demanded civilian rule, military forces initiated a violent crackdown. For
three days, the military beat and shot at demonstrators, who responded with
concrete projectiles and Molotov cocktails. Egyptian television broadcast
images of injured demonstrators carried through the streets to field hospitals. At least seven people were killed. Among the casualties was the Institut
d'Égypte, a research center and library on a corner of Tahrir Square. Black-
gray smoke rose from the building, and flames rose from gaping windows.

The institute, established by Napoleon Bonaparte in 1798, was the research
heart of the French campaign in Egypt (1798–1801). It was brick-and-mortar
orientalism in the heart of Cairo. As it burned, Egyptian television announc-
ers informed their audiences that it was home to two hundred thousand of
the most valuable and rare books in the country. As the flames did their
work, political and intellectual figures described the institute as a beacon
of Egyptian heritage and civilization (*turath wa - hadara*) and an artifact
of the richness of Egyptian culture (*thaqafa*). Protesters blamed security
forces for igniting the fire and failing to put it out for several hours. Officials
blamed demonstrators for causing the blaze and accused them of looting.
Throughout these days of violence and in the weeks and months to come, the

Figure 1.1. Street artist painting Emad Effat on a government building the day after Effat's murder as the Institut d'Égypte burns. Cairo, November 2011. The Mosireen Collective. "Emad Effat on Tahrir's Wall—2011. *Al-Shaykh 'Imād 'Iffat 'alā Jidrān al-Taḥrīr.*" YouTube. Last modified December 17, 2011, https://www.youtube.com /watch?v=AL20rNB44kY. Creative Commons.

image of this rare-collections library in flames for many came to represent the country's descent into lawlessness. Many seemed to forget that they had never known of the building's existence. The library became visible only in its destruction.

As the library burned, bystanders rushed inside to rescue books, fearing that the caved-in roof would cause the entire building to collapse. Some emerged cradling smoldering pages in their arms. Others formed a human chain around the building to protect its contents from looters. The Popular Committee for Rescuing the Institute was formed to help the National Library (*Dar al-Kutub*) collect pages and deliver them to nearby pickup locations.

Prime Minister Kamal Ganzouri, appointed by the military weeks earlier, aimed his criticism at protesters. General Adel Emara, member of the Supreme Council of the Armed Forces, referred to the fire as "a shame for every Egyptian."[1] Zein Abdel-Hady, who ran the country's main library, stated, "I haven't slept for two days, and I cried a lot yesterday. I do not like to see a book burned. The whole of Egypt is crying." Mohammed al-Sharbouni, the institute's director, told state television, "The burning of such a rich building means a large part of Egyptian history has ended."[2] In contrast to the comments made by officials, historian Khaled Fahmy observed in the literary magazine *Akhbar al-Adab*:

> The real tragedy is that nobody—not even scholars—knew of its existence in the first place, nor did those who lament the lost manuscripts ever bother to read them. The real value of a book is not its rarity or high cost, but rather the information it contains. And the significance of a library is not measured by the number or scarcity of its books, but rather by how many read those books. A library that is not frequented by anyone, and that people only notice when it is set ablaze, is worthless.[3]

For Fahmy, the value of books lies in the knowledge they convey and their accessibility, not the prestige afforded to the collection. The tragedy, as he saw it, was that the library was unknown to a general public of readers.

During these tense days, two victims were discussed alongside the burning of the library: Shaykh Emad Effat, a beloved poet, revolutionary, and senior official of Egypt's Dar al-Ifta, was fatally shot while protesting, and the beating of an unnamed woman was captured in a viral YouTube clip that depicted soldiers stomping on the veiled protester. As they dragged her, her clothing lifted above her head, exposing her body. Despite the political scandal of Effat's murder and the beating of the unnamed woman (widely referred to as "the blue bra" because of her exposed undergarments as she was being dragged), the burning of the library was cause for national mourning that united different social groups. Effat's shooting troubled revolutionaries and those concerned with the country's Islamic institutions, like the Dar al-Ifta, just as the beating of the unnamed woman raised questions about women's participation in the uprising. Yet, it was the fire at the institute that united Egyptians around a supposed shared cause—that of heritage and knowledge. To mourn the institute required taking no side at a moment when everyone had a side.

As national and international media covered the story, most Egyptians learned about the library's most valuable holding for the first time, *Description de l'Égypte*. The work was a product of the French colonial project to document the antiquities and flora and fauna of Egypt that began in 1809 and was compiled over twenty years.[4] Edward Said describes how the *Description* revealed a particular orientalist "attitude," a kind of textual knowledge that can be documented and read rather than lived or experienced (Said 2003, 84). In the same way that the French mission saw the *Description* as a way to "restore a region from its present barbarism to its former classical greatness" (86), public conversation about it echoed the orientalist view of the work as a symbol of Egypt's glorious past. The institute burned for half a day before firefighters finally put out the flames. Miraculously, as some described it, the *Description de l'Égypte* was recovered unscathed.

The national reaction to the fire revealed how books are sacred to a national and secular imaginary that regards them as objects of culture and civilization. It also surfaced long-held anxieties about the dangers of illiteracy and ignorance. While the introduction laid out conceptions of literacy, specifically as they relate to social development and modes of Quranic encounter, this chapter turns to public discourse around *illiteracy* and state programs that attempt to manage it. Illiteracy is ever-present in discussions about what kind of country Egypt should be. It is associated with moral depravity and disease and discussed as the opposite of civilization, knowledge, and order. Discussions of illiteracy feature in national articulations of anxiety around ignorance. This chapter examines how ignorance is imagined and functions as an identity through the figure pejoratively known as the *gāhil* (ignorant person). Public discussions around these terms shaped my interlocutors' worlds; it was a discourse they refuted as well as drew on and negotiated. For this reason, it is necessary to understand how discourse around illiteracy, and its association with ignorance, shaped literacy planning and implementation, which I take up in later chapters.

Talk about basic literacy and modern education is vested with religious significance. By underlining the moral and religious valences of illiteracy, this chapter probes how reading is associated with Islam and miracles. I explore how reading has been made religious. To do so, I consider how, in the modern period, new ideas about religion and education transformed both realms. The act of reading was imbued with virtue. I draw on Armando Salvatore's concept of ingraining, whereby "Muslim traditions ingrain into modern mechanisms of social governance" (2001, 11). Ingraining allows us to better understand how classical Islamic values of knowledge structure contemporary social hierarchies of modern education and social status. Two examples, one from the former grand mufti of Egypt Ali Gomaa and the other from the former first lady Suzanne Mubarak, illustrate how autonomous reading is made virtuous. The examples offer distinct iterations—one from a revered (if not highly controversial) Islamic authority, Gomaa, and the other from a (disgraced) former public figure who was once the national champion of basic literacy, Mubarak. The final section depicts the pervasiveness of religious lessons in state-run literacy classes, where literacy classes with secular state curricula become prominent sites of *da'wa*. Teachers instruct students beyond the curriculum to learn the supplicatory and ritual basics (*ta'sīs*). The state classes depict one way in which reading is made religious—by making so-called secular education the site of learning basic religious practices. The religious lessons of state classes are indicative of how religious value is ingrained in autonomous reading. The prominence of *da'wa* in state-run literacy classes suggests the meanings of ignorance and its imbrications in life skills and morality. The discussion of state classes sets up the book's tension between discourse and practice and contentions over what makes basic literacy "Islamic."

Ignorance: The Moral Valences of Education

"I'm here because I don't want anyone calling me ignorant (*gāhil*)." Salih Fathi, a twenty-eight-year-old welder, explained why he decided to attend a literacy class when it was offered to the employees of the Arab Contractors shipyard. Other worker-students nodded in agreement. We sat at a wooden desk that they had constructed to transform a welding workshop into a classroom. It was April 2012. Amid Egypt's first democratic presidential election campaign, a campaign of a different sort was afoot at the Arab Contractors shipyard. In the industrial zone of Ma'sara, some twelve miles south of Cairo's city center, over a hundred of the shipyard's workers took part in the Knowledge Is Power (KIP) literacy campaign. That day, the men lingered after class, delaying their return to their work renovating and constructing Nile cruise ships.

Salih Fathi was dressed in paint-stained coveralls. He never spoke in class, but he was the first to share with me what he saw as the value of literacy. He stopped going to school when he was fourteen and began an apprenticeship with a blacksmith in his neighborhood. When we met, he had been working at Arab Contractors for nearly a decade. Two of the older workers, Rif'at and Tawfiq, explained that they wanted to read the Quran "the proper way." They did not want to be the only ones in their family who could not read. Notably, they did not say that they did not want to *be* ignorant but, rather, that they did not want *others calling* them ignorant. Literacy classes were a way to overcome the stigma of illiteracy. While the term for a nonliterate person is *ummī*, a term to which I return below, the more pejorative term Salih Fathi and others were attentive to was *gāhil*, an ignorant person, a term that suggests more than a lack of a skill—rather, a fundamental deficiency. It is understood as a condition and an identity. Salih Fathi, typically quiet, spoke with an honesty that refused the common explanations most students gave when asked about attending literacy classes.

Anthropologists of the Middle East and Muslim societies have detailed the significance of knowledge and honor as dominant and often interrelated values in Muslim communities (Lambek 1993; Manoukian 2011; Messick 1993). As Franz Rosenthal puts it, "There is no other concept that has been operative as a determinant of Muslim civilization in all of its aspects to the same extent as *'ilm* [knowledge]" (1970, 2). While the abstract pursuit of knowledge was used to market literacy, students spoke of being motivated by its inverse, ignorance, not because they saw themselves as essentially lacking but because they knew others perceived them that way. Despite (or perhaps because of) the predominance of knowledge discourse, little attention is paid to its "shadow term," *ignorance* (Gershon and Raj 2000, 6). Ignorance is not merely the opposite of knowledge; it is widely regarded as the opposite of religion. Hourani defines *jāhiliyya* as "ignorance of the truths of religion" (1962, 6). In his description of the relationship between knowledge and ignorance, Rosenthal explains that "in the mind of the Prophet, unawareness of or opposition to his message was equivalent to 'ignorance'" (1970, 32). In contemporary Egypt, *ignorance* gains its rhetorical force in how its meanings suggest a status that brings together formal education with a sense of one's ethical formation. Education is interpolated into the ethical grounding and ontological difference of the nonliterate person.

The meanings of *ignorance*, as well as of *education* and *culture*, are many and contextually dependent. In its contemporary usage, *ignorance* means not only a lack of modern education but also an inability to perceive divine guidance. It is a powerful epithet that evokes centuries of derision in its reference to pre-Islamic Arabia: the before-revelation, the before-true-knowledge, the obstinate. The appearance of the term in pre-Islamic literature as well as the Quran suggests a meaning closer to barbarism (Shepard 2003). Islamic reformist efforts to discipline "backward practices" have focused on education and the proper methods of education, pitting rote memorization against meaning and critical thought. Modernist thinkers such as Muhammad Abduh, Rashid

Rida, and Abdullah al-Nadim saw modern education as necessary to forging an enlightened Islam (Haj 2009; Haddad 1994; Gasper 2001). They advocated for modern schooling to discipline the masses. These reformers saw peasants as ignorant of religious fundamentals (*ta'sīs*). While their reformism drew on classical thinkers like the medieval Hanbali scholar, Ibn Taymiyya, they did so in novel ways that explained ignorance as not merely stagnation in the face of progress but a sign of regression. In the reformers' works, we find the ingraining of religious and scientific knowledge that today structures what I call education-morality. Indeed, a looming assumption among contemporary adult education initiatives in Egypt is that the disciplinary techniques of modern schooling cultivate good students and pious citizens. In this way, elites, state planners, and Islamic reformers regard modern schooling—even of secular subjects—as essential for proper belief and ethical conduct.

The modern period introduced new ideas of how reading could bring about healing as well as disciplining a pious subject. This reading went beyond the Quran. Like the distinctions among the various text-reading practices described in the introduction, the distinction between *ta'līm* (modern education) and *tarbiyya* (cultivation) was similarly elided. The idea that education should have moral implications stems from the concept of *tarbiyya*, which, until the latter part of the nineteenth century, "had meant simply 'to breed' or 'to cultivate,' referring, as in English, to anything that should be helped to grow—the cotton crop, cattle, or the morals of children" (Mitchell 1988, 88). By the 1870s, under British colonial rule, it "came to mean 'education,' the new field of practices" (Mitchell 1988, 88). *Ta'līm* and its association with its central practice, autonomous reading, bears the moral weight of an education previously conceptualized as *tarbiyya*. In this way, the various practices of *qirā'a*—not only those associated with classical Quranic practices—come to have moral and religious implications. Autonomous reading was proffered as a sacred practice through the generalized pursuit of knowledge and the cultivation of a modern Muslim subjectivity.

In Egypt, Sayyid Qutb (d. 1966) popularized the term *jāhiliyya* in his writings, especially *Milestones* (1964). Indebted to the ideas of Islamist modernists Abul Hasan Nadwi (d. 1999) and Abul A'la Maududi (d. 1979), Qutb, through his famous writings on *jāhiliyya*, made ignorance the opposite of Islam, characterizing its human traits as grounded in excessiveness and immorality. Unlike Maududi, who saw Muslim societies as partially ignorant, Qutb characterized all societies of his time—Muslim and non-Muslim—as falling into *jāhiliyya*. In Qutb's introduction to Nadwi's *What the World Has Lost by the Decline of the Muslims* (*Mādhā Khasira al-ʿĀlam bi-Inhiṭāṭ al-Muslimīn* 1951), he states that "*jahiliyya* is not a limited period of time but a specific spiritual and intellectual condition" (cited in Shepard 2003, 533). His was a broad social critique that implicated not only a portion of the uneducated masses but also a social illness with its roots in an Islamic politic that could not be realized until full implementation of sharia. While *jāhiliyya* as a broader political critique is not at stake in widespread post-Mubarak discussions of ignorance, the moral weighting of the term is ever present.

The Islamic reformism that ingrained religious values in secular education in Egypt can be seen in other parts of the world, from Senegal to Turkey, yet the bringing together of colonial education practices with Islamic values is, of course, not universal. Islamic critiques of Western education abound, from the neotraditional pursuit of classical Islamic education in the United States (Kashani 2023) to the madrassas of Mali, first established in opposition to French colonial rule (Brenner 2001). Perhaps the most recognizable opposition to Western education articulated as an Islamic critique can be seen in Nigeria's militant movement, Boko Haram. The group repudiates colonial education and its influences.[5] Thurston situates this rejection in a broader context of Nigerian intellectuals' and politicians' criticism of Western education. The anxiety and critiques of colonial educational influences are a reminder that those influences have not been accepted globally as a fait accompli, with educational distinctions absorbed by or stitched into indigenous knowledge practices. The example, while dramatic because of Boko Haram's use of violence, is a counterpoint to Islamic literacy development and the broader tradition of Islamic reformism of which it is a part.

A political cartoon by artist Andeel captures ignorance talk, how ignorance is generally discussed. The cartoon was notable for its mocking depiction of President Abdel Fattah el-Sisi, uncommon in Egypt's political cartoons at that time. The image depicts el-Sisi's satisfaction imagining Egypt as greater than the rest of the world. His adviser disturbs his peace with the urgent litany of the problems in the country: "Sir, what are we going to do about the garbage, the traffic, the electricity, the hospitals, security, income, housing, the laws, job opportunities, and the future?! WHAT WILL WE DO ABOUT THE IGNORANCE?!" El-Sisi pauses and responds, "Increase the ignorance!" The adviser immediately departs, and el-Sisi is once again left to his thoughts. While el-Sisi's response to "increase ignorance"[6] lends the

Figure 1.2. "Increase ignorance." "Advisor: Sir, Sir. What are we going to do about the garbage, the traffic, the electricity, the hospitals, security, income, housing, the laws, job opportunities, and the future?! WHAT WILL WE DO ABOUT THE IGNORANCE?! Sisi: Increase the ignorance!" Andeel, *Tok Tok* #12. The cartoon was first published on *Mada Masr*, and the rights for republishing were granted by the artist, Andeel.

panel its tragic-comic punch line, many middle-class (educated) Egyptians soberly describe the state of education in Egypt in precisely these terms: the government prefers not to educate Egyptians so that it may rule with impunity over a subdued population. In this view, Egyptians with little or no schooling are both pitied for their gullibility and despised for supposedly causing the country's social and economic challenges. El-Sisi's simplistic thought bubbles and naive grin place him alongside the ignorant masses he wishes to reproduce to minimize his accountability for a litany of problems. In this view, so-called ignorant masses are the basis for moralizing discourses on the values of education that make the primary obstacle to Egypt's progress not a corrupt authoritarian political system but rather a significant effect of that system—the economically disenfranchised with little to no opportunity for formal education.

Politicians, television hosts, and the thread of daily conversation articulate ignorance as a politically dangerous moral deficiency and the greatest obstacle to the nation's progress.[7] While talk of illiteracy in Egypt has long been ubiquitous, the uprising lent the discourse new urgency. Opinion pieces regularly described a "culture of ignorance" (thaqāfat al-gahl) and the "dangers of illiteracy in Egypt" (makhātir al-ummiyya fī misr). Ignorance is widely discussed as both the cause and effect of Egypt's economic stagnation and political crises. Many Egyptians, both critical and supportive of the uprising, explained that too many Egyptians are incapable of democracy. While voting protocols took into account the sizable nonliterate population by using symbols for candidates on election campaign posters and ballots, many argued that nonliterates should not be allowed to participate in the election. Petitions circulated demanding that nonliterate citizens be excluded from the voting process. Illiteracy and general fears of nonliterate masses were a prominent argument in defense of military intervention and limits on civil liberties under el-Sisi's regime.

During the early rounds of elections following Mubarak's ouster, illiteracy was often described as dangerous not only to the political process but also to the literal health of the nation. Illiteracy was commonly referred to as a disease in headlines such as "Illiteracy: The Plague of Our Time" (al-Ummiyya Tā ūn al-ʿAsr). Illiteracy is both figuratively and literally associated with blindness, pairing the blind and nonliterate (al-makfūfīn wa-l-ummiyyīn). The connection between the two conditions has an apparent metaphorical valence, as both nonliterates and blind people are unable to decipher text.

The connection between ignorance and blindness is also associated with the prevalence of trachoma, a contagious bacterial infection that leads to blindness, found among Egypt's urban and rural poor, many of whom are also not literate.[8] Yousef describes how education was put forward in the late nineteenth century as "the ultimate social cure for all Egyptian ills" (2012, 52). Some of the solutions offered as a cure for ignorance as an illness plaguing Egypt range from religious instruction to basic literacy (and, as we will see, how these two avenues intersect). Discussions of remedies often invoke the language of miracles. Not only can classical Quranic reading practices of *qirāʾa* offer innumerable rewards for the afterlife, but autonomous reading and secular education are also described as having salvific powers.

Literacy talk that treats illiteracy as a sickness also structures identity and class formation. Educational distinctions determine how people come to think of themselves and are regarded by others. The identity of the ignorant person is part of a larger constellation of social markers around education and class, namely, the educated person (*mutaʿallim*) and the cultured person (*musaqqaf*) with whom the ignorant person is contrasted.[9] Alongside the moral and religious hues of ignorance, what it means to be educated is contingent on one's social milieu. In Batn al-Baqara, the neighborhood where I based my observations of literacy directed at women in urban slums, my interlocutors from outside of the literacy class distinguished themselves from their neighbors enrolled in literacy by telling me that they were educated. This usually meant that they had completed the equivalent of high school in the public education system. Among volunteer teachers, many of whom came from families with parents and relatives who had completed university, being educated meant holding a degree. Notably, a diploma or degree did not admit people into the category of the educated. As we will see, people in informal neighborhoods or workers, despite their level of education (or income), were often regarded as ignorant by outsiders.

The nineteenth-century shift toward modern schooling created new forms of status that marked "the Europeanization' of class structure" (Starrett 1998, 32) that scaffolded the attainment of formal education onto an individual's identity. These status categories placed education within a moral register—an education-morality that structures a sense of self in relation to others. The categories distinguished status in the Weberian sense: as a form of social stratification, where difference is premised on an "estimation of honor" (Weber and Mills 1947, 187). The role of education in social status was not novel as modern schooling transformed the country; rather, it affirmed dominant hierarchies premised on differentiated knowledge (Levy 1957; Marlow 1997).

As Shahab Ahmed explains, social hierarchy is "central to and definitive of human and historical Islam" (Ahmed 2015, 168). Brinkley Messick describes the social implications of knowledge differences as "deeply ambiguous," both rigidly hierarchical and simultaneously egalitarian (Messick 1988, 641). While sharia offers critiques of the hierarchy it structures, the polyvocality of sharia texts limits the possibilities of a critique. Modern education displaced Islamic scholars and Sufi masters from their preeminent status, in some cases, relegating their forms of knowledge and knowledge practices to the realm of "ignorant" rather than eradicating social hierarchy. In their stead, modern education placed a newly formed educated class as elites (Adely and Starrett 2011). Through ingraining, identities premised on modern education carried the weight of Islamic social hierarchies based on knowledge despite the transformations in the forms of knowledge that the hierarchies were premised on. In what follows, I explain how reading came to be a sacred practice, not only when associated with sacred texts but also through the very act itself.

Religious Reading

What makes reading *religious*? The question may appear to be a trap, the kind that the historian of religions J. Z. Smith would warn us away from, with the vague adjective *religious* raising more questions than can be answered. Taking religious reading as a self-evident category, Michael Warner distinguishes religious reading by its style—replicative, devotional, reverential (2004). These practices are directed toward cultivating a particular reading subject, one that he contrasts with the critical reader. Warner undoes Kant's formulation of a reading that cultivates "independent thinking," which Kant contrasts with "immature" reading that depends on an external authority (15). If the critical reader is instructed to distanciate themself from the text, the religious reader is instructed to revere the text and/or its author. At the same time, Warner cautions against taking the practice of recitation and audition as the putative "other" of critical reading (19). He turns to Mahmood (2004) to elucidate a mode of religious reading where, as he explains, religious reading is exemplified through recitation and memorization. While he suggests that Quran reading practices are more than merely immature in Warner's view, religious reading is not autonomous reading. I want to underline how religious reading is not limited to the reading of sacred texts. A reverence for reading itself is projected onto texts writ large.

What makes reading religious has changed over time, as different ideas about how to encounter texts, including the Quran, have changed. The emphasis on Quran education as rigid and dogmatic stresses the "religious dimension" rather than situating Quran education within a broader social context and history of literacy (Hanna 2007). Since the earliest Muslim community, reading has occupied a central place in worship, despite not being enshrined in the necessary ritual performances. The paradox of Quran reading practices is that there is at once minimum liturgical use of scripture in prescribed ritual, and yet Quran reading is a major act of worship, what Walid Saleh calls a "theology of reading" where "perusing, meditating, reciting, listening to the recitation and memorizing the Quran the most assured path for salvation" (2010, 359). Quran reading is associated with curative and apotropaic affects (Zadeh 2009; El-Tom 1987). Through the development of hadith and the *faḍāʾil al-Qurʾān* (works that detail the "excellences" or "merits" of the Quran), Muslim reverence for reading particular verses in specific formulas endows particular verses with salvific powers (Afsaruddin 2002). Some verses are believed to bring material success to people in this life; however, most of the rewards are directed toward Judgment and the next life. For example, one who reads Quran 91, "The Sun" (*Al-Shams*), is rewarded as though the reader gave the entire world of wealth in alms (Saleh 2010, 364). Quran reading as an act of worship can also be seen in material culture, from elaborate Quran stands to markings on a Quran's page that guide a reader through a monthly reading. The act of writing, like reading, is also part of a practice to transmit healing powers (Spadola 2009, 2013). The sorts of practices associated with religious reading are a part of the socialities formed around the Quran: they maintain a healthy body and body politic.

Notably, classical religious reading practices do not presume to understand the meaning of the text. Some contemporary reformers involved in literacy do away entirely with such reading practices, while others are silent or rarely mention them, emphasizing instead an intellectual engagement with the Quran's meaning. Today, much Islamic reformism stresses understanding and reflection as the necessary way to properly encounter God's Word. This emphasis is central to what I refer to as scripturalism, which I explore in chapters 2 and 3.

Significant shifts brought about through colonial reforms to Egyptian education broadened the scope of how reading came to be associated with virtue. Modern education ideals were formed under British rule in the nineteenth century when the colonial administration co-opted the *kuttāb* and attempted to create a disciplined workforce through basic literacy skills. In 1898, the British administration set up a program to bring the *kuttāb* under government inspection and receive government subsidies in return. Under this agreement, *kuttābs* were also to instruct reading, writing, and basic arithmetic. As an unintended consequence, the policy transformed the system of religious education and, even more profoundly, the way in which ordinary Egyptians understood and experienced their religion.

Modern education came to be argued for on moral grounds of performing one's religious duties in an Egyptian Islam that prioritized work, productivity, and obedience as Islamic virtues (Doumato and Starrett 2006; Kaplan 2006; Starrett 1998). Secular education was sacralized in this way so that religious reading was no longer exclusively associated with the Quran; the reformation of the *kuttābs* and the spread of modern schooling made the reading of *all* texts sacred. This new conception of religious reading and the sacralization of scientific subjects directed understandings of national and human progress. It was a new vision of education and of the person. It was supposed to cultivate a particular kind of subject for a new political and economic order.

The KIP media campaign is illustrative of this sacralization. The campaign theme song shows how books—even on scientific topics—are made to be sacred. As part of the promotional campaign, the pop song *The Greatest Miracle* (*Akbar Muʿgiza*) ambiguously refers to both the Quran and all books as "the greatest miracle." The song was composed and sung by Mustafa Ramadan, well known for singing religious songs (*anāshīd dīniyya*). The song circulated widely across Khaled's and Life Makers' social media, promoting reading as the key to all knowledge, where all knowledge starts with the Quran.

> And if you find me in a situation without any solution
> Look in my hands and you will surely find a book
> Yes, I am a weak creature, strengthened by dust
> But I fly above the clouds
> And that is not the miracle, the greatest miracle
> Of ours, oh people, was the Book.
> When you find yourself in a moment of constraint
> Medicine, science and engineering have no limits

History, civilization, literature and art
Look in my hands and you will surely find a book
(Ramadan 2012)

Islamic literacy development taught books were material objects laden with
virtuous powers of mediating knowledge, whether that knowledge was divine or otherwise.[10] The miracle of "The Book," the material form of the
Quran known as the *mushaf*, is projected onto books writ large. The depiction
of the Quran as a miracle became, through modern iterations on the virtues
of reading, a basis for regarding books as miracles. The campaign promoted
reading *all* books as a virtuous act whereby the book was a material object
laden with virtuous powers of mediating knowledge, whether that knowledge was revealed or scientific. The campaign ingrained the miracle of the
Quran into all books.

Mohammed Arkoun observes that, in Islamic milieus, books are deeply
associated with "The Book" (*al-kitāb*), which refers to the Quran (1988).[11] He
describes a movement from *the* Book (Quran) to books—what he refers to as
the Book-book—whereby the significance of the Book is projected onto all
books: "The rationalist, logocentrist activity of reason in all kinds of books is
more or less influenced, guided, and inspired by the activity of the *imaginaire*
(Vorstellung) representing the mental image of the Book-Revelation" (1988,
75–76). This logocentric view sheds light on the power of the burning of the
institute over an Egyptian public, including those who do not read and/or
never knew of the collection. Even neglected (unread) books exerted a force
of authority in their presence. As Dale Eickelman observes: "Even if only
a minority of the population read books, a much larger number hear them
spoken about—and books, following the paradigm of the Quran—remain
central to the cultural imagination" (Eickelman and Anderson 2003, 35).

Life Makers' offices always had small booklets of religious advice
(*kutaybāt*) with titles such as *A Better Life (Ahlā Hayāt)* or *For Girls Only
(Li-l Banāt wa-Bas)* on bookshelves in the front lobby. Although booklets like
these are widely circulated at mosques and by those involved in *da'wa*, as a
number of volunteers remarked after I asked about them, they are rarely read.
While they can address practical life issues facing young Muslims, the genre
of discrete written texts is less popular among volunteers than watching a
television program, attending a religious sermon, or listening to a sermon
on the radio or a cassette. The primary role of such booklets seemed to be
their sheer presence.

The value of books not only is symbolic but is also about a sense of their ability to improve one's life. In discussions about the value of reading with literacy teachers, they typically spoke about reading instrumentally—finding texts that are beneficial (*mufīd*) for one's self-improvement. A volunteer teacher remarked to me that there are only a few *muthaqqafīn* in Egypt today: "Egyptians do not read for pleasure. There's too much to do to allow for time in one's day to read for pleasure. Even my professors read only for their profession, and still, they don't read more than newspapers." Walking by a bookshop, he pointed at a copy of *The Secret (Al-Sirr)*, the self-help bestseller translated into Arabic, in a shop window and recommended it to me. He told me that he had a copy on his mobile. His interest in self-help literature was part of the broad circulation of self-help literature that includes translations of English bestsellers like *Men Are from Mars and Women Are from Venus* (*Al-Rijāl min al-Mirrīkh wa-l-Nisā' min al-Zuhara*) as well as works originally written in Arabic, which bring together popular self-help strategies with the Quran and prophetic tradition like A'id al-Qarni's bestseller *Don't Be Sad* (*Lā Tahzan*).

Cairo's bookshops and sidewalk book kiosks evidence the proliferation of the self-help genre in Egypt. In describing the rise of the genre in Egypt, Kenney observes how "self-help is not simply the glorification of the individual but, more pointedly, the sacralization of the self" (2015, 665). The values of individual self-improvement and the Islamic tradition come together to create "new discourses and practices that facilitate the emergence of different understandings of what it means to be Muslim" (2015, 665). In this way, religious reading is not limited to a specific practice (recitation) or text (the Quran) but rather is about a kind of worldly striving where the hunger for continual improvement is part of modern Muslim life that incorporates contemporary values of self-betterment. In the chapters that discuss KIP, I explore various qualities of self-help literature that were central to literacy classes, such as the focus on happiness and strategies to become more efficient.

"THE PROPHET'S ILLITERACY WAS A MIRACLE"

Prophet Muhammad is known by the Quranic reference to him as the Unlettered Prophet (*al-nabī al-ummī*). The reference has been variously interpreted over the centuries, with the orthodox position being that Muhammad never learned to read or write. On a television program created by Egypt's Dar al-Ifta, one of the major world bodies for issuing Islamic legal rulings (fatwas), former grand mufti Ali Gomaa responded to a question posed by a viewer.[12] He was asked to address the Prophet Muhammad's illiteracy. Since Muslims take Muhammad to be the ultimate human exemplar, his illiteracy has the potential to be taken as a personal characteristic to be emulated, like growing a beard or eating with one's right hand, as many Muslims do. While none of my interlocutors articulated this line of argumentation with me, Gomaa's treatment of the topic on the program suggested that the issue was either of relevance to his viewership or at least a critical distinction he saw as important to make to his viewership. He maintained the contemporary dominant understanding of Muhammad's illiteracy and denied that it was a characteristic Muslims should attempt to embody: "If a man told me 'I am illiterate and the Prophet was illiterate' this is a calamity (musība). The prophet's illiteracy was a miracle, and the illiteracy of this man is a deficiency, not a miracle. Illiteracy debases (inhitāt) and does not elevate a person. But the Prophet's illiteracy was a miracle of God that comes to us in this honorable Book, the Quran, and through the honorable and purified prophetic tradition." Gomaa distinguished between the illiteracy of everyday people, which he described as demeaning, and the Prophet's illiteracy, which he described as a miracle of God. In doing so, Gomaa disciplined the idea of the Unlettered Prophet so that it served as evidence of the authenticity of revelation—not to be confused with an attribute of the Prophet to be emulated. The command directed toward Muhammad to read and the subsequent verses are commonly understood as the ultimate miracle of his prophecy. Although Gomaa explained Muhammad's illiteracy as part of the miracle of the Quran, it should be noted that this feature of revelation is typically understood as being distinct from the doctrine of the inimitable nature of the Quran (i ʿjāz), typically associated with the Quran's style and language, which I discuss in chapter 2.[13]

While literacy organizers invoked the first words of revelation to promote autonomous reading, in the context of Muhammad's experience of the revelation, the story of these first verses often centers the emotional impact of the immediacy the Prophet felt when he heard the command—the sensation of a pressing down of the message upon him. John Bowen describes the centrality of this episode in the Muslim understanding of revelation: "This epistemology of revelation—valuing the precise act of aural revelation, repeating the act of oral transmission—derives from the ideology of absolute and unmediated presence that founds the religion" (2012, 18).[14]

The reference to the Prophet as *al-nabī al-ummī* in the Quran (7:157–158) is widely taken as justification for the interpretation that he was unable to read or write, an understanding that became foundational to the Islamic theology of the miracle of the Quran's revelation through the Unlettered Prophet. While Quranic references are ambiguous as to whether Muhammad was able to read or write, the traditional interpretation of *ummī* as "illiterate" emerged in the early second/eighth century (Günther 2002). Belief in the Unlettered Prophet has theological significance, as his illiteracy is evidence of the authenticity of revelation through the pristine vessel of his person for the miracle of the Quran. Other interpretations of the term include a reference to the Arab people (specifically, as a people without scripture) or any people without scripture. Other meanings include "Meccan," "layman," and "heathen" (Günther 2002). *Ummī* could also be one living in "an original state" (relating to the term's association with *umm*, mother).[15]

At stake for Gomaa is the idea that the Prophet's illiteracy risks being interpreted as a shortcoming (*naqs*), while he should be properly understood as perfect (*kāmil*). Alternative understandings of *al-nabī al-ummī* may take him as unlettered, but do not equate Muhammad's illiteracy with ignorance, instead privileging unmediated knowledge (in this case, *wahy*) as superior to knowledge gleaned from texts. Notably, rather than distinguish among different kinds of knowledge, Gomaa distinguishes among different kinds of people (the Prophet and all others).

Unlike *gahil*, with its long association with depravity, the concept of *ummī* has been more ambivalent—the term is at once a moniker for the beloved Prophet and central to the early Muslim community's sense of distinction in Arabia. Muhammad is reported to have said: "We are an *ummī* nation, we do not write and do not calculate" (*innā umma ummiyya, la naktubu wa-lā nahsubu*).[16] The hadith has been interpreted to indicate that the Islamic calendar should not be calculated but rather should be based on observations of the moon by the human eye, a matter that has animated Islamic legal debates for centuries. Beyond the application to calculating time, the hadith supports a notion of an *ummī* community that distinguished Muslims from other communities of the Book. The *ummī* nation gave the early Muslims a sense of identity that served as the foundation for an authentic community— authentic because of the authenticity of revelation. So while the moniker *umma ummiyya* (an unlettered people) lent the early Muslim community a sense of distinction, the significant population of nonliterate Egyptians in the modern period is a mark of the country's underdevelopment—a *watan ummī* (an unlettered nation-state). By the mid-twentieth century, literacy had become a marker of a country's economic and social development. No longer carrying a sense of cultural distinction, to be an unlettered nation became an obstacle to development. This was the period in which, in Egypt and elsewhere in the region, illiteracy came to be stigmatized. The state took on a central role in education, contributing to how what it meant to be educated was radically changing. Perhaps no single figure in Egypt's modern history has played a greater role in publicly promoting literacy than former first lady Suzanne Mubarak.

THE FORMER FIRST LADY

In March 2011, the month following Mubarak's ouster, the American University in Cairo (AUC) Press was due to release what they called a memoir by Suzanne Mubarak, *Read Me a Book: The Story of Egypt's First Lady and Her Grandson.* The book cover and description were featured prominently on the first pages of the press's spring catalog. With the demise of the Mubaraks, the publication was first postponed until September 2011 and then finally canceled.[17] The book, written in English, was Suzanne Mubarak's narration of the importance of reading in the life of her grandson, Mohamed, who died in 2009 at the age of twelve from a health crisis rumored to have been a brain hemorrhage. The AUC Press endorsed the memoir as a "personal and poignant chronicle of a child's intellectual and emotional growth through reading, of a family tragedy, and of the universal trial of mourning" (American University in Cairo Press, Spring catalog 2011, 1).

In the months following the Mubaraks' ouster, particularly around the beginning of Hosni Mubarak's trial in the summer of 2011, Suzanne came to be depicted as a mastermind behind the wrongdoings of the former regime.[18] The public libraries she had established officially removed her name; Mubarak Public Libraries were renamed the Misr Public Library (allowing the logo with the acronym MPL to remain intact).

Read Me a Book furthered Suzanne Mubarak's advocacy for reading as a way to strengthen families, a major strategy in Egypt's literacy promotion and instruction. In an excerpt from her book, she describes the moment she discovered her grandson could read: "The moment when I realized Mohamed could read took me by surprise.... At first I thought he had just memorized the words—this was a favorite story, though we hadn't looked at it for some time. It was only when he halted, then tried out the letters of the word that was holding him up, that I understood what was happening" (American University in Cairo Press, Spring catalog 2011, 1). The first instance that Mohamed autonomously read is marked as a special moment. The passage distinguishes between what would have been unremarkable—having merely memorized the story—and her grandson's accomplishment: his ability to independently read. The moment, a climax of sorts, captures that distinct relation between the person and the page as uniquely powerful. Unlike Gomaa's exhortation, the passage does not engage an Islamic repertoire. In her telling of the first moment of autonomous reading, it is a moment of transformation. Distinct from the miracle of revelation that Gomaa describes, in her telling, the miraculous moment is that of his first time to autonomously read. The moment is marked as a distinct kind of miracle, a secular one.

Both Gomaa and Mubarak illustrate how the modern period ingrained particular religious sensibilities into autonomous reading practices. Rather than set religious against autonomous reading (or religious against critical reading, as Warner does to illustrate the pieties of critical reading), the push for literacy is indicative of the ways autonomous reading is made religious, even as it cultivates a distinct style, one oriented toward the individual subject's personal encounter with text. The public discourse of two well-known figures, one a representative of Egyptian Islamic reform and the other of the former regime's gendered developmentalism, depicts literacy as being endowed with miraculous powers. Together, the examples demonstrate at once a broadening sense of the miraculous while simultaneously a narrowing epistemological horizon where knowledge is based on texts to be read and cognitively understood.

In Egypt, reading is made religious across literacy programs in several ways. In what remains of the chapter, I depict two typical state-sponsored classes that are indicative of how religious lessons were interwoven into basic literacy classes. Religious lessons were a staple of the state-run literacy classes I attended. In contemporary Egypt, literacy classrooms are critical sites of Islamic da'wa. While teachers use a state-centric curriculum, their lessons make reading part of religious fundamentals. Through the lessons of Walid, a part-time teacher and electrician, and Layla, a teacher fully devoted to her preaching, we see teachers as everyday people and reformers who make reading a basis of knowledge for the performance of essential rituals.

The Religious Lessons of Secular State Education

In Manshiyat Nasser, a dense and sprawling quarter of central Cairo, the rock-dirt alleys turned into a network of paved roads and straight-edged concrete buildings as I approached the Suzanne Mubarak Residences (*Masākan Suzanne Mubarak*). The housing development was home to residents who had been relocated from a nearby neighborhood following a 2008 landslide that killed 119 people. There, a literacy class run by the National Council for Childhood and Motherhood brought together twenty-five women who sat at desks facing the front of the class. Walid, their teacher, sat at a desk perpendicular to them. An electrician who worked as a part-time teacher, Walid, like other state-employed literacy teachers, earned up to 150 Egyptian pounds per month, although it was rare to make that much. Teachers' salaries depended on the number of students in their class. Many teachers held other jobs or taught while looking for more work. Most held a diploma equivalent to two years of training after the final year of secondary school (*sanawaya*); several were university graduates.

It was late afternoon, and Walid came to class following a house call. He addressed his lesson to the side wall, occasionally turning his head to face his students, which appeared to be a way to show respect to his female students, a gesture of not looking directly into the faces of his female students. They used the textbook *You Read to Be Enlightened (Ittalam Ittanawar)*. The book, I was told, was used by 90 percent of classes across the country. Teachers discussed how the curriculum taught comprehensive development (*tanmiyya shāmila*) for its students. The early lessons trained learners to identify themselves with the national identification card. The curriculum spoke of the importance of claiming rights and promoting "good behavior" and "life development," as one educationist from the Egyptian Authority for Adult Education (EAAE) explained to me. *You Read to Be Enlightened* had the themes of modernist state education, and yet in classrooms, education as enlightenment was continually tied to religious fundaments, particularly around the apt performance of daily ritual.

In class, the women listened to Walid's lesson, his voice rising and falling, pulling them in. The day's class moved from topic to topic. The theme that he

returned to and stressed was that humanity cannot rely on its own rationality (ʿaql). To do so, he warned, is to be led astray. "Take ritual purification
(wudūʾ) before prayer, for example," he suggested.

> If we think with our own minds that the point of wudūʾ is to clean ourselves
> before facing God in prayer (salāt), then we will think that we should wash
> the bottom of our feet. It's the bottom of our feet that touches the ground.
> So, our rationality tells us to wash there. But instead, we rub our hands across
> the top of the foot, not the bottom. This is what God has told us to do. So, in
> wudūʾ, we do as God commands, and not what our mind tells us. We were
> told how to do it, and we must follow in that way, since there is good in it that
> we cannot understand.

The lesson questioned the role of rationality, calling on the women to develop discernment (tamyīz). He stressed the need for them to create within
themselves a conscience (damīr), to be able to know right from wrong. Walid:
"It isn't the law that tells us what is right or wrong. Law can leave at any moment, like it left Egypt. We can't follow the correct path only in fear of God
or hellfire. Conscience is the direction within us, it's learning to follow the
correct direction that we know within us."

Walid emphasized the proper performance of ritual, stressing that it
should be performed by an individual with a honed sense of right and wrong.
The lesson was a critique of the autonomous subject, but troubled such a
notion, who prioritizes their rationality over what is known through God's
command. In Walid's class, autonomous reading was not for the purpose of
cultivating an autonomous subject. As we'll see, while KIP made the act of
reading itself an act of worship, religious dimensions of Walid's class made
reading an occasion to learn religious rites and inculcate a subjectivity that
warned against a kind of autonomy not dependent on God.

Another state-run class illustrates the strong influence of daʿwa within
basic literacy. Layla had been teaching literacy for the EAAE since 2004
in the hamlet of Abu al-Numros in nearby Giza. The class was held at the
Institute for Religious Propagation and Recitation (Maʿhad al-Daʿwa wa-l-
Qirāʾāt), a modest two-story building where various religious lessons were
taught to locals. She saw her work as a literacy teacher as part of her daʿwa,
which she had been carrying out for twenty-six years. "When I meet these
women, they don't know how to pray. Many don't know al-Fātiha (Quran 1,
"The Opening"). They don't know the basics of purification, so I teach them
all the different kinds."

What troubled Layla about her community was that so many nonliterates could not worship God properly. She devoted lessons to the religious basics, but she was most dedicated to the purification of the dead (*ghusl al-mayyit*). When a women in the Abu al-Numros died, Layla was keen to volunteer to prepare the body for burial. During the months I visited her classes, she reviewed the words to be said while performing the actions of the cleansing ritual on a few occasions. The high ceiling carried the women's voices as they recited a morning remembrance of God (*dhikr*). Thirty women sat in a long and narrow room on a carpeted floor facing a small cream-colored board. She supervised the students she guided through the general motions of the *ghusl*. For Layla, the practice of reading was used as a prompt to aid the memorization of short passages deemed necessary for Muslim life.

Walid's and Layla's classrooms capture the dominant place of Islamic learning in basic literacy. Teachers became state-employed everyday reformers through their literacy work. Their lessons indicate the reach of the late Islamic revival—beyond mosque lessons, Friday *khutbas*, television programs, or religious organizations—to preach through the opportunity brought about by basic literacy. They taught within the formal structures of secular state education. The role of basic literacy as a site of revival demonstrates how schooling is adapted on the ground so that a curriculum that foregrounds enlightenment values can challenge and adapt the very basis of enlightenment thinking. Many state teachers take religious instruction as a necessary part of their students' curriculum. Their literacy classes were places of religious instruction that hosted discussions of crucial Muslim values and everyday rituals. Walid's and Layla's lessons emphasized the legal category of ʿibādāt, rituals or acts of worship, such as prayer (*salāt*), fasting (*sawm*), and ablution (*tahāra*). Scholars such as Wael Hallaq highlight how the details of the ritual performance of these acts have moral weight (116). In this way, reading became a site for the education of these foundational ritual acts.

The Egyptian state defines the contours of a proper Egyptian Islam. And yet, the literacy classes are an example of how a state project unfolds in unintended ways, so that the miraculous moment of autonomous reading is not only a reading for the nation but also the basis of forming a subject literate in religious fundamentals. In this way, the scenes from the state-sponsored classes reveal a distinct mode of religious reading, one that is distinct from scripture-based programs that we turn to in the following chapter, as well as from those of the literacy campaign, KIP, and that made autonomous reading in and of itself a religious practice.

Conclusions: Anxieties over an Unlettered Nation

Ten months after the fire destroyed the Institut d'Égypte, the building—renovated and restored—was inaugurated on October 22, 2012. The minister of culture thanked the armed forces for funding the restoration project (which totaled six million Egyptian pounds). The event celebrated the military's role in rebuilding Egypt, but even as officials were touring the renovated building, the dust had not settled from the battle over the institute. It was not only that "all of Egypt was crying" over the fire at the institute, as former head of the main library Zein Abdel-Hady put it. To mourn the institute was to cry for the nation—to bemoan a lost past and a present plagued by ignorance—to face an unlettered nation.

Listening in on ubiquitous talk about ignorance, one can detect anxieties about the country's large population of nonliterates. These anxieties make literacy a marker not only of national development but also of risk to the moral fabric and state of Islam in Egypt. On the one hand, ignorance is a scourge on the nation, holding it back from development and its potential after the overthrow of the Mubarak regime. On the other, as Salih Fathi confided, ignorance talk was so overwhelming that it was the very reason why some people joined literacy classes. Conversations about ignorance involve questions about education and what kind of education is a "proper one." Ignorance is at work in ideas about "good religion" and echoed in calls for creating modern Muslims. It is also at the center of mobilizing Egyptians for massive literacy efforts.

Through the words and efforts of officials and teachers, this chapter charted distinct responses to the question: What makes reading religious? Before further excavating the place of basic literacy in Egypt's late Islamic revival, I shift to explore the place of scripture as a motivator and technique for basic literacy. As I will show, contemporary trends in scripturalism at once drive and challenge the effort for universal literacy.

Notes

1. "Amid Street Clashes, Civilians Coordinate to Rescue Rare Documents," *Egypt Independent*, December 19, 2011, accessed March 13, 2024, https://egyptinde pendent.com/amid-street-clashes-civilians-coordinate-rescue-rare-documents/.

2. Associated Press in Cairo, "Cairo Institute Burned During Clashes," *Guardian*, December 19, 2011, https://www.theguardian.com/world/2011/dec/19/cairo -institute-burned-during-clashes, accessed March 13, 2024.

3. Fahmy translated the original Arabic piece into English for publication in *Cultural Anthropology*, http:/culanth.org/fieldsights/the-real-tragedy-behind -the-fire-of-institut-degypte.

4. The original nine-volume version was housed at the institute. The original eleven-volume version is at the Bibliotheca Alexandrina; a fully digitized version is available online.

5. In Thurston's study of the group, he explains how the name *Boko Haram* is an outsider's term that limits the meaning of *boko* to Western education. It should instead indicate a broader distrust of Western institutions and culture (2017, 16). The group followed critiques of Western education articulated by their founder, Muhammed Yusuf, who argued that Western styles of education contradicted the tenets of Islam: "These foreign, global, colonialist schools have embraced matters that violate Islamic law, and it is forbidden to operate them, support them, study and teach in them" (as quoted by Thurston 2017, 14).

6. Andeel, *Tok Tok* #12.

7. For a rich discussion of ignorance in Egyptian media, see Armbrust's (1996) depiction of ignorance in television series and films that are part of a strong modernist discourse.

8. Sherine Hamdy observes that media commonly depict how ignorance brings about social conditions rather than economic conditions that lead to ignorance (2012).

9. The transliterated Arabic here represents the common Egyptian colloquial nomenclature for these social categories. In rendering the status categories into English, I leave them in their awkward English translations to draw attention to their constructedness. For readability, I do not use quotation marks or italics.

10. See Atiyeh's edited volume (1995) on the social, spiritual, and metaphorical aspects of "the Book" in Muslim societies.

11. The use of the word *kitāb* in the Quran is most commonly glossed as "book," but it also means "record" or "written page." The *kitāb* is not a "bound, written codex" but rather a symbol for God's knowledge and authority (Madigan 2001). The Arabic word is based on the verb for writing, *kataba*.

12. Gomaa, a prominent Islamic scholar, supported the 2013 coup and later retired. On Gomaa's positions during the fraught 2013 period, see Warren (2017).

13. According to the Sunni orthodox view that Gomaa relayed, the first words of revelation came to the Prophet in the year 610 when he was forty years old. The revelation took place while he was on Mount Ḥira, which he visited frequently for seclusion and meditation. The Prophet's wife, Aisha Siddiqa, is the source of two narrations of the first revelation, as relayed in the hadith collections of Bukhari and Muslim. She describes how her husband retreated to the cave of Hira:

> The angel came to him and said, "Iqraʾ!" He replied, "I am not a reader." The Prophet says, "He held me and pressed hard until I was exhausted, then he

released me and said, 'Iqra'!'" and I replied, "I am not a reader." He held me and
pressed me hard a second time until I was exhausted, then he released me and said,
"Iqra'!" I replied, "I am not a reader." He then held me and pressed me hard for the
third time. Then he said, "Iqra' in the name of your Lord who has created—created
man out of a germ-cell. Iqra'—for your Lord is the most Bountiful One, who
has taught the use of the pen, taught man what he did not know." The Prophet
returned home to Khadijah trembling and said, "Wrap me! Wrap me!" They
wrapped him and his fear subsided. He turned to Khadijah and exclaimed, "What
has happened to me?" and related to her what had happened and said, "I fear for
myself." (Qutb 1979, 194–195).

14. For an example of a different depiction of the first revelation of the Quran
to Muhammad and the tension among versions of revelation that prioritize
immediacy over mediation, see Daniel Madigan (2001), who emphasizes the
mediatory role of the angel between the Prophet and God. Notably, Muslim
theories of revelation continue to animate theological debates today, with intellectual reformers turning to orthodox versions of revelation as a starting point
for their interpretive interventions. For examples, see Arkoun (1984), and Abū
Zayd (1992, 2006).

15. See Günther (2002) for a full discussion of medieval and modern scholarly
debates on understandings of *ummī*. Joel Blecher narrates an eleventh-century
controversy surrounding the interpretation of a hadith. He describes the interpretive moves of Abu al-Walid al-Baji (d. 474/1081), who claimed, "Muhammad
did not write well, but he wrote" (2018, 21). The claim is an example of an alternative interpretation that the Prophet gained facility after the first moment of
revelation and that his ability to write in the episode of the treaty of Hudaybiyya
was one of his miracles. Despite the controversy elicited by Baji, Blecher notes:
"While he maintained that Muhammad once wrote, he just as forcefully maintained the doctrine of the 'unlettered Prophet'" (27).

16. As narrated in the hadith collection of Bukhari, chapter no. 31, Fasting
no. 137.

17. The Press declined my request to see the unreleased book, stating: "The
publication of Suzanne Mubarak's "Read Me a Book" was postponed indefi-
nitely after the Revolution last year, at the author's request. So it has never been
printed, and no copies exist" (personal communication).

18. The heavily gendered depictions were typical of the way former first ladies
from fallen regimes of the Middle East uprisings were characterized in the
media. See, for example, *Foreign Policy Blogs*, http://mideastafrica.foreignpolicy
.com/posts/2011/02/16/first_ladies_as_focal_points_for_discontent.

PART II

~

THE WORD OF GOD FOR ALL

2

The Quran and Bible as Method

Doing basic literacy with the Quran adds some complications.
—Magdy Fahmy, Egyptian Authority for Adult Education

For us, it [teaching literacy] is easy. The challenge is not
the Arabic language. In fact, it is the opposite. The real
question is: Is your heart supple, ready to receive
the Quran? This is the condition for learning.
—Shaykh Ahmed, principal of a private Islamic school

We have an Egyptian saying: "When a door is closed,
see if there is a window you can jump through."
—Ramez Atallah, general secretary of the Bible Society of
Egypt on the organization's effort to disseminate
the Bible in Egypt

The Egyptian Authority for Adult Education (EAAE), a low-ranking sub-ministry, is housed in a five-story building far from other government ministries. The EAAE is responsible for adult basic literacy, which falls beyond the purview of the Ministry of Education and the Ministry of Higher Education and Scientific Research. Literacy planner Magdy Fahmy pointed out the predicament posed by using the Quran for basic literacy. On one hand, drawing on the Quran for literacy makes sense as critical pedagogy. The technique would gain the approval of Paulo Freire himself: "Freire tells us to use the language of the learners." By that point in my fieldwork, I was accustomed to literacy teachers mobilized by the uprising referring to Freire's theory of literacy as a technique of empowerment and *conscientization*. But I had not expected his name to surface among teachers explaining Read in the Name of Your Lord (RITNOYL, *Iqra' bi-smi Rabbika alladhī Khalaq*), a state-sponsored literacy program that used Quran excerpts as curriculum. On the other hand, Magdy noted: "Doing basic literacy with the Quran adds some complications." Magdy referred to how Quranic Arabic is at once a familiar language for people surrounded by its sounds and who use it in prayer and simultaneously an elevated language, revered and widely considered out of reach to most Egyptians.

To teach basic literacy with the Quran, then, did not teach an Arabic for everyday life, as basic literacy is typically designed to do. In the past, literacy was based on a person's facility with the Quran. Perhaps nowhere was this idea most evident than with the Quran as the basis of education in the institution of the *kuttāb*. The *kuttāb* was the earliest stage of schooling primarily made up of learning the Quran through memorization, dictation, and writing. To begin literacy instruction with scripture then has historical precedent. Yet, where Magdy saw complications in using the Quran as curriculum, others saw miracles.

For Shaykh Ahmed, a Salafi private school principal, Quranic Arabic was a blessing for anyone seeking to learn to read using the proper methods. For yet another pedagogue, the Presbyterian director of the Bible Society of Egypt (BSE), Ramez Atallah, literacy starts with the Bible because the world follows on Logos—word, speech, discourse, reason.[1] Although less popular than other contemporary Arabic literacy training curricula, Quran and Bible passages are resources to encounter God's Word (*kalām Allāh*) with the skill of autonomous reading.[2] In this way, the three men led literacy initiatives that drew on holy books as a method for literacy instruction. They saw scripture as an invitation to read, and reading as a way to get closer to God, to discover how to best decipher what they each referred to as God's Word and will.[3] For them, God's Word offered the most important signs (*āyāt*) as the basis of learning, to enable students to move from Word to world.

This chapter focuses on how literacy programs articulated and managed notions of meaning in literacy programs that use scripture as curriculum. To probe the pedagogical debates that these curricula raise, I focus on teachers' and educationists' theories of language and understanding. Each of the programs offers different views in the heated debates over Arabic language literacy pedagogy. These contestations have resonance in American fights over the best way to instruct basic literacy in primary education. In the United States, in 2023, the latest "fight over phonics" led to a major overhaul of the school curriculum. These changes included school boards turning away from "balanced literacy," an approach that encourages students to choose books and read independently, learning to decipher words based on context and illustrations as they cultivate a love of reading.[4] In contrast, a movement with wide support called the "the science of reading" emphasized the use of phonics to sound out words. Phonics, advocates advance, is better supported in cognitive research as an effective method for basic literacy.

Unlike other chapters that situate literacy education in action, this chapter focuses on how literacy is directed "from above" by paying attention to the institutions (state, informal networks, and NGOs) and individuals (state employees, curriculum designers, and teachers) who seek to direct literacy for God's Word. Three literacy programs based on God's Word are illustrative of the dense field of Muslim and Christian efforts to endorse autonomous reading. I begin with the state-sponsored program Read in the Name of Your Lord (RITNOYL), then the internationally successful The Baghdadi Primer (TBP, *Al-Qāʿidat al-Baghdādiyya*), and finally the BSE program Read Your Book (*Iqraʾ Kitābak*). The BSE's efforts to reform Coptic Bible practices bring into relief polemics, mirroring, and distinction-making around the three text-centered *daʿwa* and missionary efforts. The brief treatment of Protestant literacy in this chapter does not allow space to flesh out the intra-Christian diversity and political strands raised not only by the uprising but also as a consequence of the passing of Pope Shenouda III, when he was succeeded by Bishop Tawadros (formally Pope Tawadros II) in 2012. Many Copts sought a new relationship between the church and community, as well as for Copts as citizens in Egypt (Sedra 2012).

Through their distinct reading strategies based on their approach to the Arabic language, we observe scripturalist trends in contemporary religious reform across distinct revivalist players. Their curricula are shaped by their language ideologies, what Kathryn Woolard defines as how languages "envision and enact ties of language to identity, to aesthetics, to morality, and to epistemology" (1998, 3). Paying attention to language ideology means paying attention to how linguistic form and language use shape ideas of the self as well as "religious ritual, child socialization, gender relations, the nation-state, schooling, and law" (Woolard 1998, 3).

The RITNOYL program demonstrates state efforts to direct a meaning-centered Quran engagement, one that is notably unpopular among teachers. As teachers explained to me, their efforts to instruct literacy with the Quran are stymied and fail in the classroom. The RITNOYL campaign is a telling case of how basic literacy and the Quran can make an awkward fit. In contrast, TBP, produced by the Salafi educationist Shaykh Moustafa Elgindy, as it was taught in an Islamic private school, begins with how to identify and create the sounds of Arabic letters. For those who use TBP, the curriculum offers the skills of autonomous reading made possible through the miraculous potency of Arabic as a sacred language. Finally, the BSE's Bible-based literacy program sought to establish a multigenerational community and alternative to Egyptian schooling in an effort to discipline Coptic Bible reading practices that many within the BSE perceived as too determined by an Arabic oral tradition dominated by Muslim ways of approaching the Quran. Both RIT-NOYL and RYB marshaled textbooks that drew on scriptural passages to instruct autonomous reading, while TBP deployed a method based on pho-nemes that emphasized letters and sounds, before introducing the Quran.

How are the Quran and the Bible deployed to mobilize literacy? What do pedagogical approaches to scripture-based literacy tell us about reform-ers' ideas of language and cognition? What political implications and social ramifications are brought about by these scripture-based curricula? How do the programs imagine reading subjects and collectives? In what ways do their distinct idioms of revivalism speak to and against each other? This chap-ter focuses on literacy planners' and teachers' hermeneutical aims for how scripture ought to be read and the pedagogical strategies they deployed to guide nonliterate people to do so. Looking across three groups broadens our view of distinct reformist literacy interventions—specifically, their styles of scripturalism and their conception of Logos, human cognition, and distinct language ideologies that condition social relations. Crucially, these literacy programs attempt to shape the ideal subject's relation to God.

Scripturalism in Revival and Revolution

The prominence and longevity of these programs are indicative of scriptur-alist trends in Muslim and Christian revivalism in Egypt as well as those trends born of modern education that shape scriptural encounters globally. I refer to these programs as scripturalist because of their methodology and a worldview that centers scripture culturally and politically. As I explain, there are different kinds of scripturalism—differentiated not only by religious distinctions (Muslim, Christian, and so on) but also by their hermeneutical practices that attempt to cultivate the relationship between the individual and text—a relationship that is articulated in corporeal terms. Each of the literacy programs relates and responds to a past through distinct reading practices that center the role of the body in reading, as well as the impacts of reading on the body (with attention to the eye, the tongue, and the heart). The pedagogues in this chapter focus on teaching methods as they try to implement the best technique to instruct autonomous reading. As I show, their teaching methods are premised on particular ideas of how God's Word works in the world.

Religiously sponsored literacy reveals a modern religious sensibility that measures proximity to scriptural text as proximity to God. It is a site of missionary work and *da'wa*. The twentieth century gave rise to modern scripturalism within the Islamic and coterminous Coptic revivals that deployed various educational projects to create a pious public sphere.[5] This scripturalism is imbricated in modern conceptions of the role of scripture in daily life. Following on Haeri's study of the sacred status of the Arabic language that asks, What does it mean to modernize a language? (2003), this chapter examines what it means to modernize reading God's Word.

Among Egypt's religious reformers, both Muslim and Christian, the skill of autonomous reading is proffered as a necessity for properly encountering God's Word. Despite differences in Christian and Muslim conceptions of revelation and scriptural practices, many are today united in their focus on the textual form of scripture and making that form accessible to all. To autonomously read the Quran and the Bible has become an essential, taken-for-granted practice for a modern—and heavily classed—religious sensibility. What has emerged among particular reformist strands of each of these traditions is the belief that God's Word is best encountered through autonomous reading.

Observers of modern scripturalism deploy the metaphor of "transparency" to depict how the mastery of the Arabic language is essential to reformers for deciphering the Quran.[6] The metaphor captures the significant role of immediate and accessible meaning, implying that classical modes of embodiment leave the semantic and cognitive meanings of the Quran opaque. The visual metaphor expands our attention to the senses so that audition is not the exclusive sensory mode. The language of transparency and opacity invites us to consider the Quran's language of veiling and unveiling as well as its self-reference to verses that are clear in meaning (*muhkamāt*) and others that are ambiguous (*mutashābihāt*).[7] The categories are fluid, suggesting the interpretive role of the Quran's audience, even for supposedly self-evident verses.

As we hear from teachers and through the curricula, scripture ought to be read in particular ways: it should not be recited by rote, it should be made attractive in order to be accessible, and it ought to be contemplated and applied in life. Some of the differences that underlie the different programs' approaches fuel tensions over who an ideal reader should be and the kinds of collectivities they should form among their learners. In each of these cases, scripture is deployed to different political effect. Indeed, Egyptians drew on scripture to incite, understand, and orient themselves to the uprising.

The comparative conversation I sketch between the literacy programs contributes to a new generation of scholarship that brings Muslim and Coptic interactions into focus (Baron 2014; Heo 2018; Mahmood 2016; Schielke 2012).[8] It also subverts trends in the study of religion and mediation that continue to examine Muslim societies as oral (e.g., Hirschkind 2006; Gade 2004; Eisenlohr 2009) and Christian ones as visual (e.g., Meyer and Moors 2006; cf. Schmidt 2000). Indeed, the ethnography of reading is largely centered on Christianity and the Bible (Boyarin 1993; Crapanzano 2000; Engelke 2007, 2013; Bielo 2009a, 2009b). Reformist programs are forged through spoken and unspoken polemics as well as real and imagined interactions with each other and as they interface with state institutions.

The Quran as Curriculum: Modernizing the *Kuttāb*

Like grassroots groups that emerged following the uprising to teach basic literacy, Magdy Fahmy, a senior-level educationist in the EAAE, similarly attempted to draw momentum from the uprising to make literacy a national priority. State-run literacy programs trouble a monolithic understanding of "state" education. Literacy classes are loosely organized, and, despite common training sessions, classes are as varied as the teachers who lead them. While most classrooms deploy nationalist-modernist curricula, the EAAE experimented with a novel literacy curriculum. RITNOYL, based on the shortest chapters of the Quran, was one such experiment. Despite its novelty among late twentieth-century curricula, the EAAE marshaled older methods of instructing basic literacy that were premised on the Quran. In her discussion of the first printed Quran in Egypt, Natalia Suit explains how the printing ordered by Muhammad Ali in 1832 "was most probably inspired by his need to teach the growing future cadre of soldiers and clerks to read and write. Throughout the Middle East, Qur'anic verses were commonly used in teaching literacy, so perhaps the Basha—who was himself illiterate—elected to print them with this didactic purpose in mind" (2020, 21).

Although Magdy was a major figure in Egyptian literacy programming, his colleagues were at ease around him. During our meetings, EAAE employees came and went, sometimes joining in our conversations. They would often elaborate on his explanations to help me better understand. While state teachers were often minimally trained in how to instruct in adult education, my conversations with state curriculum planners were steeped in their knowledge of education theory. In our discussions, they took on the role of patient instructor, pausing at points in our conversation to ensure I could ask questions and taking an interest in how I took notes. They were keen to see me complete the research and always interested to hear my thoughts on the classes that I observed.

Magdy: "Literacy needs to come from the lives of those who are learning. It must be a part of their own environments (bī'a). In Freire's work in coastal Brazil, this meant discovering words that had to do with the sea and fishing. For us today, in Egypt, it means the Quran." Magdy referred to Freire's emphasis on situating learning in the lives of learners. State-employed educationists spoke about the need to capture the attention of the learners and cultivate in them the desire to learn. Most explained that the Quran was the best way to motivate their students. In this way, making literacy a part of everyday life did not mean teaching vocabulary like farming implements or deciphering the expiration date of medicine (as seen in popular textbooks); instead, it meant centering the Quran.

Magdy: "The Quran is a part of their lives, and they want to know it better. This is a program for people who love religion. Egyptians clearly do: look at the election results that prove this." He referred to the success of the Muslim Brotherhood to prove the importance of religion in Egyptians' lives. Still, despite the EAAE's belief that the Quran was the best way to motivate people to learn, Magdy and other senior planners admitted that the sole curriculum that drew on the Quran for literacy posed pedagogical challenges for teachers and learners.

In the early 2000s, the curriculum was introduced by the Ministry of Endowments (*Wizarat al-Awqaf*). Classes were held in mosques by religion and Quran teachers. Magdy explained that under Mubarak, it was difficult to teach religion, which complicated implementing the curriculum. The program was moved to the EAAE in order to better align it with adult education rather than religious lessons. Written by educationist Jasim Mahmud Al-Hasum, RITNOYL was first used in Algeria and later taken up in a number of Arab countries. The program was "religious" not because of how teachers, often *dā'iyyas*, couched classes in moral and ritual lessons (as seen in Walid's and Layla's classes in chap. 1) but because of the text to which nonliterate people were introduced—the shortest chapters of the Quran, the ones most common for Muslims to have memorized. Across the EAAE offices I visited, educationists spoke glowingly of the program. But like many things to do with literacy, the curriculum existed in theory but not in practice. While many touted its innovative approach to literacy, in reality, very few teachers wanted to use it. Only when I pressed to visit classrooms did planners reluctantly share that the curriculum posed unique challenges for teachers. The curriculum that employs short Quranic chapters was based on texts that many of the students had already memorized, making it difficult to know if a student was "reading" the text by memory or reading autonomously.

In the few cases where RITNOYL was used, it was in rural areas where, planners explained, Quran lessons are less threatening to those who might see literacy classes as unacceptable for women. An EAAE teacher of sixteen years described the importance of using the Quran as a textbook among communities that do not see literacy as beneficial for women: "These classes are popular in places where women leave their homes twice in their lives: once to get married and once when they die. When you ask one of these women where she is coming from, she'll say she was learning the Quran, not that she was learning writing and reading." Another EAAE employee continued, "They come to the class knowing some Quran verses. So teachers work with this knowledge to instruct them in how to identify how the words they know look on the page."

RITNOYL did not aim to be just another literacy program. It attempted to improve Quran education through pedagogical techniques centered on meaning. In its conception, the program sought not only to resemble Quran education, as Magdy pointed out, but also to improve on it with "updated methods." According to Magdy, "This curriculum takes the benefits of religious education, and is committed to overcoming its problems, based on modern science."

> Me: "How do you know when a learner is autonomously reading or when she is reciting the verse from memory?"
> Magdy: "Now this is a good question."

THE EYE IS LIKE A CAMERA: THE QURAN'S MEANING BEFORE ITS SOUND

Perhaps because of the unique challenges of bringing autonomous reading to bear on the Quran, RITNOYL was the literacy program most self-conscious about demarcating the goal of literacy as *modern reading* (*al-qirā'a al-ḥāditha*). The opening pages of the teacher's manual describe the concept: "Reading is the process of accessing language through one's eyes, just as listening is the process of language arriving in one's ears. In reading, language does not consist of sounds as it does in listening, rather it is written symbols. While when listening, a person addresses you through articulated language, in reading they do so through written language. This is the foundation of reading" (Al-Hasum 1992, 6). The manual underscores modern reading, what I call autonomous reading, as associated with the visual, with the act dependent on the eye deciphering letters and words on a page to make meaning. The visual is what makes the activity modern, with other modes of text processing not recognized as reading. The approach captures enlightenment's ocularcentrism. Modern reading is explicitly not an oral/auditory experience. The eye is privileged over the ear to distinguish the practice. Notably, the curriculum advances modern reading as the proper mode for encountering the Quran.

The RITNOYL program emphasized the meanings of words and their cognitive understanding in a method premised on word recognition (*al-tarīqa al-kalima*). Although the curriculum makes some minor use of the phonetics-based approach (what was widely referred to by my interlocutors as *sūra basariyya*), it was primarily based on word recognition. Teachers were instructed that beginning with sounds and letters distracts the learner from understanding a word's meaning. The concept of modern reading guides teachers to instruct their students to prioritize sight over other senses (namely, sound). The teacher's guide promotes vision not for a phonetic approach to language but as a sight-based approach to it. In this way, it is "especially" visual, cuing the reader into the image of a word and not its letters.[9] In Magdy's view, phonemes slowed early readers. The thin workbook with large print begins with *al-Fātiha*, Quran 1, ("The Opening"), and then the short chapters that conclude the Quran (from 93 to 114). The ideal class is led by a teacher skilled in the proper pronunciation and elocution of Quran (*tajwīd*). Teachers are trained to begin by discussing the general meaning of the chapter, which is supposed to motivate their students to read. Students write the verses on the board, in notebooks, or on notecards. Every student must be able to see the written words. Then the teacher reads the verses several times, slowly, pointing to each of the words as they are pronounced so that students can recognize the word in its written form. The teacher recites the surah three or four times in the same way. Finally, the teacher returns to meaning, discussing individual words, and the chapter's overall message. The teacher's manual explains that this method leads with "the search for meaning and the ability to know the meaning of a word in context" (1992, 8). This, the guide explains, is what excites learners.

The meaning-centered approach prioritizes word recognition since "the whole is simpler than the part," as one teacher elaborated. The idea is that the student is first exposed to the word because it is the word they are familiar with, not the letter. In this way, instruction moves from what students are familiar with (the word) to the unfamiliar symbol (the letter), the thing without meaning. As the manual puts it: "Letters do not have meaning, words and sentences do" (1992, 8).

Magdy summarized: "The eye is like a camera. It takes the same effort for the camera to capture a small scene as it does a sprawling landscape, just as the eye can take in a letter the same way it takes in a word. We want students to work towards this visual way of learning, so that they are not distracted by sounds, but can read the word as a whole as if it were a picture." The RITNOYL curriculum encourages autonomous reading of the Quran, yet through the pedagogical challenges that it poses, we see how students are not attuned to the sensory economy of "modern reading" that they are instructed in.

Limited exercises introduced later in the program address everyday vernacular vocabulary in a limited way. As students progress through the lessons that introduce letters and Quranic vocabulary, a few examples of non-Quranic vocabulary are included based on resemblance with Quranic words. For example, *mustafā* appears beside the word *mustashfā* (which changes the meaning from "the chosen one" to "hospital" with minor changes in the letters). The focus on Quranic Arabic means students are ill prepared for the state exam that asks learners to write a paragraph about their daily lives.

The Quran is put to work as a textbook because it is a text in the lives of nonliterate people (part of their environment, as EAAE put it) with text that they recognize. While it draws on a familiar (and beloved to many) source, it does so in unfamiliar ways. The curriculum was designed as a corrective to the *kuttāb*. In stressing the need to autonomously read the Quran, RITNOYL took up nineteenth-century reformist and missionary efforts to transform Egyptians through new notions of knowledge and corollary practices that mark an epistemological distance from classical modes of Quran encounter.

Like the *kuttāb*, RITNOYL begins with the Quran; however, it does so by centering the concept of modern reading as the ideal way to encounter the Quran. The curriculum underscores the broader aims of much literacy advocacy in Egypt: to guide Quranic encounters, transforming classical Quranic practices frequently seen by secularists and reformers alike as a stumbling block to an illumined Islam. Where RITNOYL starts with meaning and moves backward to sounds, the popular method, TBP, is based on the sacred sound of the Arabic language. The curriculum is based on instructing phonological awareness, the capacity to recognize and interact with the auditory components of language. In the view of one of its teachers, through the Arabic language, God makes the difficult, even the impossible, easy.

The Children's Shaykh

Shaykh Moustafa Elgindy's voice is thin and nasal. His white beard flows down the front of a white *thawb* (ankle-length robe), and his slight shoulders curve downward with age. He is the author of several reading manuals, the most famous of which is TBP, an internationally popular reading program produced in the 1990s originally targeted at teaching children to read the Quran. The curriculum is named after a high period of Islamic civilization in Baghdad, one when Arabic grammar flourished. Across the world, the curriculum is lauded as a breakthrough method for non-Arabic speakers who find its focus on sound effective.

I met the Salafi teachers, who introduced me to Elgindy by accident. One of my roommates at the time, a German convert to Islam who learned about Islam through Salafi scholars and networks, returned home one evening to report to me that she had seen something I would be interested in: her teachers had needed to run a few errands and brought her along, making a stop at a gigantic garage filled with literacy textbooks. This group of young men who performed *da'wa* among new Muslims was also committed to expanding literacy in Egypt. They had redoubled their efforts following the ouster of Mubarak, first seeking sponsorship from the government, and when that was unsuccessful, turning to contacts in Turkey and Saudi Arabia for funding. They were passionate about a literacy program they said was unique. They approached basic literacy through what they understood as the sacred status of the classical Arabic language, emphasizing a phonetics approach to reading through sacred sound.

At a cafe in downtown Cairo, a young Salafi explained the urgency of his literacy work: "We prefer not to work with the ministry. The thing is, people don't want the country to be better. What we can do privately is much bigger. Students spend months in their lessons and most cannot read when they finish. But with us it is something totally different. Our students learn with love, and they learn quickly. What Shaykh Moustafa has created is something inspired (*wahy*). You must see it for yourself."

Many of the Salafi teachers I met spoke warmly about Elgindy, referring to him as "Shaykh Moustafa." They shared YouTube clips on their phones of their teacher giving lessons to small children. Elgindy gave parents and teachers tips on how to teach their children how to read the Quran. In one clip, a small boy sits on Elgindy's lap in front of an open Quran on a stand in front of them. A dozen five-year-olds sit nearby watching, sometimes distracted as the shaykh gives his lesson. The children play with their hands, turning to their neighbor to touch them, and the shaykh remains patient, telling viewers never to strike a child when reading, or they will associate the humiliation with reading the Quran. In another clip, a young girl comes to Elgindy's side as he opens the Quran to a random page and runs his finger along it, guiding her to display her mastery. She reads half a page. He pats her on the head and kisses her on the cheek: "*Māshā' Allah, Māshā' Allah, Allāhu Akbar*" (This is God's will, God is the greatest).

Elgindy's gentle demeanor and ease with children subvert popular images of Salafis in both European and Arabic language media as severe and unbending.[10] Among educators and many parents, Elgindy is known for his method for teaching children and adults how to read Arabic. In addition to TBP, Elgindy has written other works deploying the same theory, including *Learn Arabic Reading with Quranic Words* (*Taʿlīm al-Qirāʾa bi-Kalimāt Qurʾāniyya*) and *The Rules of Reciting the Quran* (*Aḥkām Tartīl al-Qurʾān*), and he offers teacher training courses and certification in his method. The course Teaching Arabic Reading with Phonemes directs teachers to use the method that Elgindy has become famous for over the last three decades, applying the rules of sound (*bi-l-qawāʿid al-sawtiyya*) to learning.

SOUND BEFORE MEANING

The school, Amgad, occupies half of the fifth floor in an apartment block in the sprawling concrete district of Nasser City. In one class, twenty seven-year-olds sat in small chairs facing the front board, practicing letter sounds with their teacher. In another room, eight women, most of them mothers of the children next door, sat around a meeting table, each with their own copy of the Quran. They dressed in stiff overcoats with embroidered or rhinestone patterns on the breast and loose hijabs—an aesthetic that distinguished them as part of a pious middle class. The school used money from the children's tuition to cover the costs of the women's class. The women had completed the same curriculum their children worked through and advanced directly to reading from the Quran.

The school was the project of Shaykh Ahmed, a graduate of al-Azhar University's sharia and education program. He worked as a teacher for ten years and took on the directorship three years prior to our meeting. He spoke with me in classical Arabic. Despite his formal language, he wore jeans and a T-shirt. When I began to tell Shaykh Ahmed that he was the first to describe teaching Arabic literacy as easy, he intervened: "We are teaching Arabic, which is different from any other language." He referred to the Muslim belief in the inimitability of the Quran, its *iʿjāz*. The doctrine of the miraculous inimitability attests to the divine origin of the Quran as God's divine speech.[11] Unlike other teachers who spoke of the many challenges in teaching Arabic, Shaykh Ahmed explained how if one approaches Arabic mindful of its uniquely blessed character, the students are able to learn with ease.

The community surrounding the school and those who teach from TBP curriculum do not all refer to themselves as Salafis. Shaykh Ahmed rejected the term, a distinction he made clear in an exchange one day about the possible students who might learn from TBP. I asked him whether non-Muslims can learn Arabic with TBP. Rather than directly answer the question, he stated that "Christians aren't People of the Book (*Ahl al-Kitāb*). Only Muslims." When I asked whether that understanding of People of the Book was important to Salafi theology (*aqīda*), he maintained: "We're all Salaf, *al-hamdu-li-llāh*. Egypt is *Ahl al-Sunna*. We're all *Salaf.* I do not say Salafi, since we are Muslim."

My question about non-Muslims drew him immediately to a polemic regarding who is included in the Quranic term *Ahl al-Kitāb*, People of the Book. While there is a range of interpretations, the orthodox position regards the audience of exhortations in the Quran to *Ahl al-Kitāb* as those people who have revealed scripture, Jews and Christians (as well as Zoroastrians and others).[12] His claim about who are considered within this group marked him as part of Egyptian Salafism. Salafis gained political influence in the year following Mubarak's ouster. They played a leading role in education policy between 2011 and 2013. Following the 2013 coup, some Salafis were arrested in the crackdown on Islamists, while others sided with Abdel Fattah el-Sisi against the Muslim Brotherhood. While many spoke of the increasing influence of Salafism in Egypt at the time, my interlocutors at the private Islamic school in Nasser City persistently resisted defining it. Indeed, for them, to define Salafism meant to limit it, while they understood their theology as a universal Sunnism. Notably, Salafis depend heavily on autonomous reading in their practices and studies through their production and circulation of print media.

Arabic was a preferred topic of Ahmed's. For him, like many educated Arabs, the Arabic language is celebrated for sophisticated grammar and rhetoric. Among those who celebrate Arabic, there are those like Ahmed who revere it as a sacred language. He understood the study of Arabic, including Arabic literacy, as the study of religion.[13] In this view, the study of the Arabic language is rewarded by God as the study of the Islamic tradition. Each time we met, he told me some version of the story of Ya'rub ibn Qahtan. In his telling, Ya'rub was the first Arabic speaker. He was a descendant of the prophet Hud and a great king who ruled over Yemen. He built an empire, but what made him important was that he was the first to speak Arabic. The language is named after him.

Ahmed: "It is easy for us [to instruct literacy] because of the power of the Quran's language. Our goal is the Quran and our language is not like any other. Our students learn smoothly. We have three-year-olds who can read the Quran. One of the Quran's blessings is its language. The real question is: Is your heart supple, ready to receive the Quran?"

He elaborated on the curriculum's method: "You have to hear and see the parts before you can see or speak the whole." For Ahmed, TBP was essential to opening a sensitivity to sound that enabled students with a technique to learn independently. He explained: "Working with sounds uses the brain in different ways than word recognition. We teach the letters in ten days. After twenty hours, an illiterate person can read anything in Arabic. A foreigner can learn in fifty hours over a hundred days."

The phonological training of the curriculum starts with letters and then places them side by side in combinations that do not make words. The idea is that students will get used to seeing different letter combinations that draw attention to their sounds, since they do not make up words which would allow for a learner to recognize a word and associate it with its meaning. Shaykh Ahmed explained that the method adopts practices used for Quran memorization training (*hifz*). Lessons involve detailed sound rules—how to pronounce letters properly in the mouth—distinguishing between heavy letters (*tafkhīm*) and light ones (*tarqīq*). As students advance, they read samples from the Quran. As he explained their approach, Shaykh Ahmed reminded me of the disconnected letters (*al-hurūf al-muqatta'a*), individual letters or letters in a sequence that appear at the start of twenty-nine Quran chapters.[14] Fourteen letters (exactly half of the Arabic alphabet) appear in this way. When reciting these short verses, the reader pronounces the name of each letter. Quran interpreters have spilled much ink on the meaning of the mysterious letters. For those who elaborate on the sacred (and sometimes unknowable) language of the Quran, the mysterious letters are evidence that sacredness is not only in meaning or even written words but also in the letters themselves.

In Egypt, Ahmed was part of a network of educationists using the curriculum. He had friends in Damietta, Farafra, and Mansoura with private Islamic schools similar to his own in Nasser City. For Shaykh Ahmed, the proof of the miracle of the curriculum is that the method is effective anywhere in the world. This claim of universality was part of his modern take on the classical *i'jāz* claim. The method locates a human connection to divine language that does not distinguish between adult and child, Arabic speaker or non-Arabic speaker. This approach collapses such social distinctions in a universalist view of language.

The curriculum they drew upon, TBP should not be understood as a Salafi textbook—as it is taken up far more widely—yet its method makes sense in a Salafi world. It is unashamed of rejecting modern educational methods and grounding its successes in this very rejection. It seeks to enhance and elaborate methods developed in the *kuttāb* for contemporary use, whereas RITNOYL sought to modernize those methods. Despite the rising political presence of Salafis and their relative successes in navigating the political maelstrom following the uprising, the teachers I spoke with felt embattled, frustrated by not being able to see their efforts translate into something larger than a small private school in an apartment block. They saw a world set against Islam, against truth and justice. They felt isolated from the power of the Muslim Brotherhood and alienated from ministry officials. Shaykh Ahmed was frustrated with the country, had no faith in the government, and distrusted the majority of Egyptians who, he repeatedly mentioned, did not want to make Egypt better. He took satisfaction in the belief that God's Word provides ease.

The Bible in Your Own Heart Language

Ramez Atallah reminded his audience of the possibilities for spreading God's Word in Egypt instead of dwelling, as so many do, on the country's problems. A Presbyterian who took up the leadership of the BSE in the 1990s, Ramez speaks frequently to international audiences about Egypt's Christians, 90 percent of whom are Copts, making the BSE's work the effort of a minority within a minority. At the spring 2018 meeting of the Forum of Christian Leaders, he began: "We have an Egyptian saying: When a door is closed, see if there is a window you can jump through." For Ramez and the BSE, the closed door includes Egyptian laws that restrict Christian life.[15] The closed door is also Coptic practice that stymies direct access to the meaning of the Bible. For the BSE, bookstores and literacy classes are the window to jump through. They distribute the Bible by selling it at a low cost (and as employees liked to highlight, typically losing money with each sale) at its fourteen bookshops, kiosks on saint's days (*mawlids*), and book exhibits, including the Cairo International Book Fair. They use highway billboards, youth talent competitions, and children's events with the character Kingo. The BSE reaches out to nonliterate people through illustrated works and audio and visual dramas. Among their projects to share the Bible, the BSE runs one of the country's most expansive literacy initiatives, Read Your Book, which draws on the Bible as curriculum. Read Your Book is technically a post-literacy class for those who have already completed a literacy class, so as not to be seen as competing with state literacy programming. Its focus on literacy programming underscores the program's emphasis on encountering the Word of God on the written page.

Ramez spoke of presenting the Bible in attractive ways. To do so, he drew an analogy to Egypt's economic liberalization (*infitāh*), remembering fondly how it beautified Egypt. He recalled how he once ate potato chips out of simple brown bags that were replaced with new styles: "If secular food is so attractive, we have to represent spiritual food in such an attractive way." Spiritual food: Bibles, study Bibles, Bibles that entertain, Bibles for the finger to decipher through braille and for the eye to delight in through illustrated children's editions. Literacy, in his view, should be *lectio divina* (spiritual or divine reading), a kind of "reading that enters our souls as food enters our stomachs, spreads through our blood, and becomes holiness and love and wisdom" (Peterson 2006, 4). Crucial to Ramez's understanding of what makes spiritual food nourishing is that it meets the person where they are. It is only in this way that the Bible can be transformative.

While they produced the Bible in a number of mediums, the written word was the ideal way to know Jesus. But the problem with this diet is that much of it focuses on the written word in a country with high illiteracy. For this reason, the BSE devotes much of their attention—like previous Christian missionaries in Egypt—to basic literacy. Historian Heather Sharkey relays that missionaries "vigorously promoted literacy campaigns, especially for the sake of Bible reading" (2008, 1). When American missionaries first began their work in Egypt in 1854, few Copts had a household Bible; by the twentieth century, few households did not have one (Sharkey, 46). Sharkey describes missionaries' influence on Copts as creating "something of a Coptic reformation," while Coptic Orthodox leaders saw transformations in education as a "Protestant deformation" (Hasan 2003 as cited in Sharkey, 47).

The BSE is one of 140 Bible societies in the world. Established in 1884 and currently based in Swindon, England, the organization is formally trans-denominational although generally Protestant in orientation. Its mission was forged in the confluence of the expansion of the British Empire and the emergence of the printing press. Matthew Engelke describes the organization's commitment to Bible translation and distribution:

For the first time in history a theological vision could make use of political and technological developments to imagine a global Christianity, a Christianity indexed by the presence of the Book throughout the four corners of the world. At the inaugural meeting of the Society it was agreed that the "sole object shall be to encourage a wider dispersion of the Holy Scriptures." Wider dispersion is something of an understatement: over time the founders of the Society wanted nothing less than to put a Bible in the hands of everyone on earth, ideally in their native tongue and ideally for a price that anyone could afford. It was through this book, got at by reading and reflection, that people could come to know their Lord and Savior Jesus Christ. (2013, 2)

The BSE is the largest publisher of Arabic Bibles in the world, as well as the largest producer of visual and audio recordings that transmit the Bible. The organization's bibliolatry means navigating Coptic practices that it disapproves of.[16]

Bible House sits on a quiet residential street in the upper-middle-class neighborhood of Heliopolis. It is home to the BSE's head office with 220 employees and a bookstore on the first floor that opens onto the street. The other attraction that pulls in visitors is Bible World, an interactive exhibit that teaches the history of the Bible's transmission enabled by translation and technology.

Bookshop employees described how bookshops were a space to bring Egypt's different Christian groups together. Whereas other Christian bookshops run as small stands in a corner of a church, any Egyptian can walk into an air-conditioned BSE shop right off a hot and dusty street. There were no crosses or any other Christian symbols on display. The bookstores were designed to welcome all. The sunlight through the floor-to-ceiling glass windows illuminated wood shelves where stacks of books featured bestsellers, like their recently published *Study Bible*.

Nabil began his work as a teacher and later became the director of Read Your Book. In case it wasn't clear to me, he pointed out that "*Book* means Bible—Read Your Bible." Nabil explained: "All of our work has to be done with 'context' in mind." Context was an important element of how the BSE planned its work, repeated many times by various staff. Whereas Magdy at the EAAE spoke of context to emphasize Egyptian piety and patriarchy, at the BSE headquarters in Heliopolis, context meant adapting the Bible through language and culture. Specifically, it meant knowing how to navigate Egyptian laws and how to persuade Coptic biblical practices away from habits that did not cultivate the proper reading subject for the Bible. More than anything, for BSE employees, context meant teaching Christians how to read in a country with failing schools and amid Muslim invectives against the authenticity of the Bible.

In 2004, Nabil felt that literacy should not only be for adults but also be extended to children who were not properly taught at their regular day schools. He bemoaned Egyptian schooling where children are afraid of their teachers and are forced, as he put it, to mindlessly learn "by rote" (*talqīn*). In establishing a post-literacy program, the BSE rebuffed Egyptian schools and forged a community of Christian readers parallel to and not competing with national literacy programs.

Read Your Book is made up of excerpts from the Bible. In this way, the program is distinct from the Bishopric of Public, Ecumenical, and Social Services (BLESS) and the Coptic Evangelical Organization for Social Services (CEOSS), each a major Coptic literacy programmer in Egypt. BLESS has long collaborated with the EAAE, while CEOSS, one of the country's largest social service organizations, collaborated with Vodafone on Knowledge Is Power, intensifying its efforts following Life Makers' exit in 2013. In fact, CEOSS had its very start as a literacy project in rural Egypt, underlining literacy as a pillar of the organization's activities. Both BLESS and CEOSS literacy programs adapted state programming that emphasizes citizenship, carrying out Pope Shenouda's partnership with the Egyptian state.[17] Bible House staff referred to CEOSS and BLESS literacy as secular education. Unlike Coptic literacy initiatives that sought to cultivate a pious Coptic citizenship, the BSE marshaled literacy skills that skirted the state in preference to a global Christian community.

READ YOUR BOOK, USE YOUR OWN WORDS

Teachers worried that Copts paid too much attention to the specific language and oral experience of the Bible, rather than its message. Their lessons sought to redirect attention away from the linguistic form of the Arabic Bible to instead discuss biblical themes. In the classes that I observed, students worked through the second-level workbook that drew on biblical passages that stitched together a chronological telling of the life of Jesus.[18]

In one class, students were instructed to read: "Jesus answered, The scripture says, '*Human beings cannot live on bread alone, but need every word that*

God speaks.'" The passage continued through Matthew 4–11 to describe the Temptation of Jesus. The biblical passages in the curriculum underlined three recurring themes: the power of Jesus's speech, the subversion of power and uplift of the marginalized, and doubt and reasons for faith despite uncertainty. Most of the stories centered on Jesus's speech and depicted a Jesus who willed actions and miracles through his speech. God was depicted as being on the side of the marginalized, and Jesus was shown to subvert power. Through the lesson, students were asked to reflect on the disciples' and others' inability to understand, where Jesus was the one who knew. In the lesson, the teacher discussed how easy it is to not understand—that it is through the Gospel that one gains understanding, faith, and knowledge.

The curriculum's approach to language captured common themes in a universalizing Protestant Christian language ideology that is noted by "a marked predilection for sincerity, interiority, intimacy, intentionality, and immediacy as an ethics of speech, and a privileging of the referential aspects of language" (Bialecki and Pinal 2011, 580).[19] When teachers and programmers discussed Read Your Book, these values and uses of language were contrasted with ineffective Coptic Bible habits that they saw as relying on the ritualized speech of fixed texts. Understanding was taught by facility with language, namely, the ability to describe a Bible passage in one's own words, discuss its meaning, and ultimately see it as a guiding force in one's life. As stepping stones toward this goal, activities encouraged learners to match synonyms, drawing a line between a challenging biblical word with a simpler vernacular word. A similar exercise asked students to paste a white sticker over a word from a biblical passage and write a simpler synonym on top of it. In this way, biblical vocabulary expanded into everyday language, as the Bible was rendered accessible through everyday language.

The use of synonyms was a striking departure from the Quran lessons and Quran-based basic literacy that I observed, where the particularity of the word is central to a verse's meaning. According to a dominant Muslim Arabic language ideology, the BSE's use of synonyms obscures the text. It was common for me to hear Quran teachers explain that no word can be substituted or used as a synonym because any change would alter the text's meaning. This was part of how they understood the richness of the Arabic language as part of revelation. The underlying belief is that the Muslim must bend toward the text, not the other way around. That which cannot be made understandable to the learner with reasonable effort should not be rendered in such a way that may jeopardize complexity or accuracy. For example, it is common for teachers of Islamic knowledge to tell their students: "Each context demands its own distinctive form of speech" (*li-kulli maqām maqāl*). This teaching stresses a theory of knowledge where learning is tailored to the capacities of the individual student.[20]

Turning biblical language into vernacular carried out the BSE's mission to render the Bible in "heart languages." Missionaries describe this kind of language as "the medium through which one speaks to the soul" (Handman 2015, 171). Heart language is how God communicates to a group of people. For the BSE, heart language is a way to describe what is commonly referred to in English as one's "mother tongue." Rather than describe one's first language as belonging to the tongue, the BSE places this language in the heart, stressing the importance of intimately reaching audiences through the correct language.

The BSE's emphasis on heart language contradicts the revitalization of the Coptic language led by Pope Shenouda.[21] Nabil explained the necessity of good Arabic translations of the Bible for comprehension, whereby comprehension begins as an intellectual activity necessary to impact the self. Both Nabil and Shaykh Ahmed describe language ideologies that evoke an effective response centered on the heart, although they do so through different conceptions of language. While the Quranic affective response is to an Arabic directly mediating the linguistic form of God's Word, the BSE's theory of translation situates the affective response in the potential to contemplate the text's meaning.

Read Your Book aimed to redirect the attention of students away from two common Coptic practices: the use of Bible recordings and reliance on the Van Dyck Arabic edition of the Bible. Nabil described how reading ought to provoke the understanding of scripture: "Listening promotes passivity. It can't arouse the sort of contemplation that happens when a person reads." He saw Muslim styles of Quran recitation as a negative influence on Coptic biblical practices. Neither, in his view, encouraged the proper relationship with scripture. While sound could make the Bible accessible, biblical chanting of the sort available on low-cost CDs encouraged poor Bible habits, in Nabil's view. While the BSE produced and sold these materials, Nabil discouraged their use, preferring a literate experience of the Bible.

He similarly worried about the predominance of a single Arabic translation of the Bible, the Van Dyck version that Copts highly preferred over other translations. For the last one hundred and fifty years, the Van Dyck translation has been the authoritative edition and, according to Nabil, "holy in its own right." The edition was a collaboration between the Syrian Mission and the American Bible Society in 1847. The reception history of the Van Dyck Bible shows a remarkable transformation from one met by Copts with suspicion as a missionary import to later becoming Copts' preferred translation. The majority of Copts has resisted efforts to revitalize the biblical Arabic of the Bible and replace the Van Dyck version.[22] For Nabil and the BSE, the Coptic attachment to the Van Dyck version does not support their approach to directly read the Bible in accessible language.

The BSE's efforts to translate Bibles into peoples' heart language run aground in Egypt. Their efforts underline how what makes a text speak to the heart is not limited to vernacularization. Copts "heart" the Van Dyck version. But *why* they love it vexes Nabil. The Coptic preference for Van Dyck is, at least in part, a way to rely on a single Arabic text, as Muslims do. Many Copts use a single Arabic Bible translation to inoculate against Muslim allegations of scriptural distortion (*tahrīf*). Contemporary Muslim accusations against the Bible often erroneously deem other Arabic translations of the Bible as discrepancies.[23] For this reason, many Copts have developed a sense of the irreplaceability of language that mirrors their Muslim interlocutors. The BSE teachers sought to redirect this language ideology through their focus on meaning as indicated through students' ability to use their own language to discuss biblical passages. The authority of the Van Dyck Arabic Bible reveals how Christian-Muslim polemics center not only on the authenticity of scriptures but, crucially, on how scriptures ought to be encountered and understood as well.

After completing Read Your Book, sixteen-year-old Mina's teacher prompted him to share his positive experience for an Australian fundraising campaign: "I learned how to read the Bible by myself. I also memorized Bible verses. In those four months, I came to know more things (*'arift hāgāt aktar*)." Mina's mention of memorizing Bible passages reveals how the program adopts methods of learning that are not only familiar to students but also highly valued by them. While he learned to read the Bible autonomously, he also drew satisfaction from memorizing its verses.

Nabil stressed that Read Your Book does not teach doctrine but instead teaches students how to read for themselves. The conception of God's language that he described and that Read Your Book teaches is a "transparent" hermeneutic: fidelity should be to meaning, and rendering that meaning as clearly and accessibly as possible. He did not see this as a theological position but rather as a self-evident understanding of the best way to connect the Word with the heart. As he explained, the point is to teach Egyptians how to read the Bible, not how or what to think about it. Nabil believed in the importance of the autonomous reading of the Bible as a more active mode of scriptural encounter. For the BSE, talking about the Bible, using one's own words to describe and reflect on it, is the way to see its eternal relevance.

Conclusions: The Body Deciphering God's Word

A comparative look across distinct reformist voices allows us to grasp how twenty-first-century religious revivalism makes God's Word the aim and instrument of autonomous reading. The three programs are illustrative of distinct styles of scripturalism made clear through their conception of the Word of God, and how to decipher and understand it. The programs differ in what it means to reform the classical tradition of the *kuttāb*: where the EAAE promoted meaning as a method to motivate learners, Shaykh Ahmed's school drew on repetition and sound in ways reminiscent of the *kuttāb*. Under the auspices of the BSE, Read Your Book's methods most clearly undid *kuttāb* practices, affirming instead a theory of language and learning that sought to correct Coptic Bible practices.

Across these scripturalist programs, it is not only that meaning matters but also that learning strategies presume a meaning-making subject ("meaning excites," according to the RITNOYL teachers' manual). Despite the opposing political projects that the embodied, meaning-seeking reader ideally inhabits in these three worlds, the projects converge in important ways that dissolve such clear distinctions. In each of the programs, we see that God's Word is for all, a call to make access to God's Word not only available but also essential for life. To be a believer, one must be a reader.

Each program centered on a sensing body to decipher scripture. The RITNOYL program focused on the eye, while TBP and Read Your Book located the heart as the locus of learning, albeit in different ways that corresponded with their corollary language ideologies. Shaykh Moustafa Elgindy's sound-centered curriculum not only employed a different method than that of RITNOYL but did so with a sense of sacred language that hinges on producing and hearing the sacred letter sounds of the Arabic language. The sensory involvement of TBP, then, is counter to RITNOYL's cultivation of the visually sensitive reader that the program sets out to instruct through "modern reading." While TBP is premised on the production and auditory reception of the sound of Arabic (as received in the ear and produced in the mouth with various stressed positions of the tongue, palate, and throat), Shaykh Ahmed described the supple heart as the condition for receiving the miracle of the method. For the BSE, language is a tool for transmitting the Word. The Bible must be translated and vernacularized so that it speaks the language of the sincere individual's heart. Where Shaykh Ahmed spoke of the miraculous powers of the Arabic language, Nabil focused on the sacred meaning of the Word.

Their shared centering of the heart coincides with another commonality: the inclusion of (and, indeed, focus on) children. With TBP, the focus on children takes up the *kuttāb* tradition with children best suited to learn, as Shaykh Ahmed noted, because of their naturally softened hearts. In the case of Read Your Book, the focus on children was a rejection of ineffective Egyptian schooling and aimed to form a multigenerational Christian community.

When holy books are taken up as a method to instruct basic literacy, we see various ideas about scripture made explicit: whether it should be seen or heard and whether the sacred status of God's Word is attached to its form or meaning. This chapter explored scripture as a method for autonomous reading. Chapter 3 turns away from basic literacy to explore the implications of basic literacy on Quran encounters. By exploring nonliterate Muslim encounters with the Quran, we can see that it is not simply that the skills of literacy shape Quran encounters; rather, the literate world has created relatively new conditions for encountering God's Word that redefine Muslims' relations with the textual tradition. Chapter 3 continues to explore the concept and power of the idea of God's Word through a Quran lesson made up of mostly nonliterate women. Through their lessons, we observe practices deeply indebted to written texts, even when students cannot autonomously decipher them. The women in the Quran lesson illustrate the predominance of scripturalist trends through the paradox of tracing the phenomenon among nonliterate women.

Notes

1. See Atallah's full discussion at https://www.youtube.com/watch?v=E2feY2 LvNqQ. On Logos, see Bialecki and Pinal (2011, 576).

2. For an introduction to the concept and debates surrounding the Word of God in the Islamic tradition, see Radscheit (2003). The Quranic text self-referentially uses the terms "God's word" (*kalām Allāh*) (2:75); "our Lord's word" (*qawl rabbinā*) (37:31); "his word" (*kalimatuhu*) (4:171); and "words from his Lord" (*min rabbihi kalimātin*) (2:37) (Radscheit, 541).

3. I refer to scripture when speaking about the Quran and Bible as a way to easily refer to these texts together. Notably, my interlocutors did not use the word *scripture*. The term evokes Christian and comparativist discussions of sacred writings. On the concept of scripture from a comparativist perspective, see Smith (1993). On discussions of the concepts of scripture and the Word in the Islamic tradition, see, for example, Graham (1987), Saleh (2010), Sells (2001), and Mattson (2013).

4. The method, used in schools across the country, was spearheaded by Lucy Calkins at Columbia University. It was called into question when data uncovered that as many as one in every three children in the United States cannot read at a level of basic comprehension (a trend that is racialized, with Black and Native students with lower scores). For news coverage of these debates, see Winter (2022) and Mervosh (2023).

5. Much like its Islamic counterpart, the Coptic renaissance (*al-nahda al-qibtiyya*) experienced shifts in leadership (Jirjis and Doorn-Harder 2011) and new forms of education (Hasan 2003) and media (Armanios and Amstutz 2013). Just as the impact of mass education on religious knowledge shaped Egypt's Islamic revival, similar trends in the Coptic Church brought about the Sunday School Movement (*Harakat Madāris al-Ahad*), which encouraged fasts, prayers, community service, and singing to inculcate values of sacrifice and articulate a Coptic sense of citizenship (Ramzy 2017).

6. See, for example, Reinhart (2010) and Goldberg (1991). Launay and Ware employ the visual metaphor of opacity in describing classical Quran education: "The single most important epistemic difference distinguishing adherents of the classical approach from reformists is that the former are convinced of the opacity of signs and the latter of their transparency. For reformists, the Quran can be reduced to the meaning of its words. Whoever masters its language thus has access to the content of the book and can decipher its message" (2016, 354).

7. The hermeneutical categories *muhkamāt* and *mutashābihāt* are so named based on their reference in Quran 3:7: "He is the One Who has revealed to you, O Prophet, the Book, of which some verses are precise (*muhkamāt*)—they are the foundation of the Book—while others are elusive (*mutashābihāt*). Those with deviant hearts follow the elusive verses seeking to spread doubt through their false interpretations—but none grasps their full meaning except Allah. As for those well-grounded in knowledge, they say, 'We believe in this Quran—it is all from our Lord.' But none will be mindful of this except people of reason." Early exegetes deployed these concepts in ways that animated a major strand within the Quranic interpretive tradition. While *muhkamāt* were understood to be self-evident, what

counted as self-evident verses was not settled—interpretive traditions disagreed on which verses were self-evident and which required explanation. Mustafa Shah offers an illustrative example:

> Mu'tazilite scholars, who as rational theologians advocated the doctrine of man's free will and the utter transcendence of God, insisting that he cannot be physically seen, would argue that the verse in the Qur'an, Q. 75:23, which refers to the believers physically seeing their Lord on the Day of Judgement, was simply *mutashābih*; it did not predicate that God could be seen; conversely, the verse which pronounces that sight cannot perceive him but it is God who perceives sight, Q. 5:103, would be designated by them as being *muhkam*; the opponents of such theological views would simply reverse the designation. (2012, 23)

For a discussion of the categories' impact on the Quranic commentary tradition tafsir, see, in the same volume, Kinberg (2012) and McAuliffe (2012).

8. Scholarship on the mutual imbrications of Christian and Muslim revivalism is far more advanced in other parts of the African continent. See, for example, Larkin (2008), Meyer (1998), and Soares (2006).

9. In Martin Jay's (1988) study of French hostility to visual primacy among critical theorists, he associates the rejection of dependence on the visual with the rise of hermeneutics. Notably, for French theologians, such as Jacques Ellul, the critique of vision is a move away from icons toward the Word.

10. In Egyptian and global media, Salafis are frequently depicted as a homogenous group with a distinct religious, political, and international agenda, especially during the 2011 uprisings and their aftermath. Lauzière historicizes the term *salafiyya*, locating its origins in the work of French orientalist Louis Massignon, whose scholarship made the group a distinct category to qualify religious tendencies (rather than particular theological disputes, as the term earlier indicated) (2015). On Salafism in Egypt, see Rock-Singer (2022). For an analysis of the anthropological depiction of Salafis, see Fadil and Fernando's problematization of anthropological depictions of orthodox piety (2015).

11. See Asad's discussion on the concept in relation to the untranslatability of the Quran, especially 58–61 (2018).

12. See Pregill (2021) for a discussion of the concept and its relation to *kitāb* as a signifier for scripture and the role of revelation and writing in the formation of the social groups of Jews and Christians.

13. In this understanding, he drew on ninth-century Arabic grammarians. See Chejne (1968).

14. On the disconnected letters in Anglophone Islamic studies scholarship, see, for example, Jeffery (1924), Massey (1996), Nguyen (2012), and Robinson (2003).

15. See Mahmood (2018) on how Egyptian secular governance exacerbates religious difference and discrimination against Coptic Christians in the country.

16. Estimates of Egypt's Coptic community vary. State figures estimate approximately 5–6 percent, while the Coptic Orthodox Church places the number

at 15–20 percent. Most scholarly sources estimate the figure to be 6–10 percent. Over 90 percent of Copts are Orthodox, while the remaining population is split between Catholics and Protestants. While the Coptic Orthodox Church is the centralized organization that represents Copts, Protestant churches carry a disproportionate power among Egyptian Christians (Heo 2018, 3, fn. 5).

17. See Tadros (2013) on Shenouda's relationship with Sadat and Mubarak.

18. The biblical passages were: 1. The Temptation of the Lord Jesus; 2. Miracle of healing the patient of Bethesda; 3. The miracle of healing a blind child; 4. The Lord Jesus entered Jerusalem; 5. The Lord Jesus washed the disciples' feet; 6. Trial of the Lord Jesus; 7. Crucifixion of the Lord Jesus; 8. The appearance of the Lord Jesus by Mary Magdalene; 9. The Lord Jesus meets Peter after the Resurrection; 10. The appearance of Jesus Christ to the disciples of Emmaus.

19. This view of language is also notably related to ideas of an autonomous subject.

20. See Messick (1993), especially 160–165.

21. The ancient language was displaced by Arabic with the spread of Islam in Egypt. The church translated the Bible and prayers into Arabic, and the number of those who used Coptic in the church dwindled. In his effort to revive Coptic language, Kyrillos IV called for prayers to be made in the language as well as to establish a new institute dedicated to its revitalization. Under Pope Shenouda, the Coptic Language Institute opened in 1976.

22. In one example of Coptic resistance to missionary efforts, the patriarch of Assiut ordered the burning of Smith-Van Dyck Bibles (Sharkey 2008, 37). Presbyterian missionary John Alexander Thompson, who taught at the Protestant Evangelical Theological Seminary in Cairo (where he worked on revising an Arabic translation of the Bible, as well as an Arabic dictionary), commented on the status of the Van Dyck edition. He cautioned that missionaries needed to strike a balance between a desire for a better translation and accommodating the deep love for this edition: "The Protestant and some non-Protestant people of the Near East have come to love the Smith-Van Dyck Version as the King James is loved in the English-speaking world or as Luther's translation among the Germans. Some national Christian leaders fear that an extensive revision would only confuse both Christians and non-Christians. Decisions regarding revision will require not only vision and linguistic knowledge, but also practical wisdom" (1956, 27).

23. While the concept has been variously interpreted, some Muslims buttress polemics with Copts based on the idea of a corrupted biblical text. *Tahrif*, meaning forgery, change, or alteration, is the Quranic accusation that Jews and Christians falsified their scriptures in two senses: corruption of the text (*tahrif al-nass*) and forgery of meaning (*tahrif al-ma'nā*) (Reynolds 2009, 194).

3

Scripturalism among Nonliterate Women

[The Islamic jurist] Ahmad ibn Hanbal said, "I saw God in a
dream and I asked Him: 'O Lord, what is the best way to be
near to you?'" God answered: "My Word, O Ahmad." Ibn
Hanbal asked: "With understanding or without understanding?"
God replied: "With or without understanding."

—Abu Hamid al-Ghazali, *The Revival of the Religious
Sciences (Ihyā' 'Ulūm al-Dīn)*

Samiya and her neighbors attended Quran lessons at their local community
center in Batn al-Baqara, a slum in Fustat, part of the historic district of Old
Cairo. She was one of a dozen women who studied basic literacy twice a week
in the Knowledge Is Power campaign, and on alternate days, she attended a
long-running Quran lesson in the same community center. The women gathered on the plastic woven floor mat of the prayer room three times each week
for their Quran lesson. They rehearsed the shortest chapters of the final section of the Quran (*juz' 'amma*), also known as the Seal of the Quran (*khatm
al-qur'ān*). Their lessons combined elements of Quran education that did not
typically align in lessons for laypeople but became increasingly prominent in
Egypt's Islamic revival. When Samiya and others explained to me that "there
is Quran after the late afternoon prayer" (*fīh qur'ān ba'd al-'asr*), they were referring to the variety of activities that took place in their lessons: the recitation
(*tilāwa*) and memorization (*hifz*) of short chapters, training in proper pronunciation and elocution (*tajwīd*), and instruction in authoritative interpretations
(*tafsir*). For three years, Samiya and her neighbors gathered to rehearse the
Word of God (*kalām Allāh*) in this way. They called it, simply, Quran.

94

Through their Quran lesson, the women taught me how nonliterate en-counters with the Quran are paradoxically deeply scripturalist. The emerg-ing prominence of semantic meaning among laypeople is a recent trend that has received little attention in the scholarship on Quran education, despite the epistemic ruptures it exposes. The women's lessons are indicative of the Quran initiatives unfolding in Egypt and across the world, as scriptural in-terpretation is disseminated and takes on a new and unprecedented role. Increasingly, Quran education, like that of the lessons in Batn al-Baqara, learns from a simplified tafsir in order to contemplate (*tadabburuhu*) Quranic meaning with the goal of putting its teachings into action (*al-'amal bihi*). These lessons are a component of the broader turn to Islamic education (for-mal and informal) in contemporary revivalist education trends that reach be-yond those interested in a specialized Islamic education. Women's participa-tion in expanding educational opportunities has been a hallmark of Islamic revivalism.[1] In Saba Mahmood's study of the mosque movement among women in Egypt, her analysis of these lessons delineates how women's ritual practices aimed at cultivating an ethical body unrecognizable to liberal femi-nism (2004). The women's practices of self-cultivation suggest that agency is not solely defined by individual autonomy, but rather it must be understood in relation with social, political, and religious factors that shape the women's actions and desires. My own focus is to critically illuminate the pedagogical techniques and hermeneutical practices entailed in those lessons.

The women's Quran lessons illustrate modern Muslim anxieties over how Muslims should encounter the Word of God. The lessons combined components of Quran education that did not typically align with Quran education for laypeople but that are increasingly prominent in Egypt. In their lessons, the women blended a classical pedagogical style that empha-sized memorization and performance with a reformist orientation that in-structed a particular relation to discursive meaning (a style of encountering the Quran historically reserved for scholars). This blended pedagogy is the result of a postcolonial dissatisfaction among many Muslim reformers with classical methods that they see as rote memorization, lacking a meaning-ful engagement with the Quran. The women's lessons demonstrate what historians and anthropologists have referred to as the creation of a kind of *hybrid* education and epistemology that brings together classical and mod-ern values and practices. Messick asks what happens when distinct styles of reading interact, calling this coming together of different reading modes a hybridization (1997). Robert Launay and Rudolph Ware similarly describe a "hybrid epistemology" of contemporary reformers who endeavor to merge classical and modern education. In their discussion of the epistemological stakes of reforming classical Quran education, they comment: "It remains to be seen whether such a hybrid form of Islamic education will be capable of resolving the apparent contradictions between its very different sources" (2016, 358).[2] Historian Hilary Kalmbach describes the civil-religious training of Egypt's Dar al-Ulum as a hybridity (2020). The women's Quran education represents neither the contradiction nor resolution of these blended pedagogies but rather the emergence of a specific approach to the meaning of God's Word, one that encourages but is not limited to a cognitive understanding of the Quran's content. Through the women's recitation, memorization, and group discussions of the verses, we see a hybrid Quran lesson for those uninitiated in autonomous reading.

Building on the discussion in chapter 2 of scripturalism through the use of the Quran and Bible for basic literacy, the women's Quran lessons are illustrative of Quran education for Egypt's nonliterate and semiliterate people. This chapter moves away from a focus on the drive for universal literacy to understand how trends brought about by autonomous reading are intimately linked with transmitting reformist concerns with meaning to a broader, nonliterate audience. Over the months, as I observed both the literacy classes and Quran lessons as part of the women's everyday lives, I saw how they demonstrated distinct reading regimes—different modes to encounter different kinds of texts—a kind of code-switching between different types of qirāʾa, what Messick calls "two very different sets of cultural practices (and associated genealogies) of reading and writing" (1997, 403). Chapter 4 turns to their literacy classes. By tracing literacy and Quran lessons in parallel, together the chapters render different modes of reading and their corporeal and ethical aims and practices. The women's Quran lessons point not only to oral and embodied Quran practices but also to the scripturalism of those oral and auditory Quran practices.

When I explained to Samiya that I wanted to study their Quran lessons, she balked. "How can you write about Quran [lessons]? You would need a machine to know what is happening inside us." She understood my ethnographic object to be something that happens inside the body. For Samiya, this knowledge was only knowable to an omniscient God—or perhaps a fantastical machine. At the same time, by describing their Quran practices as internal, she skirted aspects of the lessons that left their impression on me—how the lessons created a community of textual practice and interpretation that called on multiple modes of discourse, reasoning, and reflection. Samiya and the others did not trust their own words to talk about the Quran; they relied on trusted authorities to explain its meaning. Yet within their lessons, they regularly discussed their lives in relation to it.

Before turning to a thick description of the women's Quran lessons, I situate them within broader trends of contemporary Quran education and their specific sociopolitical milieu: an informal Cairo neighborhood experiencing political and economic instability. A brief history of the women's Quran lessons at the community center illustrates how, during the 1960s, recitation practices began focusing on enunciating individual words and, in doing so, drew attention to deciphering words that laid the groundwork for the contemporary focus on the discursive meaning of key words. In the first ethnographic scene, a lesson on *al-Kawthar* (Quran 108, "Abundance"), the teacher employed a question-and-answer format to call on the women to cite directly from the verses. Their responses both indexed their understanding and preserved the sacred form of the verse. The second scene, a lesson on *al-Māʿūn* (Quran 107, "Common Kindnesses"), illustrates how the women situated the Quranic term, *al-māʿūn*, within a conversation about ethical living. In the last scene, we witness a moment of failure in the recitation of *al-Fātiḥa* (Quran 1, "The Opening"), the most repeated chapter of the Quran in Muslim life. This episode of mispronunciation raises questions about the efficacy of ritual language. Taken together, the three scenes demonstrate how the women's lesson was a deeply scripturalist, nonliterate education in the Quran.

The women's Quran encounter offers an example of a community of interpretation. El-Badawi and Sanders categorize such communities as those rooted in textual interpretive practice and those shaped by experience, where the "former includes traditional forms of religion" and "the latter represent non-textual, culturally informed reimagination of what the Qur'an is and how it shapes a community" (2019, 17). Such a text/experience binary cannot capture the many Muslims untrained in the interpretive sciences and yet deeply shaped by their legacy. Niloofar Haeri (2020) and Fabio Vicini (2020) ethnographically depict learned communities of interpretation (among educated, non-Islamically trained specialists) that undo this binary through groups who read the Quran alongside and in interaction with other texts (classical Persian poetry in the former and a modern tafsir in the latter). Their contributions to an ethnography of Muslim reading depict the subtle ways in which meaning is contextually situated and in flux.[3] Taking the women's Quran lessons as a community of interpretation, I delineate the performative and discursive processes through which they recognized God's Word. An ethnography of a nonliterate encounter with the Quran uncovers the way texts are adapted by a community of readers who engage in a meaning-making reading process in their Quran education.

The women's Quran lessons depict an alternative to autonomous reading—a practice I call affirmation—as applied to Quran education. Despite interpretive conversations that revolve around key words, the women situated hermeneutic agency not within the individual but within the text itself. The goal of the lessons is to affirm the truth of God's Word. In other words, the women did not aim to discover some kind of true meaning of the verses they recited together; rather, they affirmed truth through their recitation. This aspect of their lesson echoes what Michael Lambek describes as "certain knowledge" in his observations on Quran recitation on the Indian Ocean island of Mayotte: "Correct recitation creates changes in moral states. Beyond this, the meaning is always the power, certainty, truth, the reality of Islam itself, of which the recitation is an exemplification and an affirmation rather than a description" (1990, 27). The women draw on their experiences to affirm God's Word. The meanings of key terms as authorized by a teacher's manual are taken as axiomatic; the women's experiences are thus read as affirmations of these standardized readings. Through the women's lessons, we observe three types of affirmation: citing direct quotes from the Quran, which indicates one's understanding through preservation and reverence of the Quran's language; situating Quranic concepts in daily life, which underscores the reality of the Quran through one's experiences; and actualizing Quranic study through right action.

Samiya and the others were reluctant to talk about their lessons because they saw themselves as unqualified to do so. They sometimes watched television programs with important scholars who explained the Quran. Throughout our conversations, the women were conscious of the limitations of human language for discussing anything related to the Quran. They frequently identified the insufficiency of any description they might offer of their lessons and, in doing so, further emphasized the power of the Quran in their lives. Their ideas about the limits of everyday language to describe their

Quran education tell us much about their ideas of how language works. To recognize the women's encounter with the Word of God and what it tells us about twenty-first-century scripturalism, directly questioning them about their practices, made little sense. Instead, long-term participant observation was crucial to grasp how they related to and deciphered God's Word.

The Old Cairo Quran Lesson

Batn al-Baqara was the center of the city's kiln and casting industry.[4] As such, among Cairo's slums, the neighborhood received media attention that attracted several small-scale social development projects. Fustat Street was dotted with casting and pottery wares. The entrance to the neighborhood was an opening in a line of clay pots and plaster ceiling medallions that lined the road. Batn al-Baqara was a walking distance away from the city's oldest mosques and churches in Coptic Cairo. Egyptians and tourists visited these sites regularly, which were only ten minutes from the sour scent of refuse at the entrance to the neighborhood and the audible whir of potters' tools.

The women's Quran lessons and literacy classes took place in the community center located among the narrow alleys, with three-story buildings that edged the sometimes muddy, sometimes dusty ground. The small complex included separate prayer rooms for men and women. Outside the women's prayer area was a small courtyard, about ten square feet, with a single swing and a well-worn teeter-totter. Children played and quarreled as their mothers supplicated. Adjacent to the courtyard were three classrooms with short desks, and a fourth with a carpet loom for a microenterprise project. On occasion, the courtyard was transformed into a medical clinic with plastic wicker mats strung up to create makeshift check-up rooms. While a couple of dozen men gathered for each prayer, this was primarily a space for women and their children, whose various activities and lessons drew them out of their one-room apartments into the center where they planned, prayed, imagined, and acted in a chorus of programs directed at their improvement.

In Egypt, Quran study is typically divided into different classes for distinct modes of learning, from lessons for advanced students on exegetical works (tafsir) to those open to Muslims of all educational backgrounds focused on a teacher's lesson (*dars*).[5] The most common lessons in Egyptian mosques of all sizes emphasize recitation, memorization, and proper elocution (*tajwīd*) for men and women with little to no background in Islamic education. *Tajwīd* is the foundation of Quran lessons in Egypt and a gateway to more advanced forms of study. In Cairo, prominent mosques such as Masjid al-Nur and Masjid al-Husari have daily programs of varying levels that include both group and private lessons. The state sponsors some of the world's most important Quran recitation competitions, drawing participants from across the world. These competitions discipline the performances and modes of appreciation deemed appropriate for listening and responding to recitations.[6]

Attention to the oral and discursive dimensions of Quran practices expands our approach to "understanding" beyond an exclusively cognitive process. The oral and auditory experiences of the Quran's performance are intrinsic to the affective and sensorial modes of training the body—a honing of the human senses—to embody particular virtues.[7] The Old Cairo community center's Quran lessons sponsored by al-Azhar (the preeminent Sunni Islamic institution of learning) are an example of how small prayer spaces not only bring together Quran learning strategies but also diffuse them throughout the country, even to the most marginalized spaces.

I first visited the Batn al-Baqara community center in the summer of 2011. Quran lessons became an essential site to observe not how the Quran *ought* to be read—a frequent topic of conversation in adult literacy classes in Egypt—but rather how it was *actually* encountered by nonliterate and semiliterate women. Of all the sites where I conducted fieldwork, I engaged most deeply with the students of Batn al-Baqara, where I participated in the life of the community center and neighborhood as it underwent significant changes in the months and years following the uprising. Moving between literacy and Quran classes on alternating days, I adapted my role as a participant-observer in each. I had begun my fieldwork in literacy, so it was a challenge to not be regarded as an authority. Volunteers worked in pairs, and I regularly attended classes with their teacher, Amal. She was the primary instructor, and I was the "observer" (*murāʾiba*) who watched the class and followed up with students on specific remedial exercises. To students, my fieldwork in literacy sometimes aligned me with literacy teachers. The Quran lessons, by contrast, allowed me to dissociate from the teacher and situate myself among the students. In the Quran lesson, I struggled with some of the same sounds and rules of pronunciation as my interlocutors. My susceptibility to error and frustration provided me with a learner's perspective and cultivated a familiarity with the women that eventually found its way into literacy class and my relationships with the women beyond the community center.

In the lessons, the women were under the guidance of their teacher and neighbor, Maryam. She, along with a select few from the neighborhood, was trained by an al-Azhar shaykh in 2008 to lead Quran lessons in the community center. Al-Azhar trained local teachers to instruct Quran lessons in local mosques and community centers. For the women, the lessons had the charismatic authority of al-Azhar, even as they were mediated through their neighbor-teacher, Maryam. The structure of the initiative facilitated a distinct form of mass education, one that consolidated al-Azhar as a center of Islamic knowledge, while its authority was conveyed to marginal spaces. When I sought Maryam's permission to join her lessons, she warned me that to learn the Quran is something very different than my participation in the literacy campaign. With it comes responsibility. She counseled that I would be accountable to God for anything I learned. Her students, she explained, distinguish themselves among their neighbors: "People know, this is a person who studies the Quran, so she must hold herself differently."

Each lesson typically gathered between eight and twelve students who were neighbors and extended relatives. They learned and relearned the same short chapters, directing most of their attention to the final ten chapters.[8] Maryam guided her students through a short chain of verses, strengthening each link with each repetition. I had been attending the lessons for a month before it became clear that the women repeated the same short chapters over and over. Their discussions centered on the meanings of unfamiliar Quranic Arabic vocabulary, which differs significantly from their Egyptian dialect.

The al-Azhar initiative is indicative of the spread of a particular strand of reformism in contemporary Egypt. Despite its authoritative role in defining Islam for Egypt and globally, al-Azhar is not a stand-in here for classical Islamic education. The institution plays a major role in religious, intellectual, and political life in Egypt and abroad and is both a mediator of state-sanctioned Islam and a place of intellectual diversity that has transformed rapidly since the nineteenth century.[9] Today, its authority is highly contested, particularly following the 2011 uprising and el-Sisi's coming to power. Al-Azhar's close alignment with the state has led some scholars to establish new institutions to chart a vision of a so-called moderate (*wasatiyya*) Islam independent of state interference. For example, al-Azhar graduates disappointed with the direction of the institution following the uprising established two new religious institutions: Shaykh al-Amud and Dar al-Emad (named after the beloved revolutionary Shaykh Emad Effat killed in the December 2011 protests described in chap. 1) (Bano 2018; Bano and Benadi 2018). Al-Azhar's role in the local community center illustrates the institution's emphasis on the Quran as the basis of basic education for an Egyptian public.[10]

Originally from the cities of Faiyum and Beni Suef, the women's families settled in Cairo a generation earlier. Some women were related to one another. They all lived in close proximity to each other and saw each other daily. While a few unmarried teenagers dropped in occasionally, and a couple of elderly women regularly attended, most of the students were in their twenties and had children ten and under.

The teacher, Maryam, was an outlier in her community. She had a three-year diploma in business. "It's a program people enter if they do not have high grades. I did well in it; if I'd wanted to enter university, I could have, but that was when I married." Maryam sold cotton clothing to her neighbors to make money. In her living room, a large print of the Ka'ba in Mecca faced a framed wedding photo of Maryam and her husband—he in a suit, and she in a white dress, her hair swept across the front to fall along her shoulders and down her back.

"I used to be just like the others," she explained, as she described the responsibility she felt as a teacher. Maryam always wore a tan and navy 'abāya that hung down her torso and a thick navy galabiyya, in all seasons, setting her apart from her students, who rarely wore 'abāyas, usually opting for thin colored scarves tied tightly around their head or loosely at the nape of their neck. They wore thin synthetic galabiyyas in the summer and heavy fabric in the winter.

I appreciated the women's frankness and wit as I spent afternoons with them on building stoops in the alley, their children playing nearby. One afternoon, I sat drinking tea with Umm Hazim and her neighbor, each of us telling stories about our families and the places we were raised. Umm Hazim referred to my presence in Egypt and dislocation from my parents: "See, you are like us. You are living in a place you were not born." To Umm Hazim, this was comparable to her move from the countryside to Batn al-Baqara. We were most familiar to each other when we sat reciting verses of the Quran together, when we stumbled over the same passages. Other times, I disappointed them when I did not understand a joke or I expressed surprise when a gentle friend harshly disciplined her child. This dance of discovery and the effort for intimacy stands out in my memory.

Deciphering the Word: From Cassette
Tapes to Teachers' Manuals

Before teachers came from al-Azhar, the women and men of Batn al-Baqara used to gather around a cassette player at the community center to listen to and practice their recitation. The cassette tape featured Shaykh Mahmud Khalil al-Husari, the first reciter to ever record the complete Quran in a style that came to be known as *murattal*. It is considered the model form of recitation that stresses the proper oral transmission of the text.[11] Their cassette lessons drew attention to individual words, laying the groundwork for a focus on the semantic meaning of the Quran for wider audiences. In the recording, the recitation was marshaled to convey meaning, not through an apt performance that stirs emotion (which is frequently emphasized in the literature on Quran recitation), but through a combination of enunciation, pauses for breath, and rhythm that clarified and drew attention to individual words.

The Husari recording was a concerted response by Egyptian scholars who feared that the art of Quran recitation was being neglected. Labib as-Saʿid, former president of the General Association for the Preservation of the Glorious Quran (*Jamaʿa al-Muhafiza ʿala al-Qurʾan al- Karīm*), spearheaded a large-scale project to produce a recording that would become the authoritative resource for recitation, an "omnipresent 'teacher,'" as he put it (Saʿid and Weiss 1978, 71). The ubiquity of Husari's state-sponsored 1960 recording has shaped Egyptian experiences of the Quran for nearly six decades. His voice reverberates across Egypt's soundscape, but his influence extends well beyond the country. The Husari recording is nothing short of the oral codification of the Quran; it made Quran recordings the most influential mode of transmission of the Quran in the twentieth and twenty-first centuries.[12]

In preparation for the recording, al-Saʿid observed a public recitation by Husari and remarked on its reception: "The audience was generally favorable and many remarked that the style of chanting used enabled them better to concentrate on the meaning of words" (Saʿid and Weiss 1978, 81). Saʿid cited among the justifications for the recording that such a tool would benefit women, allowing them to learn without arduous travel or having to study with male teachers, obstacles that curtailed women's pursuit of a Quran education (Saʿid and Weiss 1978, 1–12).

After practicing the Quran from the cassette for two years, in 2009, Maryam became one of only a few women in Batn al-Baqara to train with

Shaykh Omar from al-Azhar. She suspected a community center elder had selected her because she could read the teaching manual. Teachers such as Maryam were not usually authorized to teach Islamic lessons. She had memorized the final section of the Quran, whereas typically, formal licenses are issued only to those who have memorized the entirety of the Quran (known as *huffāz*) and are then permitted to teach. The Quran lessons initiated by al-Azhar introduced new methods of transmission and pedagogy that would replace the women's reliance on the Husari cassette. At the same time, it built upon an attentiveness to the significance of words.

The women's focus on semantic meaning was enabled by new forms of tafsir made accessible to wider audiences in abbreviated texts and marking a new role for tafsir in basic Quran education. The accessibility of Quran interpretations through teaching manuals that employ simple language has enabled lay Muslims to read the Quran in new ways.[13] Within Islamic educational contexts in Egypt, students and teachers described their study of the interpretation of the Quran as the explanation (*sharh*) of the text rather than its meaning (*ma'nā*), implying that they elaborate on an already established meaning from distilled tafsirs rather than engage in an autonomous interpretive act.

Maryam's well-worn instructional manual *Tafsīr al-'Ushr al-Akhir min al-Quran al-Karim: Min Zubdat al-Tafsīr* (*The Final Tenth of the Holy Quran: Selections from the Essence of Interpretation*) was the single text that guided her lessons. The author, Muhammad Sulayman al-Ashqar (d. 2009), was an al-Azhar graduate who also trained in Saudi Arabia and was known for publications such as *Al-Mawsū'a al-Fiqhiyya* (*Encyclopedia of Islamic Jurisprudence*), which was designed to distill all major schools of jurisprudence into an accessible reference for a wide audience. The booklet included the short chapters of the final three sections of the Quran (from Quran 58 through the concluding chapter, Quran 114), presented as a page from the Quran in the top quadrant of the manual's page (alternating right and left), with the tafsir occupying the rest of the page, primarily expanding on the explanation of key words.

Teaching manuals of this sort modify a history of techniques of recitation that consolidated in the eleventh century and continue to circulate among learners of all levels (Denny 1988). What made Maryam's lesson novel was the way in which it both settled and made accessible the meaning of key words in a simple format to be taken up in discussions. Tafsir scholar Walid Saleh explains how modern tafsir has radically expanded beyond its previous uses: "Muslims are now interpreting the Qur'an in order to position themselves in the world, which is a process of continuous reinvention of what it means to be a Muslim subject in an ever-evolving modernity" (2020, 696). The women's lessons were not unmediated Quran lessons for the uninitiated but rather relied on particular authorities (al-Azhar, literate community members) and strategies (print and reading) that animated twenty-first-century Quran scripturalism through simplified texts made accessible to everyday people.

The manual is part of a trend that Johanna Pink describes as "popularis-ing commentaries" (2010, 62) that do away with conventional tafsir forms through modern mediums like television and newspaper commentaries. The inexpensive manual delineates a clear and accessible meaning to its novice audience: meaning is for everyone. Further, these manuals are popular me-diators of contemporary theological discussions. Saleh notes the significance of this shift: "We now have a democratization of theology, a falling back on Qur'anic terms to recast old concepts and to develop new ones. As a result, tafsir has been repositioned as the central mode of theologizing in the Is-lamic world today" (2020, 695). Maryam's textbook, then, is illustrative of a scripturalism that takes up a new form of Quranic commentaries, shaping not only Quran education but also broader theological discourse.

The rise of tafsir in teaching manuals, in addition to other transformations in the transmission of the Quran's meaning, has had paradoxical effects: on the one hand, these manuals distribute authoritative meanings to broad audiences previously not privy to the scholarly tradition; on the other, they give rise to lessons such as the one found in Batn al-Baqara with only tenu-ous connections to trained Islamic scholars. This paradox complicates the theories of Islamic knowledge mentioned in chapter 2, whereby education is ideally adjusted to the capacities of the individual.

Basic primers, like Maryam's manual, aim to make meaning immediate and accessible, even to the lone reader. The nonliterate subject is induced into a textual interpretive tradition through new pedagogical materials that leave less room for ambiguity. As we will see, the lessons enlivened the meaning of key words addressed in Maryam's teaching manual in ways that sometimes called upon the women to revere the Word of God by cuing them to echo its form, while at other times asking them to situate Quranic concepts in their daily lives. In the following section, a lesson on the chapter *"al-Kawthar"* depicts the women's typical recitation and memorization of Quranic verses and one technique they deployed to respond to their teacher's questions about the verses—through citation, they preserved and revered the form of God's Word.

Question and Citation: Preserving the Form of God's Word

In the late afternoon, from the community center prayer room, the sound of television, sometimes an argument, and always the melody of birds could be heard as the sun began to descend. The day's lesson focused on memorizing al-Kawthar (Quran 108) and grasping the eponymous key word kawthar (which many English translators of the Quran render as "abundance"). This was the first but not the last time that I would observe the women practicing this short chapter. Maryam recited each verse separately, instructing us to repeat after her. The women repeated each verse three times. Maryam then added another verse, and the group repeated it three times. She recited two verses, and the group repeated the longer passage after her, first together and then each student by herself.

When Badriyya recited, each facial muscle relaxed as she focused. It was an expression reserved only for her recitations. As Samiya rehearsed the verses, she wanted to get them right. She could not recall the words with the same precision as her cousin. She would get distracted when someone entered the musallā. When she lost the thread, she frustrated herself, overdramatized her frustration so she could make light of it, and then hurried across the circle to sit directly in front of Maryam. As the women recited, they rehearsed the basics of tajwīd, with the aim of reproducing the sound of the word as it was revealed to the Prophet Muhammad. When Maryam detected an error within the group, she had us all repeat the verse again. Repetition affirmed the sound of the short chapter; it was a technique for stitching the verses into memory. When we faltered in our pronunciation, Maryam instructed us on where the sound should be produced in our mouths: "I seek protection with God from Satan, the outcast. In the name of God, the Lord of Mercy, the Giver of Mercy. We have truly given abundance [kawthar] to you [O Prophet]—so pray to your Lord and make your sacrifice to Him alone—it is the one who hates you who has been cut off." The women continued to string together verses. They began in synchronicity, and when a single voice strayed, the small imprecisions caught in the ear like a misplaced note. Tajwīd was a critical component of the women's efforts to affirm God's

Word. After repeating the verses with proper *tajwīd*, Maryam then focused on the word *kawthar*. Consulting her manual, she explained that *kawthar* is a river in paradise.[14]

She then quizzed the group: "What did God give?" The question and answer format was typical of her lessons. Women shouted different answers over each other. She asked again, "What did God give?" Each time she posed the question, her voice gradually rose at the end of the sentence. She prompted their response by offering the first verse that held the answer to her question: *innā a'ṭaynāka al-kawthar* (We have truly given abundance to you). A few of the women picked up on her cue. Badriyya responded: *kawthar* (abundance). Maryam was satisfied. Her question was intended to elicit an answer from within the verse.

Kawthar is a Quranic Arabic word that is not used in the Egyptian dialect. In Maryam's lesson, no explanatory interpretations or synonyms were used to describe the idea of abundance. According to Maryam's explanation, *kawthar* describes a specific physical place, and it is also an image for the idea it represents—abundance. The discursive meaning of the key term was not elaborated through a definition but through a specific instance of God's generosity. Through citation, Badriyya's response preserved the form of God's Word.

Maryam deployed pedagogical styles of modern Egyptian schooling in the Quran lesson. Through the method of question-and-answer, Maryam searched for a clear and concise response for the women to indicate their learning. The style of question-and-answer was familiar to the women from their primary education, just as the subtle forms of praise that she used were reminiscent of Egyptian schooling.[15] On this particular day, Maryam's question "What did God give?" called for a direct quotation from the Quran. Maryam relied on the tafsir in her manual to render a Quranic Arabic term to her students; however, the question called on them to respond not from the tafsir but from the verse itself. In this way, the women were induced into the interpretive tradition even when the teacher's style of questioning called on them to maintain the linguistic form of the verses. By preserving the word itself in the form it appears in the verse—*kawthar*—the women were solicited to regard Quranic Arabic as irreplaceable.[16]

The conceptual claim underpinning the lesson's approach to the Arabic language is part of a long-running theological dispute. In one of the formative debates of Islamic theology, the Ash'arites (whose ideas are now the basis of

Sunni orthodoxy) supported the idea of Quranic Arabic as an immutable sacred language, while the Mu'tazilites (an eighth-century rationalist school whose positions have gained traction among both Muslim reformers and secularists) maintained that Quranic Arabic was created, like all of God's creations. According to the latter position, then, an orientation toward the text that privileges form obstructs free and critical thinking and, worse, obscures the very idea of God's Word.[17]

In his discussion of religious language, Webb Keane describes citation as "more deferential to the text" than the practice of paraphrasing, which involves more interpretation on the part of the person responding. He explains that quotation "tends to sharpen the distinction between the quoter and the person quoted" (2007, 439). The women's citation from the Quran demarcates their own language from that of the Quran. Notably, Maryam did not ask "What is *kawthar*?" which would anticipate an explanation of the word's semantic meaning. Maryam called on the women to demonstrate their understanding by echoing the chapter directly. She framed her question to elicit one of God's words, not an extrapolation of the word's meaning. Her question was not an open-ended prompt to elaborate on instances of God's abundance. The question called on the women to participate in an authorized dialectic that demonstrated their understanding. The style of question managed a possibly overwhelming consideration of God's abundance with a manageable single-word response, concretizing the meaning of *kawthar*. Rather than discern citation as always deferring to or reinforcing authority, by preserving the form of the word, Badriyya's response left open the vastness of the response's potential referents.

Citation was a form of repetition, a major component of the women's lessons. Repetition was also a part of maintaining the responsibility of preserving previously memorized verses. The need to remember is an obligation that calls attention to the significance that an internalized verse is supposed to have on the individual: one must continue to carry the memorized verses. Forgetting is careless and indicative of a laxity with revelation. In this way, the relearning of the simple chapters is not a failure to progress but a shouldering of the responsibility of learning. Maryam reminded the women of this responsibility, citing a hadith that a forgotten verse is like an abandoned house. Other times, she cautioned that the Prophet warned Muslims that verses can escape the memory like a camel freeing itself of its rope. The women's reward (*thawāb*) is not only from the amount of Quran

SCRIPTURALISM AMONG NONLITERATE WOMEN   109

they memorize but also in the effort they exert to learn and retain it. As we will see in chapter 4, their literacy classes followed the forms of repetition established in their Quran lessons, so that rather than moving toward completing the curriculum, due to lapses and disruptions, literacy classes took on a cyclical learning and relearning like their Quran lessons. In the lesson on *al-Kawthar*, the citation indexed one's understanding and affirmed the form of God's Word. In the women's reading of another short chapter, *al-Māʿūn* (Quran 107, "Common Kindnesses"), we will see how Maryam's questions could make a key term the basis for discussions of ethical living.

Question and Contemplation: Applying Quranic Concepts in Daily Life

The words of *al-Māʿūn* flowed easily from the women as Maryam reintroduced the short chapter to them verse by verse. She began: *bi-sm Allāh al-raḥmān al-raḥīm/ araʾayta alladhī yukadhdhibu bi-l-dīn* (In the name of God, the Lord of Mercy, the Giver of Mercy. Have you considered the person who denies the Judgment?). The women repeated the lines until the group recited in unison. Maryam introduced more: *fa-dhālika alladhī yaduʿʿu al-yatīm/ wa-lā yaḥuḍḍu ʿalā ṭaʿām al-miskīn* (It is he who pushes aside the orphan and does not urge others to feed the needy). They continued, and Maryam corrected their vowel sounds. She strung together four verses to conclude the chapter. Many stumbled over the extra lines:

> *fa-waylun li-l-muṣallīn/ al-ladhīna hum ʿan ṣalātihim sāhūn*
> *al-ladhīna hum yurāʾūn/ wa yamnaʿūna al-māʿūn.*
> [So woe to those who pray but are heedless of their prayer (*sāhūn*); those who are all show and forbid common kindnesses (*al māʿūn*)]

Maryam explained that there is a valley in hell for those who are heedless in prayer (*sāhūn*). She described two different kinds of heedless people: those who are not regular or punctual in their daily prayers and those who pray to be seen but are not present or are insincere in their prayer. She stressed the problem of not maintaining regular prayers. Yasmin, who always sat with her infant daughter in her lap, joked about her laziness and how she never performed her daily prayers. Another woman shared that she usually prayed all of her prayers at the same time in the evening instead of at their appointed times throughout the day. Maryam related how she herself, busy with chores and children, also often did this. Another woman, Rabab, joined in: "Today, when I woke for *fajr* (the predawn prayer), I was happy with myself. But I knew it was Satan (*shaytān*) making me pleased with myself. I know that's wrong. Satan comes and spoils even the good things I do."

Maryam continued: "And what are *māʿūn*?" When no one responded, she explained: "*māʿūn* are the little things we do for each other, so small we don't notice them, but when we aren't aware, we think they are big. We are so far away from God in our bad habits and neglect that we can't even do the very smallest thing for our neighbor." The women discussed the simple gestures they could do for each other to make life easier. They complained about the lack of common kindnesses that people in the neighborhood were willing to give. Aya, who lived in a first-floor apartment beside a small shop, complained that she had no space to hang her family's wet laundry because her upstairs neighbor refused to let her use their clothesline. The others agreed that this would be something easy to allow one's neighbor to do. More joined in. One woman was agitated because her cousin was too quick to strike her child. When Maryam sensed the conversation straying, she reined it in: "So, what is *māʿūn*?" She called on Umm Ahmad, who answered: "*māʿūn* are the nice things we forget to do for each other." Maryam was satisfied and carried on with the lesson to individually test the women's recitation.

Maryam's question prompted contemplation, which stirred discussions about how to apply the Quranic concept in their social interactions. The women's reflections were guided by the meaning of the words authorized by the favored interpretation of the manual and taken as axiomatic. The students drew on their experiences to elaborate the standardized explanations of *sāhūn* and *māʿūn*. Their discussions were responses to the meanings established by religious authorities that they then located in their lives. In this process, they described the Quranic term *māʿūn* in their own vernacular, employing the word *khidma* (a small favor) as they considered neighborly gestures. The conversation illustrates a momentary dissolution of the sharp distinction between sacred and mundane language as a technique to render the meaning of the Quran relatable. By way of concluding the conversation on small kindnesses, Maryam returned to the authorized meaning of *māʿūn*. The women's discussion did more than veer away from the lesson; their conversation made a Quranic concept real. Meaning was a deliberative process focused on Quranic vocabulary.

The women's frank conversation regarding *sāhūn* and the challenge of maintaining regular and sincere prayers underscores their education as a process. They articulated the gulf between the ideals of their Quran education and their perceptions of their shortcomings. Their reflections on prayer raise the question of the impact of their Quran education on their actions. Indeed, proper understanding of the Quran is ideally embodied in the actions of the learner through what Ware describes as "actualized knowledge" (2014, 4). In the following section, an episode of mispronunciation reveals divergent views regarding the stakes of an error in Quran recitation. The episode raises questions about the efficacy of religious language as a means to induce one to pray and as a matter of the validity of prayer. The mistake opens a space to contemplate meaning beyond the semantic meaning of words, and to inquire into the ritual effects of the women's lessons. The episode further depicts the disjuncture between the ideals of their Quran education and what transpires in and outside their afternoon lessons.

Mispronounced Sacred Language: Ritual Implications of an Improper "T"

At the end of each lesson, Maryam called on the women to individually recite the day's verses. She corrected and evaluated them, scribbling observations in her notebook. When a woman successfully completed the recitation without Maryam's prompting or correction, she was free to leave. One day, Maryam returned to the most repeated chapter of the Quran, *al-Fātiha* (Quran 1). Seven verses in length, the chapter is central to prayer, as it is a part of each prayer cycle (*rakʿa*).[18] Samiya and I were regularly the last to leave. She tended to the women's space of the community center for a small monthly wage and was responsible for locking the padlock on the wooden door to the women's prayer area at the end of each lesson. Maryam was clearly distracted during Samiya's recitation. When she was finished, Maryam said she had made a mistake that day: she had taught the group to say the word *al-ṣirāṭ* (path or way) with a plain or nonemphatic *tāʾ* rather than the correct letter, the emphatic or pharyngealized *ṭah*, two distinct letters in the Arabic alphabet.[19] She worried that the error would render the women's prayers void.

> Maryam: "If they learn it incorrectly because of me, I receive a sin each time it is recited this way."

Samiya tried to reassure her: "Just tell them at the next lesson."
Maryam: "It will be too late; they will be praying for days incorrectly."
Samiya: "None of the women pray anyway. They won't recite the chapter before our next class."

I laughed and asked how Samiya knew this. "I'm the one with the keys. I know when they come and go. And when we're in our homes, I see who moves to pray when it's time." She named the women who prayed, most of whom were the elderly attendees of the lessons.

Maryam was clearly worried about the implications of the error that would spread through the homes of Batn al-Baqara, invalidating the women's prayers. She finally smiled at Samiya's identification of the women who pray and suggested we visit each of their homes to make the correction. We went to the front doors of their buildings. They were surprised to see us, but they recited the chapter when Maryam asked them to do so. She ensured that when they said ṣirāṭ, they vocalized the correct heavy ṭah. They did not appear to be bothered by the difference between the two pronunciations. After visiting half a dozen buildings and listening to the women recite the verses again, Maryam's worries were assuaged.

What is at stake in an error of pronunciation? Maryam was so troubled by the mistake that she continued to dwell on it even after learning that her students did not maintain regular prayers. The problem, as she saw it, was not that the incorrect letter altered the meaning of the word, rendering it nonsense, but that the mispronunciation corrupted the correct form of prayer. Her focus remained on pronunciation—form—rather than the general obligation to pray (salāt), the foundational Muslim practice that is the second pillar (rukn) of Islam (after the first, which is bearing witness to the oneness of God and the prophethood of Muhammad, known as the shahāda). She later explained that this was because the women's proper pronunciation was her responsibility, whereas performing regular prayers was their own obligation.

Maryam and her students had different orientations toward the significance of the form of sacred language and its impact on prayer. Maryam was troubled because she understood her role as a teacher to be to transmit—intact—the Quran so that the women could properly perform their obligatory prayers. Emphasizing the classical model of Quran education that places form over content, Launay and Ware describe the implications of an error in pronunciation: "A botched recitation is at the very least inefficacious and at worst impious" (2016). Ṣirāṭ should be pronounced as it was pronounced when it was revealed, the way it has been properly repeated for over fourteen centuries—the necessary form for the performance of prayer. Maryam was troubled by her role in creating the error. She had been instructed by her teacher that, just as she would be rewarded for each of her pupils' correct recitations and prayers, she would be punished for their errors.

The requirement of proper form to apt prayer is dealt with in Islamic jurisprudence (*fiqh*) under the category of the performance of prayer. As we see from Maryam's anxiety, reaction, and remedy to the error, the difference between *tā'* and *ṭah* is grave not only because of the distortion of meaning but also, and most importantly, because of the juridical position regarding errors in recitation that state that it can invalidate prayer. Three of the four legal schools (the Malikis, Shafiʿis, and Hanbalis) state that the proper recitation of *al-Fātiha* is an integral component (*rukn*) of ritual prayer. To support this position, these legal schools cite the prophetic tradition (hadith): "Whoever does not recite *al-Fātiha* in his prayer, his prayer is invalid." The fourth school (the Hanafis) takes a different position: such an error is a deficiency, but it does not invalidate the prayer. This position is based on a line from the Quran: "So recite as much of the Quran as is easy for you" (73:20). Although there is consensus that an error in pronunciation is consequential, jurists have debated what type of error jeopardizes the validity of the prayer itself. Many fatwas have determined that a mispronunciation that alters a word's meaning (*maʿnā*) is such an error, while others explain that the validity of prayer depends instead on the sincerity or effort of the person praying.

Maryam took the former (majority) position. In doing so, she eschewed the opinion of nineteenth-century Hanafi jurist Ibn Abidin (d. 1836), for instance, who differentiated between errors that can be avoided and those that are unavoidable. For Ibn Abidin, the substitution of the Arabic letter *tā'* for *ṣād*, such as uttering *al-tālihāt* (not a word) instead of *al-ṣālihāt* (righteous deeds) is inexcusable. However, according to Ibn Abidin, pronouncing *tā'* instead of *ṭah* (like the women did) does not invalidate a prayer because it is difficult for many to hear and to distinguish between these sounds; the error instead falls under the legal category of a "general hardship" (*ʿumūm al-balwa*). This position is especially popular among non-Arabic-speaking Muslims, but it is important to recall that the women were learning to distinguish between letters of the alphabet that non-Arabic speakers often struggle with.

The mispronounced *tā'* crystalizes what anthropologists of Christianity have called the "limits of meaning." Engelke and Tomlinson explain how modern Christianity's emphasis on the production of meaning can also reveal when meaning cannot be found: by looking at a moment of failure, "scholars can approach meaning not as a function or a product to be uncovered, but as a process and potential fraught with uncertainty and contestation" (2006, 2). We see the complex relation between form and content at work in a pedagogical approach that tries to fuse the two. Maryam's urgent attention to form (not shared by her students) underscores affirmation as an ideal that the women do not always achieve. The episode calls into question the efficacy of the women's Quran education in two important ways: when the Quran lesson does not lead to correct action—in this case, the performance of regular prayer—and when the form of the language is not precisely articulated. The error, then, reminds us that the Quran is not always correctly affirmed. Indeed, for one to affirm the truth of the Quran in habit, behavior, and comportment is a struggle. Rather than offering a third instance of affirmation, the episode allows us to appreciate how Quran lessons do not always play out as they supposedly should.

Conclusions: A Nonliterate Community of Interpretation

Months later, looking over pages of field notes, I rediscovered the frenzy of late-afternoon birds and the sun falling through the prayer space window across a circle of women. During these lessons, I would try to discreetly write in my notebook, but I felt their eyes on me. I wrote as though if I could plot these scenes in my notes, there would be a fragment to return to help me better understand what I had been a part of for so many months. I stuffed my notes into my bag, embarrassed and worried that they would be a barrier between me and the others. In this chapter, I have tried (through writing) to repeat, cite, and echo the women of Batn al-Baqara in their encounter with God's Word. Yet in doing so, I risk misunderstanding.

One possible misreading of their lessons is to take them as an illustration of rote memorization. One might observe that Samiya and the others neither questioned their teacher nor challenged her interpretations. They did not endeavor to create their own interpretations through a personal intervention in the exegetical field. However, such an expectation does not admit the significance of the form and agency of God's Word itself. Neither is it sensitive to the contemplative discussions that related the Quran to the women's lives. As a community of interpretation, the women made sense of the Quran through authoritative texts that prompted them to reflect on their lives. They demonstrate how texts are accessed and grappled with without autonomous reading.

The "reader" in the Batn al-Baqara Quran lessons is not autonomous but rather depends on a teacher who in turn relies on the authority of al-Azhar and her manual, all to effectively mediate the potency of God's Word. *Qirā'a* here is not about the powers of an independent subject. Instead, the individual is subordinated to the text, which is the proper relation between the Muslim and God. The reader does not act on the text but rather is acted upon by it. While not an explicitly civic project like literacy programs, the women's Quran lessons are of public consequence. Maryam sometimes reminded the group that as women studying the Quran, people in the neighborhood held them to a higher standard than others. She told them to carry their lessons in their comportment. Affirming the Quran, then, is not only a witnessing and reiteration of truth but also the propagation of the Quran to others through their self-presentation.

For the women of Old Cairo, the truth of God's Word must be recognized and affirmed through various modes of Quranic encounters: the performance of the recitation as well as the deliberative practices that center on meaning. The felicity of the women's practice was measured in its mimetic reproduction of sound, a determined dialogic of question and answer, and the discussion of key terms authorized in the teaching manual's gloss (*sharh*). Together, the three Quran lessons bring to light conceptions of God's Word as it is lived, adapted, rehearsed, forgotten, and neglected. In their late-afternoon circles, the women engaged in practices of memorization, discussion, and community that aimed to remember God. They connected the truth of the text to their lives and in doing so affirmed God's Word and their place in the world.

What we see in the women's Quran lesson is a scripturalist trend that does not rely exclusively on autonomous reading, but rather, on a hybrid practice. The Old Cairo Quran lesson is a project to modernize and localize Quran instruction. In this way, it resembled the aim of scripturally based literacy programs (discussed in chap. 2) that sought to make the Word of God available to all. The women conceived of their recitation and discussion not as a redress of their illiteracy but as practices that facilitated the correct reception of the recitation. From the Husari cassette tape, with its vocalization that renders each word audible and distinguishable, to the al-Azhar initiative, which employed a simplified explanation of words, we see the Quran made accessible. Maryam—keeper of the teacher's guide and the literate neighbor—directed the women in the authoritative meanings of words that they echoed through their discussions. These discussions were part of a contemplation predicated on a distinct orientation to the Word of God.

Their lessons challenge notions of *meaning* and *understanding* in Muslim encounters with divine speech, especially as these encounters are part of reformist attempts to center both the sacred form of Quranic language and its content. The women's Quran lessons also remind us that scholarly approaches to understanding that foreground the sensing body may risk imposing classical models of Quran education, even when those models are subverted as they unfold in real life. A mispronounced *tā'*, then, makes audible the dissonances between ideal and practice.

Chapter 4 shifts to the women's basic literacy classes in the Knowledge Is Power campaign. The campaign made literacy an Islamic imperative to ideally cultivate a particular type of modern Muslim subject. By alternating between spaces of the community center for basic literacy and Quran lessons, the women structured how they moved between reading modes with distinctive ethical aims and conceptions of mediation. The distinctive reading regimes each involved oral and bodily repetitions that aimed to cultivate specific subjectivities. In their Quran lessons, we see practices they adopt to interiorize the Quran and "apply it" to their daily lives, whereas the women's basic literacy classes we now turn to depict an Islamic literacy development intent on shaping responsible mothers. While their Quran lessons demonstrate textual encounters without the skill of autonomous reading, the women's literacy classes instruct a sense of development that attempts to forge individual and national improvement through a modern conception of "religious reading."

Notes

1. On women's religious education, see the important work of Kalmbach and Bano (2011), Alidou (2013), Doorn-Harder (2006).

2. The volume edited by Robert Launay explores the epistemological gulf between European-influenced education and classical Islamic education, drawing on the pedagogical objects of "writing boards and blackboards" (the subtitle of

the volume) to illustrate the distinct educative practices animated through those objects (2016). Writing boards are the wooden planks used in classical Islamic education where students worked individually on a text, typically Quranic verses, with their teacher. The blackboard was essential to the emergence of modern mass education, with teachers instructing groups of students at the front of the class.

3. See also Tawasil's ethnographic account of Iranian *howzevi* women reading Guy de Maupassant's novel *Claire de Lune* (1895) (2019). She depicts a reading hermeneutic that not only questions secular norms of reading for women's freedom but does so through understanding the novel in relation to the women's knowledge of the Quran and Islamic scholarly texts. Beyond the Quran, Azar Nafisi's international bestseller *Reading Lolita in Tehran: A Memoir in Books* (2003) demonstrates an intense interest among popular audiences in Muslim women's reading communities. Nafisi's account of women reading Western literary classics suggests reading as a site of women's agency. The work was widely critiqued within the academy for decontextualizing Iranian culture and politics as well as for supporting the US-led Global War on Terror. See Dabashi (2008), Donadey and Ahmed-Ghosh (2008), and Mahmood (2008). The bestseller attests to the power of reading communities as an analytic in relaying readers' worlds through their textual encounters, particularly when the message is that of women reading for liberation.

4. Cairo's urban quarters that developed in the Fatimid period were first developed around "ethnically organized military units" and later became known by particular trades (Abu-Lughod 1971).

5. The Ministry of Endowments (*Wizarat al-Awqaf*), the government body that oversees the regulation of religious affairs, regulates formal initiatives to train teachers, issue instructional licenses, and conduct religious lessons.

6. I am indebted to the late Abdel Mustafa Kamel, a prominent teacher of the art of Quran recitation (*maqāmāt*) in Cairo, who instructed me in recitation for several months as part of my research. In addition to his generosity in teaching a novice (he typically instructed advanced students), he shared his concerns for the devaluing of recitation and the increasing control of its art by Muslim neotraditionalists.

7. See, for example, Hirschkind (2006), Nelson (1985), Osborne (2014), and Frishkopf (2009). Scholarship on Quran practices among non-Arabic speakers is particularly attentive to affective understandings of the Arabic Quran (Rasmussen 2010; Ware 2014; Gade 2004). The critical attention to questions of language and cognition among non-Arabs and the paucity of challenges of understanding Quranic Arabic among native Arabic speakers reaffirm notions of a literate Arabic-speaking world set against a more creative, experiential Quranic encounter among the vast majority of Muslims who are non-Arab.

8. These are: *al-Nās* (The People), six verses; *al-Falaq* (Daybreak), five verses; *al-Ikhlās* (Purity [of Faith]), four verses; *al-Masad* (Palm Fiber), five verses;

al- Naṣr (Help), three verses; *al-Kāfirūn* (The Disbelievers), six verses; *al-Kawthar* (Abundance), three verses; *al-Māʿūn* (Common Kindnesses), seven verses; *al-Quraysh* (Quraysh), four verses; *al-Fīl* (The Elephant), five verses; *al-Humaza* (The Backbiter), eight verses.

9. For a general overview of the history and social transformation of this institution, see Dodge (1961) and Inan (1958). On educational reform in the late nineteenth and early twentieth centuries, see Ali (1974). For sociohistorical and sociological studies of twentieth-century al-Azhar, see Eccel (1984) and Zeghal (2007). In addition to the mosque and university, over two million students attend school through the al-Azhar institutes (*maʿāhid azhariyya*). On the global influence of these primary schools and their modernizing effects on African Islamic education, see Babou (2016).

10. Al-Azhar University is itself in the process of negotiating how classical texts can be made more accessible to their own students. Most students today are not prepared to work directly with premodern texts and instead rely on simplified texts, much like the simplified teacher's manual that Maryam drew from in her class (Cardinal 2005; Nakissa 2019).

11. The second general recitation mode is *mujawwad*, which employs the dramatic use of melody and register to heighten the emotional experience of the listener. It is the form of recitation often performed publicly in Egypt. Only the most advanced students study this style.

12. On the material Quran (*mushaf*) on which the 1960 recording is based, see Reynolds (2009) for a discussion of the 1924 Egyptian royal edition of the Quran. The textual compilation of the corpus of the Quran is known as the Uthmanic text, named after ʿUthman ibn ʿAffan (d. 656), the third caliph to rule the early Muslim community following the death of Muhammad. The standard sources on the Uthmanic compilation are the Nöldeke et al. (2013) collection, especially "The Genesis of the Authorized Redaction of the Koran under the Caliph Uthman," 252–276, and Bell and Watt (1970). For the most up-to-date analysis of the canonization, see Comerro (2012).

13. On the influence of mass print culture on the production of accessible Islamic publications, see Eickelman and Anderson (1997), Robinson (1993), and Ingram (2014).

14. The manual succinctly reads: "*Kawthar* is a river in paradise created by God. It is a miracle for the Prophet and his *umma*" (al-Ashqar 2006, 61).

15. Mandana Limbert similarly describes the use of modern schooling techniques in a women's religious lesson in Oman (2005).

16. On Muslim discussions of the Quran's meaning in prayer, see Haeri (2013, 2017).

17. The distinction is significant because if the Quran were eternal, it would be on the same plane as God. My depiction of the debate in broad strokes is

intended as a heuristic to contrast differing language ideologies, each grounded in a philosophical/theological tradition. For a rich discussion of Muʿtazilite theories of language, see Vasalou (2009). For an analysis of the political stakes of Islamic reformist hermeneutical strategies, see Mahmood (2006).

18. *Al-Fātiha* is ritually significant; it is the foundation of *salāt* and is recited to commence and bless important transactions and events. Michael Sells depicts the chapter's meaning as "a microcosm of basic Quranic beliefs in the compassionate creator, the day of reckoning, and the need for guidance" (2001, 173).

19. In Egyptian Arabic, the error would be heard in the vowel preceding the consonant—in the quality of the *a* rather than the emphasis on the *t*.

PART III

~

THE VIRTUES OF BASIC LITERACY

4

Making Mothers Read

It, of course, remains an open question whether, when Egyptian women are educated, they will exercise a healthy and elevating influence over the men. . . . If it can be once admitted that no good moral results will accrue from female education in Egypt, then indeed, the reformer will despair of the cause of Egyptian education generally in the highest sense of the word.

—Earl of Cromer, *Modern Egypt*

Here, literacy classes are a painkiller.

—Aya, resident of Batn al-Baqara

The women sat on child-sized benches that lined the walls of the community center classroom. In the morning, the room was filled with kindergarteners, while by afternoon, women from the neighborhood used the space for their literacy class. On a pale blue wall, cardboard circles with letters of the alphabet made a cartoon caterpillar. Since the women were typically responsible for watching over their children, the literacy teacher, Amal, encouraged them to bring their children along with them to class. The children played in a small courtyard next to the classroom, often disturbing the class, to Amal's frustration.

Samiya leaned over to pick up on our earlier conversation. "There isn't any point." She was explaining why she did not send her five-year-old daughter or nine-year-old son to school regularly. Samiya described how far their schools were: her daughter's school was on the far side of the metro station two stops away, and her son's—a school supposedly equipped for his physical and mental disability—was even farther away. "There are too many in the class for the teacher to even speak. And they don't know how to handle his needs. And the expenses! There is the uniform, the supplies, and I don't even know what else. Sometimes I send them just so they can get out, but that's it. They don't learn anything there."

Samiya turned back to the whiteboard. This was her fourth month in the Knowledge Is Power (KIP) literacy class. She had finished primary school at the age of fourteen but had never learned how to read a paragraph. While few of her female neighbors and cousins worked—few of the men had jobs either—Samiya was paid a modest wage each month to open and close the community center between prayers and activities. It was a job she inherited after her husband left her and her two children. She was twenty-six and had moved to Batn al-Baqara from Beni Suef with her family when she was young. Much of her extended family also made the move, and they lived close to each other in Batn al-Baqara.

Her cousin, Badriyya, sat on my other side. She was the most advanced in the class. Her daughter ran into the class to complain about her twin brother. Badriyya tried to ignore her and focus on Amal at the whiteboard. The women repeated the letter with different vowels following it, practicing how to recognize the difference between short and long vowel sounds. Badriyya was typically the only one who came to class with a notebook. She had attended school up until the age of fourteen. She spoke of her intelligence in the past tense but with pride. She was regretful that she had stopped school at such a young age—the same age that the men and women in her family stopped. She was twenty-four and the middle child of four siblings. Like Samiya, her parents moved to Cairo from Beni Suef, and she married shortly after at seventeen to a man who worked at the local pottery.

Badriyya strained to hear Amal, who shouted over the young voices shrieking outside the door. Amal paused, exasperated, waiting for the action to settle. One of the women stepped out to quiet the children. Amal tried to coax the room back into the lesson. She instructed the women to connect letter sounds together to build words, and not to memorize words as whole units, as she was once taught. She called on Samiya. She had been trying for weeks to direct them to raise their hands to answer questions, but the women saw the lesson as a group activity. Badriyya and a few others called out their answers. Some did it gently to tease Amal. The women's literacy instruction bent with the vicissitudes of when Amal arrived in the neighborhood, their children's moods, and many other factors that made classes sometimes rushed, often spontaneous, and always raucous.

In March 2011, the KIP campaign opened its first five classes in Batn al-Baqara. At that time, a wide range of activities were underway in the neighborhood, all run by mostly young volunteers, some of whom had been working in the neighborhood for years, while others were part of new undertakings born out of the uprising. By the time of my departure, after eighteen months of literacy instruction—three times longer than the Egyptian Authority for Adult Education's (EAAE's) official determination on the period of study needed to become literate—the women varied in their abilities to sound out words independently. None of them took the state exam. Amal wanted the two most advanced students, Badriyya and Rabab, to take the EAAE's test and earn the certificate, but they were hesitant to do so without the rest of their classmates. The arrangements seemed too complicated. One obstacle was the need to present a national identity card to take the test. Technically, students must present the card to enroll in classes, although this procedure was always overlooked since many nonliterate people did not have the card. Neither Badriyya nor Rabab had one. They never took the test. For nearly two years, attending literacy classes had become a part of their lives—not because reading or writing became routine but because discussing its importance had.

While I participated in community center activities and observed several different classes, I closely followed a single group that met three times a week. The dozen women in this class were brought together because many of them were in the same Quran lesson (discussed in chap. 3). These women became my closest interlocutors. They were neighbors and extended relatives who lived near the community center. Originally from Faiyum and Beni Suef, their parents settled in Cairo in the 1990s and early 2000s. There were a few mother-daughter pairs as well as cousins and in-laws. When everyone came together, the older generation was often indecipherable from the younger one.

This chapter follows the primary targets of urban literacy campaigning—women in slums. By paying close attention to their classes and situating literacy development within students' social worlds, I show how basic literacy in contemporary Egypt is so often frustrated. Though pointing to this failing, the chapter does not offer recommendations on how to rewrite a better curriculum, as some of my interlocutors had hoped. Instead, I draw attention to the epistemological, social, political, and material realities that make autonomous reading nonessential to so many Egyptians' lives. Literacy programs attempt to measure and recognize progress through government-issued exams, certificates, and statistical data, but a close look at literacy in one neighborhood illustrates the less tangible goals of literacy campaigning: the justification for literacy in the first place. For their teacher, Amal, and the women, the transition from nonliterate to literate was not an end in itself—a transformation that is difficult to quantify. Literacy's promises were always greater, just beyond.

Batn al-Baqara crystalizes what Starrett calls the charisma of schooling, even (and perhaps especially) when education cannot deliver on its promises (2009). This chapter describes how, through KIP, Islamic literacy development tried to manage students' ambivalence toward their literacy through moral lessons that associated literacy skills with the women's ability to mother. Literacy teachers attempted to cultivate the desire (*raghba*) for literacy, especially reading, in their regular lessons. In Batn al-Baqara, autonomous reading was taught as a skill essential to producing a particular kind of relational subject—a modern Muslim mother. In this way, literacy in Batn al-Baqara was gendered.[1]

I begin by introducing the KIP campaign, outlining the literacy sponsors and their faith development project centered on autonomous reading as a virtue. The implementation of KIP offers yet another version of Islamic reformist efforts to mobilize literacy. While previous chapters sketched distinct reformist efforts through basic literacy (as a site for instruction on religious fundamentals in chap. 1 and as a technique to bolster scripturalist approaches to the Quran in chaps. 2 and 3), KIP was reformist in yet another way—it promoted literacy as essential for Muslim civic life. I then trace the women's ambivalence toward literacy as they responded to lessons that instructed literacy as wholly transformative, to their lives, families, and neighborhood. In the final section, I consider the slum as a location of intensified development motivated by the revolution, drawing together media and campaign discourses and conceptualizations that make "slum eradication" and "the eradication of illiteracy" mutually imbricated projects for urban development. Nearly ten years following the women's experiments with literacy, after years of living with the threat of government relocation, in 2021, the last residents of Batn al-Baqara were relocated to a new development. Their homes were destroyed to make way for a new megaproject that combined commercial real estate and green space. It was my time in Batn al-Baqara that most clearly revealed the tragedy of literacy campaigning. Batn al-Baqara is a prism through which to see contending notions of "development." While residents directed teachers' and other NGO workers' attention to the material needs of the neighborhood, they were frequently met with reminders of the powers of literacy to improve their lives.

Knowledge Is Power

KIP was the largest literacy campaign launched during the euphoric period following Mubarak's ouster. The campaign was financially sponsored by Vodafone Foundation Egypt and implemented by half a dozen major NGOs, including the leading NGO, Life Makers.[2] Vodafone funded the campaign, and Life Makers took the lead in recruiting and training teachers, developing the curriculum, and establishing classrooms. Volunteers were mostly college students and unemployed graduates.[3] With Life Makers leading the campaign in the early months, classroom lessons brought together a standard developmentalist curriculum called Make Your Life, which teachers combined with their own Amr Khaled–inspired teachings.[4] Rather than traditional Islamic values, such as cultivating modesty or a fear of God, which are emphasized in the literature on the Islamic revival, KIP cultivated reading as an Islamic civic practice, promoting a classed, Egyptian Islam. Basic literacy, as taught through KIP, was directed toward developing one's role within the nation: to inculcate values of responsibility and culture.

Neither Vodafone nor Life Makers had any experience with literacy prior to 2011, so they called on Dr. Reda Hegazy, one of the country's experts, to be the lead technical consultant. He had recently been appointed as director of the Arab States Fundamental Education Centre (ASFEC) to revitalize the institution and its place in Egyptian literacy programming. (In 2022, he became the deputy minister of education and, later, the minister of education in the Mostafa Madbouly cabinet under el-Sisi). In our conversations, Hegazy outlined his pedagogical philosophy that, at least formally, animated the campaign. The techniques of instruction combined phonetics and word recognition with the ultimate aim of literacy as a means to build confidence, self-awareness, and self-reflection.

Vodafone promoted the use of a mobile app for literacy instruction that could be used on inexpensive handsets. The application was officially launched in October 2013, although I never saw a class or student use the app. It was featured in KIP promotional materials shared with investors and was employed in demonstrations at KIP training camps. The use of mobile phones in basic literacy is part of a development trend that incorporates technological solutions to major social and political issues.[5] A literate clientele advanced Vodafone's profit in a country the company referred to as an "emerging market" (along with India) through the sale of data.

Life Makers, founded and led by Khaled, evolved from a nearly defunct disparate collection of activities and offices during the Mubarak era into a nationally recognizable, revitalized good-works (*khayr*) organization in the wake of the January 25 uprising. The organization was the product of Khaled's television program of the same name that aired in 2004. The series sparked thousands of young people to get involved in grassroots organizing and marked the introduction of Khaled's message that civic responsibility is an Islamic duty. This was a significant shift from his previous stress on righteous etiquette (*akhlāq*). The series appealed to bored youth by calling them to replace the humiliation and frustration of unemployment with the purpose and dignity of volunteerism. Beginning with the establishment of Life Makers, Khaled's main message changed direction, calling on viewers to develop Egypt through grassroots community work. The program aimed to convert television viewers into actors mobilized by faith.

Life Makers emerged as a component of Khaled's work at the same time as a national shift in policies on charitable giving. Their activities responded to the Ministry for Social Solidarity's appeal to charitable organizations to adopt developmental values and practices through microfinance projects, capacity-building, and other methods (Atia 2013; Mouftah 2017). In this way, Life Makers was exemplary in taking up the government's effort to supplant charity with development. Although the organization ran traditional good-works activities, such as their annual distribution of food bags during the holy month of Ramadan, organization leaders typically downplayed these projects, emphasizing what they saw as their more innovative programs, like their campaign to stop school drop-outs. Literacy efforts fit within the scope of their dedication to principles of development.

From its beginnings, Life Makers had a tumultuous history with Egyptian authorities. The main source of the conflict was over how the organization mobilized Islam in their activities in a state wary of so-called political

Islam. Life Makers volunteers honed a distinct ethics and politics of faith development (*tanmiyya bi-l-īmān*) that sought to redefine traditional Islamic alms practices while critiquing the entanglements of politics and religion. Volunteers were mostly college students and unemployed graduates, and they distinguished their good-works activities through innovative projects that supported long-term social development. Their most potent critique of Islamic good-works organizations was in their emphasis on faith rather than mere religion. Their emphasis on faith was indicative of a reformism characterized by its apolitical stance that tried to avoid state sanction, as well as its marshaling of self-help and neoliberal discourses and practices. In their understanding of faith development, they rearticulated what made an act virtuous.[6]

Amal was among the first volunteers to join KIP. She opened the first class in Batn al-Baqara. Like other Life Maker volunteers, as a teacher in the campaign, she worked through her own stifled ambitions to find meaningful work; participating in the campaign was part of her efforts toward self-improvement. The uprising came during a long spell when she felt stuck. She was twenty-nine, living with her mother and two brothers in a low-income neighborhood at the end of the metro line. They lived on remittances sent from her father, who worked in Saudi Arabia. Amal had completed most of her schooling there, returning to Cairo to study law at Cairo University. Eight years after graduation, she continued to look for legal work. In our conversations, she would think through different career possibilities. Her experience with KIP and her inability to find legal work inspired her to consider the teaching profession.

With her students, she was friendly but guarded. Samiya and Badriyya pointed out how she was always careful to leave the neighborhood before sunset, revealing her discomfort and worries about safety in Batn al-Baqara. Amal explained that when she first started teaching the women, she wanted to do more than teach skills—she wanted her students to discuss matters of personal development (*tanmiyya dhātiyya*): "At the beginning they used to ask to focus on the alphabet. But with time, they came to enjoy our discussions. It makes me feel useful to give these classes." As she explained, discussions were a chance to offer advice and teach them culture. Her classes instructed women in manners and behavior (referred to as *tahdhīb*, self-edification, or *al-diyanna wa-l tahdhīb*, religion and self-edification), subjects that appeared in Egyptian curricula at the start of the twentieth century.

This, for her, was what she saw as education. She worried at times, however, that her students might not be interested.

Ambivalent Desire

Noha Saad, manager of Vodafone's Corporate Social Responsibility (CSR) team and Vodafone Foundation Egypt, spoke in an open-air hall perched on the Nile in the upscale neighborhood of Zamalek. She was recruiting volunteers for the KIP campaign. She explained how the campaign came to be, its early accomplishments, and the obstacles it was facing.

> We never imagined that our most basic challenge would be to attract illiterates to the initiative. At first, we imagined that when we would tell people we have a literacy campaign, any person—I mean it's very natural to believe—we thought that anyone given the chance to learn would participate. But the reality was much more difficult. The greatest difficulty is that they feel they must "keep up the costume," as they say. They do not want to admit their weakness. So, the illiterate person requires a catalyst, requires something to overcome the awkwardness they will feel in their family, with their children, when they go to learn, at the age of thirty and forty, how to read and write. We found the difficulties we faced strange, but they opened our eyes to the experiences and reality of development life in Egypt that we didn't previously know.

Much of what Saad shared about the campaign's challenges were the concerns narrated to me by KIP campaign teachers. Teachers were shocked that their students did not seem to want to become literate. One teacher from Batn al-Baqara understood this lack of a desire for literacy as part of the residents' state of ignorance: people could not want what they did not know was good for them. KIP's literacy activism focused on instructing potential students on *why* they needed to gain the skills of basic literacy.

An episode of the first post-Mubarak television series, produced by Amr Khaled, *Tomorrow Is Better* (*Bukra Ahlā*), is indicative of how educated classes assume a universal desire for literacy. (As Noha Saad explained, "It's very natural to believe" that nonliterate people will want to learn basic literacy.) Khaled filmed the episode in Batn al-Baqara, where he toured the famous kilns of the neighborhood and one-room apartments and spoke with people on the streets about their daily troubles. He distinguished the reality of what he saw in "the heart of the slum" from their cinematic depictions and negative stereotypes ("*Bukra Ahlā*" 2011). Sad music played as he evoked pity from viewers. The thirty-minute clip was designed to be a peek into the life of a slum that offered hope, with the shift to upbeat music in the literacy classroom scenes. Women were brought together from different classes for the filming. Khaled sat among them while a teacher wrote on the board. Khaled asked: "Why did you want to learn to read?" Some women offered responses, each over top of the other. None of their responses were intelligible. Khaled appeared pleased, smiling at them and the camera. The episode's conclusion was hopeful, promoting literacy as a way to transform the bleak urban conditions the episode depicted.

The clip of the KIP campaign in Batn al-Baqara is an example of what Lila Abu-Lughod calls "development realism," an Egyptian media aesthetic that "idealizes education, progress, and modernity within the nation" (2005, 81). For Khaled, the necessity of literacy was self-evident. His question to the women was rhetorical: *Why did you want to learn to read?* He focused on their desire for literacy, but his and many of his viewers' expectations for the women's responses overwhelm the scene. No real response can be heard. The answer is supposedly so obvious that it does not need to be articulated. There are a variety of reasons that lead people to literacy classrooms that cannot be articulated as wanting to read. The seemingly straightforward query assumes desire. The untold story of the episode is that daily lessons are dedicated to teaching students this desire.

Early in my fieldwork, I often made the same mistake as Khaled. Most of the responses to "Why do you want to read?" came from the early manuals of literacy curricula. A common reply referred to a lesson based on the image of a sick child: "I want to read so that I can tell if my medication has expired." Another: "I want to read because I want to read the Quran." Or: "Because I want to help my children with their homework." What I did not immediately realize was that by asking this question, I put their personal desire to read at the center. I quickly learned to abandon the assumption of learners' desire for literacy and to pay attention to the ways that teachers attempted to produce this desire in their students.

Amal worried that the women were less invested in the classes than she thought they would be. Months into the campaign, she decided to face their ambivalence head-on with an exercise. She scooted the children out of the class and shut the door. "Close your eyes and listen to me." This was not one of her usual lessons. Umm Hazim watched Amal as the others closed their eyes or covered them with their hands. Amal started: "You wake up in the morning and wake your children. You review their homework with them as you prepare breakfast. The news is on and you can read the words at the bottom of the screen. You take your children to school and then go to the market. You can read the cost of tomatoes and can count your money. You know how to pay the right amount for everything." By the end of the visualization, Amal had the women making their own money by starting up a small microenterprise project. In her description of their day, the women went to bed tired and satisfied. Then she told them to open their eyes. Umm Hazim was grinning at her teacher's idea of a lesson. This was her third time registering for a literacy class. She knew the sounds of some letters before she began her latest effort. But others in the room looked exhilarated.

Amal's visualization attempted to create the desire to read by presenting a vision of their transformed selves. She tried to teach the women to desire a better life, one that is clean and dignified. At times, the women put their faith in the power of reading so that with thin notebooks and a lot of practice, they could be more supportive mothers, more efficient managers of their homes, and better-informed Egyptians who could vote and participate in civic life. Still, they did not see how the ability to read could change their most immediate concerns. Their friends could not sell the small kilims they produced on the community center looms. Their husbands struggled to sell their casting work. They had no confidence in their children's schools. Community members I spoke with were often cynical about literacy efforts in their neighborhood. The women in the classes were ambivalent about literacy and the kind of changes it could bring about.

Reading Mothers, Forgotten Fathers and Sons

Motherhood was a trope shared by statist, Islamist, and neoliberal conceptions of gender that made reading a basic feminine responsibility for the nuclear family and the nation. In her study of literacy in turn-of-the-century Egypt, Hoda Yousef describes these "gendered uses of literacy" (2016, 6) in a context where there was a sharp distinction between the skills of reading and writing. Women were excluded from writing even when their reading was allowed and at times encouraged (what Yousef refers to as "inert or read-only literacy" [64]). Women who engaged in literacy practices typically learned to read and became consumers of print media, while men were scribes or held positions that required them to write. As historian Wilson Chacko Jacob explains, a woman's skills were directed toward the performance of familial and civic duties, whereas men's education "sought to produce a sovereign individual subject capable of governing others" and also oneself (2011, 297, fn. 82). Literacy was gendered not only in the practices that were emphasized in literacy classes but also, significantly, through the moral implications attached to it.

Literacy efforts in Batn al-Baqara resembled literacy programs across the Global South that focus on women as primary subjects for literacy. Contemporary development frameworks associate a country's development with women's education. Specifically, Arab and Muslim women are regarded by an international development regime as particularly in need of saving, especially through education. This commonsense development framework has been thoroughly critiqued by scholars who point beyond education as an explanation for social problems, highlighting geopolitical contexts shaped by colonialism, war, and other forms of oppression (Abu-Lughod 2005, 2008; Adely 2009, 2012; Khoja-Moolji 2018). Khoja-Moolji explains how the Muslim girl/woman "has functioned to incite fear of societal degeneration as well as hope for the future. She is passive but embodies energy and power, which if not harnessed properly through education, can spell the destruction of society. However, when educated appropriately, she can inaugurate familial, national, and civilizational progress. Thus, the education of Muslim women and girls has been intricately linked with governing them and molding them into ideal subjects" (2018, 13). The figure of the Muslim girl/woman homogenizes women, making no distinction between national, class, or other differences that shape women's lives. In all cases, a woman's education is seen as a tool of empowerment. In her critique of education as women's empowerment, Adely is attentive to women's articulations of progress that they locate in relation to family and morality, not in opposition to them (2012). This important intervention disrupts unitary notions of progress and complex ways in which women imagine the role of education in their lives. The women's literacy class in Batn al-Baqara offers a different vantage point from which to view literacy because the women are ambivalent and, at times, even skeptical about the value of education in their lives. Their classes, like Egyptian literacy efforts, promoted and instructed literacy as a skill to enhance women's contributions to the home.

At the end of the nineteenth century, political leaders and intellectuals articulated the need for women's education, making girls' and women's education key to building the modern nation. Historian Lisa Pollard describes how in this period Egyptian education made the private realm have political implications. New national curricula imagined the progress of the nation through the cultivation of women's role within the family.[7] As Omnia El Shakry observes, "Both secular nationalist and Islamist texts on proper mothering and child rearing identified women as both a 'locus of backwardness' and a sphere of transformation essential to the nationalist project" (2007, 174). The gendered implementation of adult education (like all levels of education) by the state, Islamist, and leftist feminist groups stressed literacy as essential to motherhood.

By the twentieth century, the family became a focal point for social planning that made it "a microcosm of the desired moral order" (Eickelman and Piscatori 2004, 83). The family was depicted as a sacred domain to reorient Islamic politics. The modern family was defined as a husband, wife, and children; polygamy and living with extended family were regarded as backward. Arguments in defense of women's education among Islamic modernists centered the value and necessity of her education for the family (Najmabadi 1998; El Shakry 1998).[8] Women were seen as having the privileged role of overseeing both the biological and ideological reproduction of the Islamic community. To this end, their education was not only tolerated; it was deemed essential. Modernists like Qasim Amin (d. 1908) advocated for the primary education of women to enable them to reshape themselves and their families. Zaynab al-Ghazali (d. 2005), founder of the Muslim Women's Association (*Jamāʿat al-Sayyidāt al-Muslimāt*), a group closely allied with the Muslim Brotherhood, argued that women could be educated as long as they dedicated their skills to their families. She warned of the harm caused by women who do not stay at home until their children have become independent.[9] At the same time, the emphasis on motherhood was also a hallmark of Egyptian nationalism since Gamal Abdel Nasser's family planning programs sutured domestic relations with the nation (Baron 2005). The theme of motherhood in nationalist and Islamist discourse is historically well documented, and yet the ways in which women and families have encountered this messaging are widely overlooked.

Amal's lessons drew on a long history of nationalist and patriarchal imaginings of the family—particularly the mother—as a moral grounding for the nation. Her classes taught women to embody their knowledge as frugal housekeepers, supportive wives, and instructive mothers. Amal, like most volunteer teachers, was single and without children of her own. In several classes, she encouraged the women not to spank their children and to instead use persuasive language with a gentle tone. In a lesson on basic arithmetic, she discussed the importance of saving money, even if in small amounts. When the women laughed at the suggestion of saving money, Amal tailored her advice: "Even one or two pounds a week."

In each of the women's homes and within the buildings they shared with extended family, I observed how the lessons on motherhood were ill suited to the realities of their families and households. Students' families did not adhere to the ideal forms of the family unit modeled in literacy lessons. Instead, their kinship attachments beyond the family unit, as well as their reliance on neighbors, disturbed the roles and responsibilities of the gendered family as taught in a classroom (that echoed the messaging of Egyptian social development projects). The focus on women left many men feeling excluded. Badriyya described the residual problems associated with social programming that targets only women. She explained how literacy classes sometimes put her at odds with her husband. When she tried to save a small sum of money one month, as Amal had encouraged the women to do, her husband complained and spent the money. She was concerned that, through their lessons, the women became more conscious (wa'ā) of social issues than the men in their lives, which resulted in marital tensions and disputes.

Umm Hazim had previously completed a literacy class. She was forty-eight, the oldest in the class, and technically too old to participate in the campaign. She was married at sixteen and lost her husband a few years prior to enrolling in the literacy class again. She was Samiya's maternal aunt and lived on the first level of the same building. She lived in her apartment with her only unmarried children, two sons—eleven-year-old Rady and twenty-three-year-old Hazim. Hazim sometimes worked with neighborhood artisans at the kilns. He was typically away whenever I visited his mother; on the couple of occasions that he returned home while I was there, he stood at the doorway to talk with me so as to maintain an appropriate distance where he could be seen by others in the building. One time, he arrived as his mother was preparing tea, and he joined us. She scooped water out of a large plastic barrel into a small metal kettle on a gas burner. She poured equal amounts of tea pellets to sugar into two cups, one for me and one for Rady. His pants were stiff with clay from the kilns. He asked me if there were any plans to start literacy classes for men. There were already five classes at the community center, all for women, and I was not aware of any plans to open any more. I told him that I would mention his interest to a KIP coordinator. He described how the men were having difficulty selling their goods. He looked down into his cup: "Maybe they think the men are too busy at work."

Samiya had a cautious sense of possibility in the early months of the literacy campaign. "Tahrir," as she and others put it, referring to the central point of demonstrations, was for their unoccupied sons—not in school and without work—while the women tended to housework and childcare. Most of the women urged their husbands to work rather than get caught up in protests. Among women in the class, some stayed at home and did not earn any wages, while others participated in projects that allowed them to make money, like Samiya, who performed a maintenance role at the community center; Maryam, who ran a small business of selling baby clothes; and Aya, who taught the morning period at the community center's kindergarten. These women had more secure incomes than the men in the neighborhood.

Two posters from two literacy campaigns sixty years apart are illustrative of the mother figure in literacy promotions. Both posters show mother and son. The black-and-white image displayed in an exhibit at the Literacy Museum at ASFEC, in Sirs al-Layyan, Menoufia, comes toward the end of the exhibit, among half a dozen similar black-and-white posters from a literacy campaign in the late 1950s or early 60s. The literacy museum is a showcase of mounted wall placards, photographs, paintings, textbooks, and dioramas that tell the story of literacy in Egypt starting with the establishment of the United Nations and UNESCO (United Nations Educational, Scientific and Cultural Organization). A woman in a *gallābiyya*, the traditional Egyptian everyday garment, with a scarf tied around her hair, reads to her son. In Modern Standard Arabic (MSA), the caption states: "*Ummī laysat ummiyya*" ("My mother is not illiterate"). The wording plays on the words *umm*, "mother," and *ummiyya*, "illiteracy," which come from the same Arabic root. The poster depicts the idealized image of a mother reading to her child. It takes up the voice of a boy who has learned the lessons of Egypt's modern education that, as Pollard summarizes, "a reformed, educated, rational mother would teach him the kinds of morals, virtues, and behavior suitable to an Egyptian in all his affairs" (2005, 122).

The color image comes from a Vodafone CSR brochure. The publication reports on the successes of the company's social responsibility accomplishments and is distributed to Vodafone investors. The glossy booklet reported

Figure 4.1. Poster from literacy campaign in the Literacy Museum, Regional Centre for Literacy in Rural Areas for the Arab States (ASFEC), Sirs al-Layyan, Menoufia. "My mother isn't illiterate." Photo: Author.

السـت دى قـدرت تتعـلـم
تقــرأ وتكـتـب ودلـوقـتـى
بتساعد أولادها فى المذاكرة

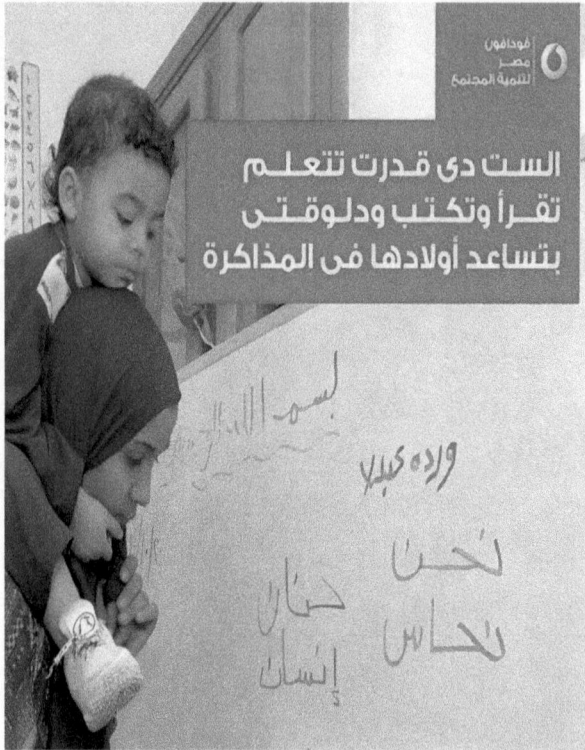

Figure 4.2. Vodafone promotional media for Knowledge Is Power. "This woman was able to learn to read and write and now helps her children with their studies."

on the KIP campaign. An entire page was dedicated to one of the women from Amal's class. Her son sits on her shoulder as she writes on a whiteboard. In colloquial Egyptian, the caption reads: "This woman was able to learn to read and write and now helps her child with their studies." The photograph captures her lesson, while the caption projects how this lesson will enable her to use this skill for her children.

In the black-and-white poster, the voice of the son proudly narrates that his mother is not shamefully illiterate, while Vodafone's promotional material is narrated by a third voice. Neither caption attempts to capture the woman's perspective on her (il)literacy. The posters also reveal tensions over what form of language should be used in literacy through the shift from MSA used in the first poster to dialect in the second, a shift undoubtedly related to campaign sponsors. Compare Vodafone's colloquial "this woman" (*as-sitt dī*) with the formal language of the black-and-white poster, which was produced during Gamal Abdel Nasser's pan-Arabism when literacy efforts were made on a national level to enlist MSA as a uniting and culturing force. Vodafone's "this woman" speaks the language of the women themselves, the everyday language of Vodafone, employing the vernacular of telephone calls and text messages.

The KIP campaign sought to bring the nonliterate into a conversation of political participation and responsibility, emerging markets and citizenship. The campaign turned to mothers amid a failure of state institutions to provide education for their children. In this way, KIP, like other campaigns and programs, had the mother replace public schooling as the support for the nation's overburdened and little invested-in education system. The motherhood dimension of the campaign raised the stakes on the moral imperative of literacy: failure was not just a personal matter but meant the sacrifice of one's children and family.

Recall from the first chapter, Suzanne Mubarak's unpublished memoir was told through the lens of reading bedtime stories to her grandson. *Read Me a Book* was a maternal call to the nation to read, and the memoir continued the tradition of pedagogical-didactic *tarbiyya* treatise through the genre of memoir and the relationship between a grandmother and her grandson.[10] Suzanne Mubarak, sometimes affectionately referred to in the media as "Mama Suzanne," promoted reading as an activity of familial bonding. In guest appearances on the Arabic *Sesame Street* (*'Ālam Simsim*), just as in her libraries, Suzanne Mubarak's literacy advocacy was that of a mother to her children. During the uprising, the reified mother of nationalist discourse was an important figure for state media, NGOs, and revolutionaries alike. The campaign maintained the historical continuity of the trope of the mother.

While women participated in lessons that made reading essential to motherhood, in conversations outside of class, they questioned the benefits of literacy classes at a time when their neighborhood risked threat of dislocation and suffered from poor waste disposal and other material problems. The trope of the self-sufficient mother in literacy classes offered a theoretical solution for Egyptian education—one that starts and ends in the home. But this was not an ideal the women strived for, even as their own images were used to promote it through campaign media.

The Limited Powers of Autonomous Reading

Traveling on main thoroughfares that pass the edges of Cairo's slums, I frequently heard Egyptian friends pity the people who lived there. In Batn al-Baqara, sitting on a stoop in the afternoon, the women pitied their friends from nearby neighborhoods who were forced to leave. When I arrived in Batn al-Baqara, some residents had already been relocated to a new desert development. Neighbors debated these relocations. While a few described their improved situations in new buildings with running water, most commiserated with those who had moved away from the place and people they knew. Aya, a kindergarten teacher, described their dislocation as lonely and without life. She had a friend who had been relocated three months earlier. Her friend complained to her every day—the small apartment, the empty neighborhood. There was no market, no life. Among my interlocutors, there was a looming fear that they too would soon be relocated. Batn al-Baqara had problems, yes, but it was home.

Residents were accustomed to the influx of middle-class NGO workers and volunteers visiting the neighborhood following the uprising. Most saw literacy as better than the food bags they received as alms. The presence of outsiders in the neighborhood allowed them to discuss long-term problems, such as the insufficient sewage system. A few members of the community plied young activists and volunteers, educating them on "the real needs" of the neighborhood in an attempt to direct their attention toward infrastructural projects. In my early days in the neighborhood, some asked if I was collecting information for the government. At first, I worried that this meant they were suspicious of me; however, I soon realized that some wanted me to be such a researcher in the hopes that I would report their needs to the government.

In Cairo's damp winter months, the shifting mud on the street caused problems in some of the buildings' foundations, and the occasional light rain was enough to bring down roofs. During these months, I was asked to visit homes and witness the destruction. I told them that I would contact an organization that does home repairs. After weeks, I finally got through to an NGO worker I had met in the neighborhood. She explained that she turned her phone off most of the day because of the number of calls she received from residents notifying her of roof collapses and other building troubles.

One afternoon, I sat on Aya's couch in a darkened living room. She lived around the corner from the community center where she taught kindergarten in the mornings. My conversations with her were more relaxed than with others because there were no children nearby to be disciplined. At twenty-two, she had spent her whole life in Batn al-Baqara. She reflected on the influx of new projects in the neighborhood following the January 25 revolution. Most of the initiatives revolved around education such as adult literacy, tutoring, and a new Montessori school that had recently been built. She was one of the few women in the neighborhood who had graduated from the equivalent of high school, and she was the most skeptical of the intense focus on education. "I'm a teacher, and look at me, here I am carrying this bucket to the road like everyone else." She referred to the cesspool at the entrance to the neighborhood where residents collected their waste.

"The first problem everyone here will tell you about is the sewage. It is a ditch that fills, and once a month, a man comes with a machine to drain it. He takes 150 pounds. Sometimes, when we call because it is filled, he doesn't come for days. Do you know how we know when it is filled? When it overflows." She stopped to watch my reaction to this. She wanted me to absorb the indignity. "We need a local oven with affordable bread; we have to walk too far for basic goods and then the price is high. And a pharmacy, we need a pharmacy. The cost of marriage is high, and it is difficult for women to collect all the things they need to start a household." A neighbor stopped by, and as she settled in to join us, Aya prompted me to ask her friend what the greatest problem was in Batn al-Baqara. Before I could say anything, her friend responded: "It's the sewage." Aya nodded at me.

Aya said, "Here, literacy classes are a painkiller (*maskan*). The problems are deep. We would need to be powerful to do anything." Her criticism of literacy was not a critique of all education but of the limits of education to improve their lives. For Aya, knowledge, not even formally recognized knowledge in the form of diplomas, was power. Power came from connections. It came from a family name; it was the prerogative of people in well-to-do parts of the city, those on television and who wrote in newspapers, those who visited Batn al-Baqara to do *khayr* work. As she and others saw it, the benefit of the campaign's focus on the neighborhood could be found not in educating mothers but rather in attracting attention to basic infrastructural needs of the community, needs that were too often overlooked for more ideologically attractive projects like education. It was not only that literacy could be implemented inexpensively, while sewer lines cost money. Literacy perpetuated the lessons of a civilized society: that "the problem" is education—access to it and the quality of it. Literacy, as Aya and others saw it, was part of an education system they did not trust, no different following Mubarak than it was during his thirty years. In the context of social transformations underway in Batn al-Baqara and places like it, literacy, as Aya put it, was a painkiller.

In the Old Cairo neighborhood, adult literacy classes came to resemble the schools where residents sent their children. One may or may not learn. Amal met this challenge by investing in the ideal of transforming lives through didactic lessons. Women tried, on and off, in their literacy studies. The *why* was rarely spoken of. But the students' ambitions were more modest than those of their teachers. Power was not accessed through a skill. It could, however, be prodded through outsiders.

Both the women of Batn al-Baqara and their teachers saw literacy as an opportunity that could improve their material worlds; however, they imagined this in different ways. Some of the women saw the intense focus on literacy in their neighborhood as a possible way to connect them to people with influence. Teachers, however, saw education itself as capable of having transformative impacts on the neighborhood. The stigmatization of slums and the people who live there is similar to the stigmatization of illiteracy. The discourse that constructs the categories of illiteracy and slum are related.

The Project of Eradication

Following an afternoon lesson, I left Batn al-Baqara with two volunteer teachers. Down the main road, a cluster of high-rise apartments was under construction. Unlike the uneven edges of Batn al-Baqara's streets, the new blocks were eight or nine stories high, symmetrical, and perched on a plateau overlooking their older neighbors. I asked whether the development was considered part of Batn al-Baqara. Sarah told me it would be called New Fustat, but it would likely soon resemble its surroundings. She said: "A slum is not a neighborhood (*bi-manti'a*), it is a state of mind (*bi-fikr*)." Amal agreed but was bothered by her own pessimism: "How can they change if they can't even live as human beings?" We walked together quietly for some minutes, past the ceramics and pottery vendors that lined the road and through a cloud of burning refuse. As we made our way to the metro station, they began to talk about a recent Life Makers event. While in the classroom, they stressed the transformative effects of education. Outside, as they confronted the cesspool and fumes, they worried that the city's slums were irremediable.

The eradication of slums and illiteracy are interrelated projects that understand the person and place as codependent. Timothy Mitchell describes this view of education through a Foucauldian understanding of "methods of ordering" (1988). Major educational transformations of the nineteenth century created new institutions that introduced modern education, while, at the same time, Cairo's cityscape was planned to minimize alleyways and build grand boulevards. Commenting on these simultaneous projects, Mitchell observes that educational reform and the demolition and reconstruction of the city "conformed with prevailing medical and political theory. The disorder and narrowness of the streets that open boulevards eliminated were considered a principal cause of physical disease and of crime, just as the indiscipline and lack of schooling among their inhabitants were the principal cause of the country's backwardness" (Mitchell 1988, 66–67).

National development and urban planning discourses reveal how both the space and the people who inhabit informal settlements are elided, so Sarah's comment—that the slum is more than a place, but a state of mind—is an observation that naturalizes the relationship between those who live in slums with their physical spaces. The focus on slums in literacy development is part of a broader national effort to take up the cause of urban development. Until recently, Cairo slums have been largely neglected by government policy that privileges rural programs. The country's social fund explained the direction of resources to villages as a response to the most severe cases of poverty and argued that urban interventions would accelerate rural-to-urban migration. Such a policy is not supported by statistics but appears to be part of a preconceived understanding of "third world poverty," which contradicts the Egyptian case (Sims 2010).

Of Cairo's seventeen million people, eleven million, or about 63 percent, live in informal developments built since the 1960s (Sims 2010, 91).[11] The 1992 earthquake caused major damage to informal neighborhoods and raised the profile of the need to address urban poverty. While Cairo's slums expanded over the last thirty years, it was not until 2008 that a presidential decree established the Fund for the Development of Slum Neighborhoods (FDSN).

Both the FDSN and the EAAE are similar in their function as government bodies that address "failures" of national planning, one in urban planning and the other of education; they each operate as a backup emergency body for the Ministry of Planning and the Ministry of Education, respectively. In their capacities to produce policy and programming, they speak of "eradication" in their plan for Egypt's future—the eradication of illiteracy and informal spaces. For example, a February 2013 headline in the major daily newspaper *Al-Masry Al-Yawm* read: "Executive Director of Slum Fund: Egypt without slums by 2017." Egyptian newspapers frequently run stories on the persistent dangers of rockslides, crime, and disease in slums. In the years following Mubarak's ouster, newspapers reported on the general worsening conditions and failures of bureaucratic endeavors at relocation. With security as the basis for intervention, slum removal programs are couched as benefiting those in the neighborhoods as well as being in the service of the greater good of Egyptian urbanites whose safety is threatened by unchecked urban squalor.

The organized apartment blocks that emerged down the street from Batn al-Baqara were only the beginning of intensifying urban developments that transformed Fustat and Islamic Cairo. In June 2021, all thirty-two acres of Batn al-Baqara were evacuated and seized by the New Urban Communities Authority to build Fustat Hills Park, a megaproject of green space, shopping malls, and restaurants.[12] Nearly two thousand families were removed from their homes. Media outlets widely spoke of the furnished apartments with modern appliances that awaited them. By order, all residents were relocated to Asmarat, some eight miles east of where Batn al-Baqara once was. The official name of the development, a grid of identical concrete buildings, is *Tahya Masr* (Long Live Egypt), a slogan of the revolution. For many of Egypt's middle class, the development is a testament to the country's progress. By the time of the evacuation, none of the phone numbers for my interlocutors in the neighborhood worked. It was not uncommon for phone numbers to change, but over the years, I was no longer in contact with any of the women in Batn al-Baqara. None were on social media, where I kept in touch with other interlocutors. I asked KIP teachers who worked in the neighborhood to help me make contact. They, too, had fallen out of touch. I felt I had failed them. They had been the heart of my fieldwork and grounded me in my life in Cairo.

As I tracked the news on life in Asmarat, I imagined Aya, Badriyya, Samiya, and Umm Hazim starting anew with their families. Residents who had once owned their properties, even those in poor condition, lost them with little or no compensation. Rent in Asmarat was expensive.[13] I wondered what the men who had worked the kilns did now that their workshops were destroyed along with the home demolitions. I wondered if they lived close to each other and what it meant for a nonliterate woman to sit in a new apartment she never wanted to move to.

Thinking about urbanism in conjunction with literacy reveals some ironies. Although Aya and her neighbors prioritized an improved infrastructure in their neighborhood over the promises of education, their forced dislocation was also not what they wanted. Egypt's massive urban planning projects are key to the neoliberal planning politics of contemporary Egypt. So, too, are the limits of what Islamic literacy development can bring to a place like Batn al-Baqara.

Conclusions: Reading for Modern Muslim Motherhood

Literacy classes in Batn al-Baqara reveal the different and sometimes conflicting constellation of expectations of teachers and learners. KIP endeavored to cultivate a desire for literacy in the face of women's ambivalence about its potential in their lives. Amal and other volunteer teachers attempted to introduce a new habit of reading into the women's lives, to remake their lives. Instructing women to desire literacy became the main objective through lessons that taught the women to imagine literacy as a step toward hygienic, pious, and responsible living. In Batn al-Baqara, where basic material needs were more tangible and pressing, the teachers' case was a difficult one to make.

In Batn al-Baqara, women saw the family-focused lessons with an emphasis on motherhood as disconnected from their realities. The focus on women created family tensions. It left some women feeling isolated from other members of their families who did not partake in similar classes. Beyond their immediate practical concerns, there was a profound distrust in the education system, for those of their children and, more broadly, in terms of the power of education to be in any way transformational. Literacy was seldom what was asked for, and yet it was a priority among activists and *khayr* organizations. In this way, literacy did not fulfill the desire of the person to be developed but rather sought to instruct them in how to desire the correct things.

The KIP campaign taught reading as a sacred practice not because of a connection with sacred texts but through how they made reading a virtuous act for the liberal state—a practice upon which a pious nation depended. These ideals were part of regular literacy classes in Batn al-Baqara and beyond. Chapter 5 turns to the secondary recipients of literacy: male workers. At a shipyard in an industrial zone south of Cairo, literacy classes revealed the contradictions of literacy as revolutionary action. By tracing the moral lessons of the literacy campaign that made literacy virtuous, namely, the emphasis on creating happy, cultured, and productive laborers, chapter 5 inquires into how literacy classes became sites to navigate social hierarchies between teachers and students, as well as administrators and workers. While worker-students were skeptical of KIP's upbeat message of development through faith, they invested in the lessons in an attempt to gain respect.

Notes

1. On women's gendered literacy in the Arabic-speaking Middle East, see, for example, Agnaou (2004) and Khamis (2004).

2. As the financial sponsors of the campaign, Vodafone's involvement was indicative of decades of Egyptian neoliberal development (Atia 2013; Elyachar 2005; Mitchell 2002). Vodafone has an expansive international CSR division as well as country-specific and administered Vodafone Foundations that work closely with national partners on local projects. The CSR activities are typically company initiated and work more explicitly on company objectives. In Egypt's Vodafone structure, employees work between the Foundation and CSR departments.

3. They volunteered during a period of high national unemployment, felt particularly by those under the age of thirty-five. According to Egypt's Central Agency for Public Mobilization and Statistics (CAPMAS), unemployment rose to 13 percent at the end of 2012, up from 9.8 percent at the end of 2010. The growing number of young people entering the workforce, particularly those with a higher education, increases national unemployment figures annually (Assaad 2008, 133). My own foray into international development as a Canadian International Development Agency youth intern involved working on a program that specifically targeted youth unemployment as a demographic problem and sought to transform it into one of the country's major assets for development. The United Nations' International Labour Organization and its subgroup, the Youth Employment Network, isolated the social and economic challenges of unemployment faced by youth. As fewer young people find jobs and are thus forced to postpone marriage for a number of reasons (including limited funds to cover its high costs), the period in one's life known as "youth" extends into and through one's thirties. Following the earliest events of the Middle East uprisings, the focus on Arab youth sparked journalistic and scholarly interest in young people in the Middle East. For scholarly works, see Deeb and Harb (2013), Jung et al. (2014), Sukarieh and Tannock

(2014) as well as the collected essays in Khalaf and Khalaf (2011). For an overview of the anthropological study of Arab youth, see Joseph (2013).

4. The name of the campaign uses the word *'ilm* (knowledge) in its broadest sense, including "scientific knowledge." *Ma'rifa* is sacred or mystical knowledge; it is God knowledge. See Rosenthal (1970) on the major role of knowledge and its pursuit in the Islamic tradition. At the time of KIP's launch, Vodafone had much to gain from the positive image of collaborating on a development project with Life Makers. Like other major mobile and internet networks, Vodafone cut their services for five days, starting on January 28 (although some activists had their lines cut for several months). The unpopular decision led to protests in front of Vodafone branches in the United Kingdom. Vodafone Egypt CEO Hatem Dowidar publicly defended the company's decision to suspend service, affirming its compliance with the laws by which its networks operate and claiming that the state could have cut connection in their stead, which would have prolonged the reconnection. The company drew further criticism for broadcasting a commercial celebrating the revolution and suggesting that it inspired protests in Tahrir Square.

5. See Moore's (1980) study of the engineering profession as a key factor in Egypt's theoretical modernization launched with Nasserism.

6. I refer to affect, emotions, and feelings not as emotional or psychological states but rather as social practices (Lutz and Abu-Lughod 1990; Ahmed 2004). In doing so, I tend to the ways that my interlocutors understand a language of emotions to create and communicate positive feelings through the literacy campaign.

7. See, especially, Pollard (2005, 100–131).

8. Referring to modernists like Al-Tahtawi, Abduh, al-Afghani, and Qasim Amin, Cuno observes: "The most important reason for the education of women was their role in childrearing and household management" (2015, 106). Ellen McLarney locates the significance of the Muslim family in Islamic politics: "The private sphere of intimate relations has been the site of a particularly intense process of creative self-fashioning, a place for cultivating the techniques of self so critical to Muslim piety in the age of the Islamic awakening" (2015, 3). In this view, she continues, "Women are interpreted as having a privileged role in overseeing the transmission and reproduction of these techniques of self" (2015, 3).

9. See Hoffman (1985) for a discussion of al-Ghazali's position on women's education.

10. See Baron (1994), El Shakry (1998), and Pollard (2005) on Egyptian *tarbiyya* literature.

11. The rapid construction of informal settlements in Cairo began in the mid-1960s (Sims 2010, 11). Sims explains how the term *slum* is employed to discuss urban margins in a globalized discourse of urban planning that associates Cairo's informality with vastly different conditions in other major cities of the South.

12. The New Urban Communities Authority is another state body, alongside the FDSN, whose work includes the building of new urban settlements to relocate residents from informal settlements.

13. For a typical Egyptian media depiction of Asmarat, see *Al-Watan*'s coverage at https://www.elwatannews.com/news/details/6511628. Mohie (2018) provides a rare critical depiction in the Egyptian independent *Mada Masr*: https://www.madamasr.com/en/2018/06/18/feature/politics/asmarat-the-states-model-housing-for-former-slum-residents/. On media depictions of Asmarat as a way for the state to consolidate power, see Elmouelhi et al. (2021).

5

Workers Writing toward Dignity

I use my time to work in order to build Egypt
And I like to work to protect my country and my family
And I work well for the sake of God not in fear of anyone

—Tawfiq, Arab Contractors, Maʿsara

Tawfiq had a complaint. He did not want anyone teaching him happiness.

That day, Tawfiq's literacy class was interrupted for a special seminar. Teachers gathered the worker-students into one classroom. A Life Makers volunteer tried his hand at motivational speaking. He stood at the front and wrote the word *saʿāda* on the board. *Happiness*. For forty minutes, he spoke about gratitude to God and how to appreciate God's blessings. The smell of salty sweat hung over the crowded room as many of the men fidgeted. The speaker encouraged them to live with hope and optimism in the face of instability. Other teachers joined in with examples of how they chose to live happily despite setbacks. When they finished their lesson, the workers filed out of the makeshift classroom to return to their regular classes.

In a hallway made of long sheets of wood that the workers had built in the workshop-cum-school, Tawfiq spotted his teacher, Omar, and confronted him: "What is this? I don't come to literacy class for happiness talk. Happiness? This is not why we leave our work and come to literacy. I come for my abcs. In these seminars they try to tell us how to vote, but we discuss politics among ourselves, we don't need the opinion of this youth. I work all day. When I go home, someone wants thirty pounds for this, another wants fifteen pounds for that. Happiness! He wants to talk about happiness!"

Teaching about happiness was part of the cultural programming embedded in the literacy classes at the Arab Contractors shipyard in an industrial corridor of Maʿsara, south of Cairo. There, Knowledge Is Power (KIP) aimed to instruct the workers to be cultured and productive subjects.[1] The lesson, however, was an embarrassment to Tawfiq, who wanted to learn literacy skills, not lessons in faith and happiness. He ran errands for company administrators, while most of his classmates were laborers. He spoke with clear diction, unlike his colleague Salih Fathi (mentioned in chap. 1), who said he did not want anyone calling him ignorant.

Complaints like Tawfiq's were not common at the shipyard. Omar was embarrassed by Tawfiq's objection. The student's eloquent rejection had disrupted the typical rhythm of literacy classes at the Arab Contractors' shipyard. Still, days after the confrontation, Omar wrote a sentence on the board as part of a writing exercise: "Don't search for happiness; create it yourself" (*lā tabḥath li-saʿāda wa-ṣnaʿhā ʿan nafsik*). Each of the men, including Tawfiq, copied the sentence into their notebooks.

Workers (predominantly male) are the secondary targets of literacy development in the Global South.[2] In Egypt, literacy has long been directed toward educating agricultural as well as industrial workers. The KIP campaign continued in that tradition, integrating faith lessons into its classes across dozens of factories participating in the campaign. As an affective pedagogical project in Life Makers' faith development, KIP sought to cultivate productive workers in ways that drew on and magnified class divisions between the ignorant (*gāhil*) and the educated (*mutaʿālim*). KIP lessons enjoined workers to imagine positive futures in ways that workers sometimes argued were out of touch with their realities.

Reading was the literacy skill emphasized among women, as seen in chapter 4's discussion of literacy development in urban slums. In contrast, writing was the focus of factory lessons that were directed toward guiding male worker-students to pass the final exam. To demonstrate literacy's effectiveness to the shipyard's human resources department, literacy had to be made legible through the written word—written paragraphs, successful exams, and government certification. The campaign carried out a global trend of directing men's literacy toward writing and a form of autonomy that made them self-possessed subjects.[3] Not only was writing the masculine skill of literacy but, as I depict, it was deployed for men's claims for a masculine dignity.

For many workers, literacy was a tool to gain respect from others. As Lila Abu-Lughod notes in an aside on literacy among women in rural Egypt, the paternalistic methods implemented in classrooms undermine the potential

laudatory effects of education initiatives (2005). Her observation underscores the predicament of the giving and withholding of respect in adult
education programs that structured the literacy campaign at the shipyard. I
use the terms *respect, dignity,* and *honor* interchangeably, despite the height-
ened prevalence of talk about dignity in the context of the Middle East uprisings. Several scholars of the region have noted the significance of dignity
(*karāma*)—and its politicization—in the period leading up to and including
the uprising (Hamdy 2012; Singerman 2013; El Bernoussi 2021). I include
the terms *respect* (*ihtirām*) and *honor* (*sharaf*) within a constellation of my
interlocutors' vocabulary, as these are values that contrasted against feelings
of shame (*'ār*) and humiliation (*dhull*)—sentiments that workers described
as the motivation for their participation in the campaign. As I show, literacy
classes provided the space and opportunity for men to experience occasions
that prompted these feelings.

Teacher-student interactions reveal the challenges of using literacy as
a technique for social transformation. Because workers were required to
present themselves in normative structures of self-representation, they were
obliged to reflect on their lives in unfamiliar ways in order to construct and
portray those lives as ideal workers.[4] In their early experiments with the
written word, neoliterate workers mobilized circulating scripts of the virtues
of work and happiness to respond to and participate in their literacy classes.
By taking up the tropes of productive labor, they were taught to employ the
very discourse used to discipline their productivity in order to make claims
to their personal dignity, one of the central claims of the revolution.

Shipyard classrooms offer a crucial site to observe a major challenge to
revolutionary action—the negotiation of recognition between social classes
brought together through literacy campaigns—worker-students and volunteer teachers. This chapter explores the (mis)communication between workers and teachers, paying close attention to how workers navigated face-to-face
communications and their incipient writing. *How did workers (en)counter
literacy as cultural capital and an ethical project of self-formation? How did literacy classes (dis)enable workers' communicative strategies, particularly amid a
new chapter of Egypt's workers' movement? What communicative strategies did
workers deploy to navigate interactions with their employers and the campaign?
How did burgeoning literacy skills shape workers' negotiation for respect?*

Workers did not depend on writing to make political demands, nor did
they employ their nascent writing skills as a tool for "self-expression," as

educationists like Reda Hegazy, director of the Arab States Fundamental Education Centre, envisioned for literacy. Instead, they continued to privilege face-to-face communication as a means of complaining and negotiating with authorities. While those who learned to read and write during the literacy experiment at their workplace had the potential to use their new skills to further the workers' movement, to assume that literacy enables such political participation is to follow the fallacies of linear literacy development from the illiterate to the literate.

It may seem obvious that workers would be wary of writing as a new form of communication and be more confident in the spoken word. But it is important to note that just as illiteracy is highly stigmatized, how a person speaks and the language they use is indicative of one's social class. As literacy studies scholar Lesley Bartlett explains, "speech shaming" comes from any deviation from the way that the social group believes is correct speech. Deviation creates "linguistic insecurity" among those with little or no formal education who fear that they do not know the "correct" way to speak (2007, 556). Noting the ways in which speech reveals social class, it is significant that distinctions in speech were far less inhibiting for workers who navigated their literacy lessons at the shipyard in ways that sought to protect their dignity. By strategically shifting communicative practices, workers navigated not only the powers exercised by teachers and shipyard administration but also the powers of communicative technologies (Abu-Lughod 1986; Caton 1990; Cody 2013).

In this chapter, I situate KIP at the Arab Contractors shipyard and within the broader context of the workers' movement. By placing workers' communicative practices within their broader political context, I pay particular attention to workers' expressions of shame and their overtures to gain respect as a primary motivation for their participation in the campaign. I then turn to the moral lessons of the campaign, returning to the happiness lesson described in the chapter's opening to understand the campaign's message of faith development through lessons on optimism. The remainder of the chapter examines workers' adaptive and sometimes strategic shifting communicative practices—between the use of images, the spoken word, and the written word. As I show, the act of writing hamstrung neoliterate workers who employed the moral lessons and vocabularies of literacy to assert their dignity in their writing.

Gender dynamics at the shipyard were markedly different from any other space I navigated in Egypt. On the grounds of the male-dominated shipyard,

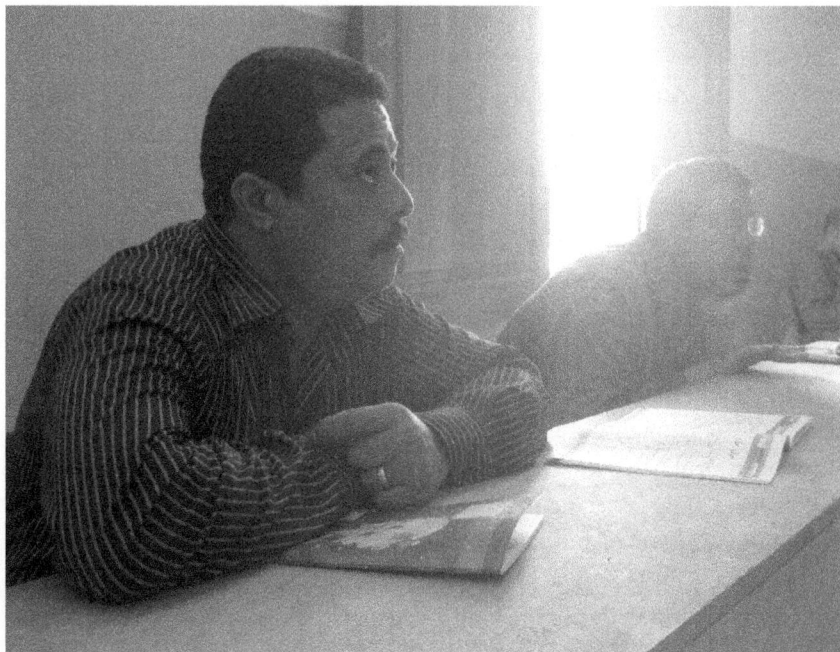

Figure 5.1. Tawfiq (*left*) and Rif'at (*right*) in Arab Contractors classroom. Ma'sara, June 2012. Photo: Author.

I was defined less by my gender and more so by my education. Some worker-students were self-conscious in front of me as an advanced graduate student on my way to earning a doctorate. I tried to minimize my involvement in the classes, which took the form of occasionally grading exercises. Whatever I did or did not do in the classroom, what was most crucial was that I demonstrated respect for the men.

Literacy at Work

In 2012, KIP was implemented at Arab Contractors sites in Cairo as well as Pepsi Egypt and a number of factories located in the Sixth of October industrial area. Regular, regimented classes and monitored attendance at factory settings made literacy classes the most effective sites for ushering students through the state literacy exam. Still, at the Ma'sara shipyard, after eight months of classes, few students passed the state exam. Three times a week, shortly before one o'clock in the afternoon, workers at the shipyard laid down their equipment to attend a two-hour literacy class. They participated in KIP at a moment when managers at AC—the largest construction company in the Middle East—were coping with unprecedented workers' organizing. AC's involvement in KIP was symbolically and strategically important given the company's central role in major national projects. Since literacy had become a major development goal in the 1950s, Arab Contractors had been a key partner in the country's industrialization. Opening literacy classes at Arab Contractors sites in 2012 was a patriotic gesture initiated at a moment of increased worker organization and mobilization.

Arab Contractors is a symbol of Egyptian industry and national development. The company was behind the construction of several of President Abdul Fattah el-Sisi's high-profile megaprojects, including what was touted as the world's largest suspension bridge, as well as mosques and government buildings in the New Administrative Capital (built outside of Cairo). Its role in the country under el-Sisi's leadership is a continuation of a long history of prominent Egyptian development projects, including a Suez Canal causeway and the new Alexandria Library. Arab Contractors founder Osman Ahmed Osman established the company in 1955, and from the beginning, it was closely associated with Egyptian industrialization and modernization. Its minor role in the construction of the High Dam under Gamal Abdel Nasser was widely advertised and established a reputation for the company. Anwar Sadat contracted Arab Contractors to renovate two presidential palaces; throughout the renovations, Osman and Sadat formed a close relationship that eventually led to Sadat naming Osman minister of construction in 1973.

Osman continues to be a major reference point for the company's philosophy. His memoir, *Pages from My Experience* (*Safḥāt min Tajribatī*, 1981), sold out a first printing of sixty-five thousand copies, and bookstores continue to sell the book. A Life Makers and KIP administrative leader began a meeting for Arab Contractors volunteers by citing Osman's memoirs and holding him as an exemplary figure of a self-made man.[5] Osman is so closely related with building projects in Egypt that people made up a joke about his importance to Egyptian history: "Who founded the Ottoman (*Osmanī*) Empire?" "Osman Ahmed Osman."[6]

Work at the shipyard included building and repairing Nile cruises, mostly floating hotels and restaurants. The shipyard was situated along the Nile, some twelve miles south of Tahrir Square, where I would catch the microbus for the long commute down the corniche to the industrial zone of Maʿsara. The shipyard is surrounded by cement factories and other production plants. The guarded entrance opens onto a compound of office buildings, workshops, and heavy machinery. Workers arrived from across the city each morning, many traveling over an hour. Classes were held in a workshop-turned-school. The men were compensated for their time in the classroom and promised bonuses if they passed the final exam, with prizes for top students. Of the 1,500 workers at Maʿsara, 109 were enrolled in the literacy classes. Supervisors nominated workers they knew could not read or write. The human resources department closely followed the progress of the classes. An employee took regular attendance, and the HR manager visited periodically to observe classes. Each time the HR representative would exit the room, he would encourage the students he referred to as *awlād* (children), *shabāb* (youths), and *rigāl* (men). The diminutive terms were part of how status at the shipyard was produced.

The worker identity was reproduced in interactions with teachers and was part of the men's negotiations for respect. Samer Shehata's ethnography of shop floor culture at a textile factory examines how "working class identity emerges at the point of production" (2009, 2). A working-class identity is produced simultaneously with products through processes that create modes of interaction that shape how people understand themselves and others. At the shipyard, literacy became a site through which the worker identity was not simply reproduced but was renegotiated through cross-class communication where workers articulated their own meanings and goals for literacy.

In Egypt, the working class emerged in the 1910s, when terms such as *worker* and *workers* (*ʿāmil* and *ʿummāl*) as well as *the working class* (*al-ṭabaqa al-ʿāmila*) were first used in public discourse (Lockman 1994, 158; Goldberg 1986). The emergence of these categories was the result of capitalist modes of production as well as political and ideological changes that created new notions of nation and citizenship, in which the worker was a significant player (Lockman 1994, 187). Literacy development's emphasis on individuation was attenuated by the celebration of a collective workers' identity, especially one that was reanimated in complex ways with the revolution.

Egyptian workers have been both a support to governing legitimacy and a challenge to authoritarianism.[7] While the worker has been an important figure for nationalist causes—a patriot and builder of the nation—unionists, scholars, and activists depict the Egyptian worker as a patriot precisely through their resistance to power. Long a figure of national pride and a symbol of the country's industrialization, workers are simultaneously regarded by an "educated" class as simple, aggressive, and even violent—notions that clearly shaped literacy class interactions.

Egyptian workers labor in varying conditions that have been criticized internationally as unfair and illegal. The International Labour Organization has kept Egypt on the blacklist of countries violating labor rights since 1957. This decision was made following the announcement that a government-sponsored union, the Egyptian Workers Federation (later known as the Egyptian Trade Union Federation, or ETUF), would be the only representative of workers' rights. The decision to form the ETUF was somewhat ironically announced on the occasion of Nasser's oft-quoted position that represents the Egyptian state's stance toward workers to this today: "The workers do not demand; we give."

The country's first independent union, the Egyptian Federation of Independent Trade Unions (EFITU), was formed during the 2011 uprising in a move to overthrow the government's stronghold over worker mobilization. It rapidly grew to 1.6 million workers in its first year with several hundred other new unions. The EFITU was formed at a moment when the role of workers in the uprising was debated (Beinin 2012). Some leftists, such as Ahmed Maher, cofounder of the April 6 Youth Movement, claimed that workers did not contribute to Mubarak's overthrow because their narrow claims did not include broader political demands.[8] Others, such as 2012 presidential candidate and labor rights lawyer Khalid Ali, saw the momentum of workers' protests in the years leading up to 2011 (particularly the 2006 Mahalla al-Kubra strikes) as inspiration for the 2011 uprising.[9] The strikes in Mahalla al-Kubra were the culmination of an increase in collective strikes in the early 2000s, particularly among textile workers whose factories were scheduled to be privatized. New methods of protest emerged during this period. Instead of participating in factory occupations where production continues as normal, protesters chose to employ a method of protest initiated during the Nasser era—they halted production altogether. This method was controversial, as it was understood to be an affront to Egyptian industrial development. Throughout 2011 and 2012, worker strikes and high-level organization grew at a rapid rate never seen before in Egypt, although the strikes were seriously curtailed under el-Sisi's severe antiprotest laws. This was the backdrop for the implementation of literacy education in the Arab Contractors shipyard.[10]

While KIP taught literacy as the first step to Egyptian development and democracy, the very techniques of revolution that brought about the fall of Hosni Mubarak's regime were successful precisely in their bodily methods, rather than the use of formal channels of opposition dependent on literacy. Arguably, one of the most effective strategies of worker protest is withholding labor. In addition to workplace protests, laborers demonstrated in front of sites of symbolic power, like the People's Council and the government-sponsored ETUF. Creative tactics included mock funerals and beating on empty pots to demonstrate hunger as a result of low wages (Ali 2012, 24). One reason that complaints were made orally and protesting was expressed through physical acts was a possible mistrust of writing. Not only was writing a symbol of inefficient and oppressive bureaucracy, but it could also form evidence against the workers. Even workers' contracts that could protect their rights and give them official status within a company were used against many in company practices that pressured their employees to sign away legal protections.[11]

In Ma'sara, workers had long abandoned the idea of forming a union. While the uprising gave rise to some new forms of agitation for pay raises at the shipyard, none of my interlocutors were a part of those efforts. As they explained, if there was a union, it would only be for appearances. There was a significant difference between older laborers who had worked at the shipyard for at least a decade and younger workers. The older generation spoke of stable contracts. Their salaries helped them to marry and raise families. Most of their children were in public universities or on track to attend one. The younger generation had less stable contracts. The men in their twenties were saving their money to be able to afford to marry. Still, even they saw their employment at the shipyard as fortunate. Mustafa, a twenty-four-year-old solderer, began working at Arab Contractors in 2008 but was forced to leave when work dried up. He went on to install transmission towers for Mobinil for a year before he was able to return to the shipyard. He explained that, despite an occasional work shortage, he preferred Arab Contractors to other jobs because he was paid decently and given better benefits than those offered by other companies where he performed similar work.

Despite the relative quiet of the shipyard while workers elsewhere organized and protested, HR was distressed by a rise in complaints. The Arab Contractors administration I spoke with described literacy as essential for culturing shipyard workers. Most shipyard administrators began by describing how literacy would increase workers' efficiency, but—even more important than their work—they saw literacy as a technique with psychological and behavioral benefits. Literacy, in their view, was a way to culture brute (ʿasabī) workers and a remedy to what they saw as rising tensions on the jobsite following the uprising. Abir worked in HR for thirty-two years. She described what she saw as the deteriorating respect afforded to authority and the challenge of placating workers' demands: "Here we have many problems. After the revolution, the workers want everything—an increase in salary— they want more." She said that the workers' monthly salaries (ranging from 1,000 to 2,000 EGP) were good, but because the workers complained and it was a time of "people taking rights," salaries increased anyway. "Yes, things have changed after the revolution. Nobody respects any other person. [...] I am by nature calm. We are taking all of their complaints, all of their words, and we are really working on them. Because now, after the revolution, you can't just say 'no' to anyone, even if it isn't their right, you are forced to respond and give them something. The revolution has really changed people from within."

For the shipyard's administration, literacy was a form of action to respond to changes taking place in the country. Literacy classes were another service to offer workers (along with company restaurants and intramural sports). But they were also something more. For Abir, literacy had the power to manage workers at a moment when social order had been disrupted.

Make Your Life: Happiness as Virtue

Fatima, a volunteer teacher, strained to be heard over the sound of a nearby saw. She paused and turned to the board, writing: *maʿan naṣnaʿ al-ḥayāt* (Together, we make life). This was Life Makers' slogan and a lesson she repeated in her classes, which echoed the campaign curriculum, *Isnaʿ Ḥayātak* (Make Your Life). The men copied the phrase into their notebooks. When the saw stopped, Fatima pointed at each letter, asking students in turn to make the corresponding sound. Below it, she wrote: *dhikr Allāh yurīḥ al-qalb* (The remembrance of God eases the heart) and proceeded in the same way until the class of ten men sounded out the phrase together. Next, she turned to the lesson, *aḥlāmna* (Our Dreams). She asked students to share their dreams for the future and assisted them with recording their goals, discussing what steps they might take to achieve them. Fatima extended Amr Khaled's self-management techniques, so prominent among Life Makers KIP volunteers, to the campaign's students. The lesson was typical of KIP literacy instruction.

When Tawfiq rejected the happiness lesson at the seminar, he was responding to more than a singular lesson but to an effort by KIP volunteer teachers at the shipyard to suture positive affects to Islamic faith. For Life Makers, happiness was the virtuous expression of Islamic faith and central to its teachings, both in how its members were trained as volunteer teachers and in how they instructed their classes. Volunteers taught hope (*amal*), happiness (*sa'āda* and *farah*), and optimism (*tafā'ul*) as expressions of faith in their revolutionary actions. Change, as they saw it, needed to be grounded in positive feelings.

One day at the shipyard, Salih Fathi asked that I pass along a message to Amr Khaled: "Tell him that students graduate from high school and still don't know how to read. What does he plan to do about that? And what happens when they graduate? Does he know that here we have students who graduate from high school and don't know how to read?" A teacher overheard our conversation and announced to all within earshot that it was important to be optimistic at this time and not lose hope. Salih Fathi said nothing and returned to work. His "message for Khaled" was a departure from the more characteristic deference he offered his teachers, even when their lessons seemed out of step with the men's lives.

KIP campaign teachers saw themselves as providing a more comprehensive education for cultivating Islamic faith. The campaign curriculum Make Your Life extended the familiar themes of self-representation, health, and hygiene seen in state curricula like *It'allam Itharrar* (Learn and Be Free) and *It'allam Itnawwar* (Learn and Become Enlightened) with Khaled's lessons on dreaming, happiness, and goal-setting. KIP resembled national literacy programs with lessons on how to read a national identity card and the presentation of jobs (farmers, factory workers, etc.) as a way to fulfill one's role within the nation, but it also drew together those lessons with Khaled's Islamic *da'wa* that preached happiness as a crucial part of building faith and developing positive emotions. Additionally, teachers improvised beyond the curriculum, stressing the need to cultivate a positive outlook as part of a faithful life. Short Quran verses and hadith were woven into lessons to instruct an Islamic faith of positivity.

The message of the volunteer teachers contrasted with many of the affects commonly articulated at the time, such as everyday expressions of worry, despair, or anger.[12] Their happiness lessons echoed developmentalist social programs in Egypt that were a pointed departure from the atmosphere they worked in. Graffiti in Tahrir Square declared: "I'm angry" (*ana ghadbān*) with an incitement to continue demonstrations. Evening talk shows implored viewers to recognize various threats to the security and unity of the country. As Fatima explained to me, happiness is something a person *is* as well as what a person *does*. For Life Makers, optimism was not a state of mind but rather was integral to the realization of faith through action. Volunteers drew on a wide repertoire of self-help literature. Their persistent positivity at that political juncture made their critics perceive them as naive and willfully disconnected from what was happening in Egypt.

Volunteers spoke of the more pious disposition of hope (*amal* and *rajā'*), but the emphasis on happiness and optimism as virtuous affects predominated the lessons. While *amal* and *rajā'* describe a longing for God and the afterlife, optimism reflects patterns in personal development that were also part of global marketing trends and popular culture. Following the events of 9/11, happiness was promoted in the region through public relations campaigns that regarded Arab and Muslim cultures as obsessed with death in initiatives like the 2008 Culture of Optimism campaign launched in Egypt (Sukarieh and Tannock 2014; Sukarieh 2012).

The cultivation of specific emotions for ethical ends is a dominant feature of contemporary Islamic reform. Life Makers' promotion of happiness contrasts with Islamic rhetorical strategies in Egypt that emphasize fear of God (*taqwā*) and fear of the afterlife (*tarhīb*) through detailed images of death and punishment. Teachers aimed to cultivate particular virtuous sentiments, although they set themselves apart from this major trend. So while optimism was not unique to Life Makers, it was a technique to cultivate a particular kind of piety that distinguished them from other revivalists.

Happiness lessons were integral to volunteer teachers' faithful implementation of literacy at the shipyard. The happiness seminar that day captured the tenor of Life Makers' affective pedagogy and the politics of the campaign. Lauren Berlant's felicitous "cruel optimism" (2011) illuminates the political effects of KIP's affective pedagogy. For Berlant, optimism is cruel when the desire for an object impedes the very aim of initial attraction. Life Makers' optimism was not only cruel in how the campaign filled in where state programs were lacking or failed. It was cruel in its support of the state while the organization was surveilled and regulated by authorities in ways that would soon make their work precarious. The campaign's insistence on optimism was cruel in its bind to support the state through good works, while subject to the whims of state power.

Life Makers created a form of Islam that eschewed not only political ambition but also the claim to religion. For volunteers, faith development was not an alternative to the machinations of Islam for political power; it was an authentic version of Islam. Teacher-student interactions gave rise to experiments on how to communicate across social classes. Volunteers saw these interactions as edifying experiences, while for students, exchanges between teachers and students could be fraught.

Images of Hierarchy: Omar and Hisham

Hisham kept to himself. Unlike the others who came to class directly from work, Hisham changed into street clothes for class, shedding his blue coveralls for a worn collared shirt. At thirty-six, he had been a company driver with Arab Contractors for nine years. After literacy class, he often drove volunteers in the company's van to the shipyard gate. He seemed satisfied to offer the favor. He had paid for his literacy certificate in order to get the license necessary for his position. Each drive to the gate was a reminder that "to become literate" was a formal recognition available for purchase. The media regularly covered scandals of people purchasing literacy certificates. The Egyptian Authority for Adult Education acknowledged these stories in its communications; in 2012, it confirmed a case of students procuring licenses for 800 EGP (equivalent to 130 USD at the time).[13] Hisham explained that he was in literacy class this time because he wanted to learn "for real" and not just for a certificate. Several other workers expressed the same ambition— that this time, they wanted literacy to not be "for show."

Despite Hisham's efforts to earn his certificate this time around, he quickly grew frustrated with his classes. In our conversations, he shared how he usually felt lost and did not understand why lessons seemed easy for others. One day, as I graded his quiz, another student looked over my shoulder and teased him about his errors. In embarrassment, Hisham yelled at his classmate and shoved him. His teacher, Omar, tried to separate the men; a shipyard administrator eventually arrived and pulled Hisham away. He missed the following two classes. Hisham and I never spoke of the altercation or his absence. I sensed he did not want to. For weeks, he did not speak in class and avoided talking with me.

Omar was known among the workers for being patient and friendly with his students. He asked them not to use *ustāz* ("sir," a formal way of addressing a male teacher). It was a notable request that was part of what made him different from other teachers. He was a twenty-four-year-old graduate of the Faculty of Architecture at a small private university. He enjoyed photography and was a consummate observer who struggled to make decisions. When we first met, he had recently graduated but was waiting to be called to serve in the army, a rite of passage for most Egyptian men. Omar was less confident than many of his Life Makers friends who were more committed to the organization's ethic of development based in faith. He explained that while Khaled was "a little bit religious," he watched his television programs because they made him feel better when he was depressed about school.

Omar made a distinction between his teaching work at the shipyard and his involvement in other organizations he joined in 2011. When he worked with a small neighborhood grassroots organization, Maʿadians, and another established good-works organization, Resala, he met other people like him. Fellow volunteers lived in similarly comfortable neighborhoods and went to similar private schools—better than public schools but not as exclusive as international language schools. With these volunteers, Omar sorted and distributed food bags, but he rarely interacted with the recipients. Through his work with the campaign, he explained, he got to know people from different social classes: "I wanted to help the country after the revolution. I asked myself: Should I continue to protest with others? I thought the first step should be education. There is poor etiquette (*akhlāq*) among the lower class, and literacy can help with this."

Teaching turned out to be a source of anxiety for him. He struggled with how to instruct adults and found himself speaking to them like children. He recalled with embarrassment how early in his teaching he had scolded a student, grabbing a pencil from the man's hand. Both he and the student were flustered by the episode. The altercation with Hisham also shook him, but as a result, he tried to improve his relationships with his students. He thought that by sharing his interest in photography, he might make himself more approachable and form some sort of bond with the men.

After class one day, the men gathered to take photos with Omar. Most took pictures on their mobile phones of the equipment and occasionally together in groups; Omar, however, mainly took portraits of the men. He spent the most time with Hisham, who posed for his portrait in front of a company sign posted beside the entrance to the workshop. Before Omar took the photograph, he read the sign to Hisham, turning the company placard into an impromptu lesson.

> Your Dignity Comes from the Dignity of Your Country
> Donate a day's work to the Egyptian economy
> It is better than raising our hands to our enemies
> And God said about alms:
> "And in heaven is your provision and what you are promised"
> Make optional deductions today for two months
> Whoever wishes to do so, register your name with the Director of Human Resources
> Raise Your Head High, You're Egyptian

The sign asked workers to turn their labor into alms. The donation is voluntary, an invitation to give up a portion of one's wages. By invoking a chant often heard during the uprising (*Raise your head high, you're Egyptian*), the placard—with its call to see one's dignity through Egypt's—turned the workers' financial support of their employer into a patriotic act. In the photo, Omar captured Hisham's full body, dressed casually with no uniform. Arms at his sides, he abandoned his usual cigarette for a pencil that he gripped in his right hand as he looked into the camera.

As a student himself who was struggling to pass his final exams, Omar was aware of the frustrations his students experienced. His photo of Hisham was an attempt to dissipate a strain that stemmed from his power over his student. With his camera, he tried to create camaraderie. And yet the photos with the uniformed men revealed the image of the worker-student and the ambiguities of respect entailed in that position. Months later, when he failed the state exam, Hisham said little. He would continue his job without the interruptions of a class that regularly humiliated him. Omar shared his photos, which the men circulated by text message. Through his portraits,

Figure 5.2. Hisham poses for a photo by his teacher. Maʿsara, August 2012. Photo: Omar ElKady.

he sought to diffuse teacher-student power relations. And yet, as I saw the pictures shared on Omar's Facebook page, the portraits created the image of a worker-student—dignified yet diminutive, and through the likes of his friends, they became evidence of the campaign's success. Similar to the portraits, the workers' early written passages that we now turn to depict the self-conscious poses of worker-students as they represented themselves to their teachers and also themselves.

RECOGNITION THROUGH WRITING

When students who learned to write began composing sentences and, later, short passages, they employed the vocabulary and themes they had learned in class. A few weeks after Salih Fathi's expression of cynicism, he wrote his first sentence, spending twenty minutes recording a common prophetic saying: *inna Allāh yuwaffiq man yuḥāfiẓ ʿala waqtih wa-yaqūm bi-adāʾ ʿamalih bi-itqān* (God grants success to those who conserve their time and do their work well). While literacy programmers and teachers spoke of writing as a way for neoliterates to express themselves, students rarely deviated from their lessons. To do so would have required a facility with writing that few, if any, mastered.

Within literacy development, writing is an idealized form of self-expression. On the state literacy exam, the ultimate (and only legal) arbiter of literacy, the final section prompts students to write a paragraph about themselves. What makes an individual literate, according to state testing, is their ability to write a paragraph about their daily life. To prepare for the question, teachers assigned various writing tasks such as composing a letter to a friend, writing about Ramadan, or describing the value of work. The workers' early written passages capture what Laura Ahearn describes in her study of Nepalese incipient writing as a window on "social transformation *as it is occurring*" (2004, 306). In their early written passages, neoliterate students mobilized circulating scripts of the virtues of work. By representing the tropes of productive labor, they employed the very discourse used to discipline their productivity.

Rifʿat was among the most advanced students at the shipyard. He brought booklets with him to class that he sometimes read while his teacher covered a lesson he was already comfortable with. In response to a writing prompt asking students to reflect on the proper use of time, he brought together common class themes of efficiency and piety with his own gestures toward self-respect:

> *ana asta ʾmil waqtī fī al-ʿamal min agl an nabnā maṣr*
> *wa uḥibb a ʾmal min agl an nuḥāfiẓ ʿalā al-waṭan wa-ahlī*
> *wa-atqana fī ʿamalī li-wagh Allāh wa-laysa khawfan min aḥad.*

> I use my time to work in order to build Egypt
> And I like to work to protect my home and my family
> And I work well for the sake of God not in fear of anyone

Rifʿat used a lesson on time management to respond in a way that would satisfy his teacher and yet also assert his own self-sufficiency. In the writing exercise, he portrayed himself as someone who went beyond the conventional expectations of worker loyalty through personal courage. Like other early written passages by the few students who gained skills in writing, Rifʿat's sample associated a worker's dignity with his labor: his commitment to "build Egypt" and work for God. Yet, his relative skill enabled him to modify classroom scripts by including his pride in caring for his family. Workers frequently spoke with me about how they hoped new literacy skills would help them feel more at ease with their literate families. Worker-students were taught that their literacy was essential to their roles as workers—not within the domestic realm. Despite this, the men shared with a mix of pride and shame how they were the only nonliterate person in their family. Their employment at the shipyard enabled them to marry "educated women," as they described their wives, and send their children to school and university. Their wives and children's education subverted the hierarchy of the nuclear family patriarch, even though education did not undo the father's power through his role as the family's provider.

The workers' writing was a way to stage masculine ideals. Indeed, masculinity was integral to the sort of recognition they sought. As Farha Ghannam explains: "Acquiring a masculine identity is not simply an individual endeavor but is deeply connected to the recognition granted by others" (2013, 3). While literacy programs imagined men to claim masculinity through their labor, men were instead eager to discuss how their literacy would allow them to play a greater role within their households: by helping their children with their homework, for example, and more generally, by belonging in a family where they were no longer the only person who was not literate. They explicitly evoked literacy skills as valuable to their roles as fathers.

SAYYID'S COMPOSITION

Sayyid wore glasses but still needed to sit close to the board. He rarely participated in class and seldom spoke to his classmates, who were mostly young contract workers. Everyone felt a certain affection for him as the mild-mannered elder of the class. When we first met, Sayyid spoke proudly about his educated family: a daughter who worked as a teacher, one son who was graduating from the Faculty of Law, and another in his final year of high school. His wife taught Arabic at a private school.

As the temperature rose in late spring, it became difficult to sit at the wooden desks in the midday heat. After four months of literacy classes, Sayyid came to class with a passage he had written at home. He described how, after the Friday prayer, he had left his family to sit in a room by himself and write. As he showed me the composition, two of the younger workers, Mustafa and Muhammad, listened to our conversation. Soon, Fatima overheard and came over to see his work. Mustafa and Muhammad teased Sayyid that he was the only one in his family who could not read. He only nodded and repeated that he wrote his paragraph without any of their help.

Sayyid's foray into writing turned into a classroom event. Typically reluctant to use my camera because of the disruptions it often caused, I asked if I could photograph his paper. He was pleased with the request, but insisted that he copy out his passage in better handwriting. I explained that I liked the one he had produced at home, but he insisted on one with better penmanship. Throughout the class, he diligently reproduced his work on a clean sheet of paper from his notebook. The endeavor took two passes, but by the end of class that day, Sayyid shared his fresh copy.

kānat thawrat al-khāmis wa-l-ʿishrīn min yanāyir hadifa wa-mubāraka. tilka hiya al-thawra allatī fajjarahā shabāb ṭumūḥ min agl al-khurūg min al-ẓulumāt ilā al-nūr li-l-wuṣūl ilā al-ḥurriya wa-l-dimuqrāṭiya wa-l-ʿadala al-ijtimāʿiya wa-tilka hiya al-thawra allatī adhhalat al-ʿālam ajmaʿ fa-ashādat bi-l-maṣriyīn alladhīna al-ʿazīma wa-l-iṣrār min agl al-nuhūḍ bi-baladihim. wa-kāna al-shabāb hum al-sharāra allatī awqadat tilka al-thawra al-ʿazīma min agl taḥqīq maṭalibihim al-mashrūʿa al-jadīra bi-l-iḥtirām min agl taḥqīq mustaqbil afḍal. wa-lam nansa bi-l-dhikr shuhadāʾ tilka al-thawra alladhīna qaddamū arwāḥahum fidāʾan li-l-waṭan min agl an taḥyā maṣr ʿazīza karīma ḥurra mustaqilla li-dhālika nabʿath li-kull al-arwāḥ al-ṭāhira allatī fāraqat

*al-ḥayāt li-tamnaḥunā al-ḥurriya wa-l-karāma wa-l- 'izza wa-l-dimuqrāṭiya.
ḥāfiẓ Allāh maṣr.*

Name: Sayyid ʿAbd al-Munʿim Muhammad, carpenter
The 25th of January Revolution had specific goals and was a blessed
revolution. This revolution was sparked by ambitious youth in order to move
from darkness to light to reach freedom, democracy, and social justice. This
revolution amazed the world who praised Egyptians who persist and insist
on raising their country up. These young people were the spark that started
that great revolution to achieve their legal and honored demands for a better
future. We do not forget the martyrs of this revolution who gave their souls as
a sacrifice for the country of Egypt to be precious, free, and independent. We
send blessings to all the pure souls who left life in order to give us freedom,
dignity, honor, and democracy. May God protect Egypt.

After he completed the final version in his best handwriting, his teacher left
her own mark on the page. She drew a red star and wrote: *rabbinā yukri-
mak* (May God honor you). The process of rewriting the paragraph returned
Sayyid to the position of a student seeking the approval of his teacher, and
yet his effort marked a departure from all other writing at the shipyard until
that day. Sayyid took pride in the composition, even in its performance (the
rewriting, my photograph, Fatima's red star). The content of his passage di-
verged from the usual topics and forms of worker-students' writing. Instead,
he participated in a revival of the language of political poetry underway with
the uprising.[14] In his celebration of the uprising, Sayyid depicted how expressions of nationalism articulate an Egyptian masculinity.[15]

The composition was reminiscent of mid-twentieth-century workers' poetry that took up the poetic form known as the *zajal*. Leftist intellectuals
adapted the form in their literary circles and political struggles, first writing about the worker and later incorporating workers' own *zajals* into their
literary magazines (Beinin 1994). Written in colloquial Egyptian, the *zajal*
employs themes and rhythms typical of oral poetry. Rather than celebrating
the worker-patriot, Sayyid's passage praised *youth* as heroes of the revolution.
And yet, in marking himself as author and carpenter, in both content and in
its very formulation, the composition dignified the writer.

Sayyid's composition was citational, like the Quran lesson described in
chapter 3 in which the women offered answers—verbatim—that they were
given by their teacher. His composition was not a revelatory "account of the

self" but instead repeated what was commonly stated at the time. In this way, his writing recognized "the value of the already-said" (Foucault 1983, 68). For Sayyid and other neoliterate worker-students, writing was neither the ideal of self-expression their teachers spoke of nor was it the medium of opposition by which literacy activists are often motivated. Sayyid's passage identified the revolution as a youth revolution, one harnessed by people like campaign teachers. At the same time, it drew learners into the "blessed revolution" not only as problems to be solved through literacy but also as actors. His passage depicts nouveau literacy, a concept Dana Sajdi deploys to describe the entry of nonelite people into the practice of writing historical chronicles, a genre previously reserved for scholars. She explains how nouveau literacy is not about everyday people's *attainment* of literacy skills but rather how those people gain a new *authority* in entering the discursive field of the genre, using their writing "as a means for self-presentation and/or preservation" (2013, 6).

Rif'at's and especially Sayyid's passages depict how workers subtly employed writing as a technique for recognition. Sayyid, like the others in his class, understood himself, in part, through the eyes of others. Workers saw their teachers' lessons as naive, and yet they carried on the dialogue necessary to be understood by them. While most were cynical of Khaled's reformism, they recognized that they were indeed dependent on the campaign for their own aims. Their engagement in literacy demonstrates how those deemed ignorant skillfully negotiated their recognition—a recognition that they understood may be politically inconsequential but could afford them dignity.

While Sayyid's composition offers a rare instance of literacy-in-process, his composition was not a culmination of the campaign to make workers legible through writing. Instead, Rif'at and Sayyid's written passages are indicative of the kinds of scripts found in incipient writing. While workers sought dignity through recognition as people who are not roundly deemed ignorant, the actual ability to write was no guarantee of transcending stigma. What constitutes the sign of literacy and the literate person is a moving target.

By participating in the campaign, workers negotiated status through various strategies to circumvent the stigma of ignorance. In their literacy classes, the men performed an identity they knew to be intelligible: the worker. It is through these interactions—the gaps between the spoken and the written—that we better understand the fragility of respect, a fragility that has political reverberations beyond the shipyard on ongoing protestations for personhood on the national stage.

Figure 5.3. Sayyid rewrites his first composition. Maʿsara, July 2012. Photo: Author.

A younger generation of Arab Contractors workers took up their burgeoning literacy skills in different ways from Sayyid. After two months of
literacy classes, I received a Facebook message from Mustafa: "Hi Nermeen.
Why didn't you come [to class yesterday]" (*hay Nermeen, inty magīsh lā*). In
his Facebook photo, he wore a suit and tie. He listed his favorite television
show (*Xena: Warrior Princess*) and pop musicians (Mohamed Mounir, Ramy
Sabry, Mohamed Hamaki), as well as his preferred soccer team (Al-Ahly).
He was friends with only six others, and under his personal information,
the only category he filled in was the name of his employer. His curated
lists of favorites and memes with Islamic advice demonstrated how he put
his new literacy skills to use in ways that were a departure from the written
paragraphs of his coworkers Rifʿat and Sayyid. Mustafa's Facebook page
resonated with a global culture of self-identification through the features of
an online social network that offered a format that created space for him to
break with his teacher's lessons. Mustafa's occasional postings crystallized
the shortcomings of the moniker "Facebook Revolution" to describe the

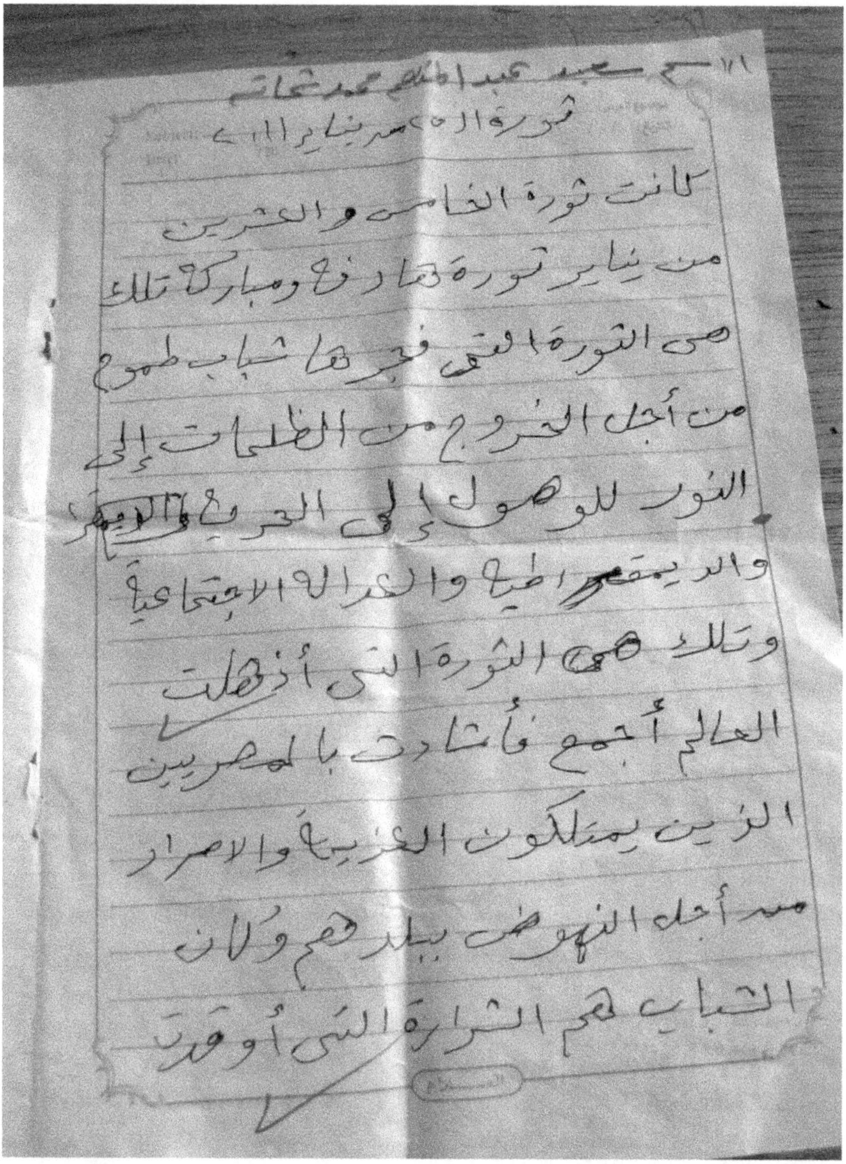

ثورة ٢٥ يناير ٢٠١١

كانت ثورة الخامس والعشرين
من يناير ثورة هادفة ومباركة تلك
هي الثورة التي فجرها شباب طموح
من أجل الخروج من الظلمات إلى
النور للوصول إلى الحرية
والديمقراطية والعدالة الاجتماعية
وتلك هي الثورة التي أذهلت
العالم أجمع فأشادت بالمصريين
الذين يمتلكون العزيمة والإصرار
من أجل النهوض ببلدهم وكان
الشباب هم الشرارة التي أوقدت

Figure 5.4. Sayyid's composition after being graded by his teacher. Ma'sara, July 2012. Photo: Author.

Middle East uprisings. Access is restricted to those who are literate and with internet access. At the same time, discussions about the power of a "social media revolution" enticed neoliterates to participate in its form as leisure and a site for communication. Through his Facebook profile, Mustafa created and shared a version of himself I had not known through our interactions in the classroom, one that addressed an audience of "friends."

Conclusions: Reading and Writing for Respect

At the shipyard, the contradictions of literacy as revolutionary action were apparent. Volunteers taught literacy not as a technique to further workers' mobilizations but instead to lift their spirits and guide them to be more dili-gent and dedicated employees. They did this through lessons that revealed a middle-class Islamic reformism that envisioned and implemented the skills of modern education. Teachers and students put care into how best to com-municate with each other. Through their relationships, we glimpse literacy's limitations as a platform for revolutionary change. Their interactions reveal the societal divisions that impeded literacy activism. The workers under-stood literacy as a valuable set of skills that could allow them to transcend the stigmatized category of the *gāhil*. They deployed the very discourses used to discipline their productivity in order to make claims to their personal dignity.

The workers' persistent use of face-to-face communication to articulate de-mands suggests that, for neoliterate workers, writing was neither a technique of self-expression nor a tool for political opposition but rather a way to acquire cultural capital. By performing what was expected of them in their composi-tions, worker-students claimed their dignity. Teachers instructed a sort of individuality through literacy that was persistently reined in by the strong role of the worker as a social category, a category that, while central to the men's self-identification, was also limiting. Although literacy promoted a sense of self to be represented and reflected upon, at the shipyard, literacy's individu-ating power was in tension with the idea of treating workers as a collective.

For Tawfiq, Salih Fathi, Rif'at, and the others, literacy was an opportunity to gain respect. It is in this way that Islamic literacy development stuttered in its revolutionary aims. Literacy classes were places where status was affirmed and reaffirmed through teachers' lessons, verbal exchanges, and gestures. In their early experiments with the written word, worker-students mobilized circulating scripts of the virtues of work and the image of the worker-patriot. By representing revolutionary sentiments and the value of productive labor, the men drew on the very disciplinary discourses of their instruction in order to make themselves legible to their audience. In their incipient writing, the men presented themselves to teachers, shipyard administration, and would-be state examiners through the very identity that both diminished respect for them and through which they were recognized.

At the Arab Contractors' Maʿsara shipyard, Tawfiq complained. He offered his teacher a sweet black coffee before class and enjoyed those spare moments away from the responsibilities of reporting to his manager. He took a drag off his cigarette to prepare for class and then spent the next two hours preparing to help his children with their homework. For him, these lessons, his effort—none of it had anything to do with happiness.

Notes

1. On the cultivation of cultured subjects in Egypt, see Winegar (2006). She notes how culture "as defined in particular ways and created through certain government institutions and discourses—has become an important feature of state projects to manage Islamic practice and identifications" (2009, 190).

2. See, for example, Clark (1995) on the role of workers' unions in a 1923–27 Russian literacy campaign.

3. Historically, literacy campaigns typically emphasize writing (over reading) among men. See Furet and Ozouf (1982) and Limage (1987).

4. *Workers' Expressions* (1992) by Calagione, Francis, and Nugent explores workers' lives beyond their work conditions to take into account interrelations between work and social life.

5. In May 2014, a court found Mubarak and his sons Gamal and Alaa guilty of embezzling public funds for private Mubarak properties. Arab Contractors, with its long-standing relationship with the presidential palace, was implicated in the case, and two low-level employees were charged (Bahgat 2014).

6. Ibid.

7. On the role of workers and unions in Egypt's political economy, see, for example, Beinin (1987), Lockman (1994), and Posusney (1997).

8. During the 2012 Egyptian presidential elections, four of the candidates were prolabor, including Hamdeen Sabahi, who gained 21.5 percent of the vote, the third highest, in the first round of voting.

9. See, for example, Ali (2012). For more on developments in workers organizing in post-Mubarak Egypt, see Beinin and Vairel (2013), Beinin (2015), Makram-Ebeid (2012), and Sallam (2011).

10. In 2012, there were nearly two thousand labor strikes in both government and private sectors, including those by teachers, doctors, public transportation workers, post office workers, and public taxation authority workers. With the advancement of the workers' movement, under the military, a new law was passed to criminalize labor strikes that disrupted production.

11. See Beinin on unfair contract practices (2012, 24).

12. See Winegar (2013) on the emotional registers of *ihbāt* in the early years following the uprising, describing its meanings as frustration, heaviness, and "dashed hope."

13. For an example of how these cases are discussed in Egyptian media, see coverage in *Al Jumhuriya* of a particular 2012 incident: "800 Pounds: The Price of Literacy Certificate" and "Review of Literacy Certificates after Discovery of Forgery Incidents."

14. On the use of poetry during Egypt's uprising, see Saad (2012), Colla (2012), and Schielke (2016).

15. Jacob describes how pride of country was part of an Egyptian *effendiyya* masculinity: "The ability to win hearts and minds over to the nationalist cause made for a great man" (2011, 51).

Postscript

Around the same time that the Institut d'Égypte was set ablaze, another scandal involving books circulated the media. Newspapers reported in alarming tones that Arabs were reading, on average, a mere six minutes each year. I heard the figure mentioned at cultural and literacy events in Cairo. I discovered that the claim had been circulating before December 2011, although news outlets had recently picked it up. One opinion piece contrasted Arabs' lamentable six minutes with "Westerners" who were said to read twelve thousand minutes a year. The article claimed that the average Arab reads a quarter of a page a year, the average Brit reads seven books, and the average American reads eleven books.[1] While *Al-Akhbar* investigated and debunked the statistic, the wide circulation and discussions it sparked indicated a sense of crisis in the region—how a lack of reading contributes to a deeper malaise.[2]

The myth of six minutes is illustrative of a discourse around literacy that regards reading as a balm for all social ills. By articulating the problem—a lack of reading—a solution was implied: the power of reading. The statistic found fertile ground at a moment rife with abstract calls to read for religious edification and national progress. The circulation of the myth of six minutes is more than a story of misinformation at a time of conflicting news narratives. The erroneous statistic is an example of the durability of "the literacy myth," the belief that literacy can bring about social progress, order, and morality, whereas illiteracy creates the social conditions of disorder and authoritarianism and hobbles economies (Graff 1979, 2010). The myth of six minutes portends hope that if Arabs read more, democracy will flourish, the economy will thrive, and people will enjoy a better quality of life. The myth evades challenging power, critiquing inequalities, and questioning rigid class distinctions. Instead, it places the blame for social and economic problems on "non-readers."

By focusing on illiteracy and the mass efforts to eradicate it, the story of Islamic literacy development may be misunderstood as contributing to anxieties surrounding illiteracy and panic over education in the Muslim and Arabic-speaking Middle East. It is all too common to find depictions of Muslims and Arabs as obdurate and backward, like the myth of six minutes. Illiteracy is blamed for religious violence despite evidence that militants are more highly educated than the average person in their home countries. For example, a World Bank study based on leaked Islamic State of Iraq and Syria resources reports that 69 percent of recruits had at least a secondary-level education, only 15 percent did not complete high school, and less than 2 percent were illiterate.[3] The assumption that violence stems from ignorance imagines the nonliterate person as easily malleable and recruitable to a cause, rather than a politically engaged agent with a cause.[4] Instead of furthering stereotypes of ignorant masses or ill-informed Muslims with violent proclivities, I have tried to consider how literacy—and the desire for it—structures particular forms of knowledge and subjectivities, how it forms rigid social hierarchies, and how it shapes social groups and distinct reading communities.

By calling attention to the ways Muslims interact with the Quran without autonomous reading, some readers may find evidence that religion discourages critical thinking or a sincere engagement with scripture. These persistent tropes of a naive religion project rationalist and sometimes Protestant notions of how to read onto a Muslim encounter with the Quran. Various Egyptian institutions, such as the Ministry of Endowments and Al-Azhar, as well as foreign support from the United States, have been at work to promote a style of scriptural reading and interpretation that engenders a moderate and "enlightened" Islam (Mahmood 2006). Considering Quran education alongside basic literacy, I have elucidated Quran practices such as citation to make legible modes of Quran encounters within a constellation of text practices. In doing so, I have tried not only to underline multiple Arabic literacies but also to sketch the ways that distinct textual practices are embedded in particular ways of knowing. An ethnography of various modes of text processing (guided by an attunement to the multiplicity of *qirāʾa*) asks us to recognize the personhood and knowledge of nonliterate people. It challenges modern secular sensibilities that relegate classical modes of religious reading to the past. At the same time, I have depicted the ways that so-called modern modes of text processing, namely autonomous reading, are ingrained with religious value.

By tracing the ideals and implementation of Islamic literacy development, I did not set out to critique or advise teachers or literacy planners. Important practical planning for basic education is underway at various institutions in the country, including ones discussed here, such as the Arab States Fundamental Education Centre, as well as others not mentioned, such as Ain Shams University's Adult Education Center. Rather, my interest in basic literacy, from campaigning to the classroom, has been to probe its ideologies, pedagogies, and associated politics. By tending to the unanticipated consequences of the 2011 renewed push for literacy, I drew attention to the knowledge hierarchies exacerbated through literacy campaigning, as well as the hermeneutical implications of literacy pedagogies.

At first blush, the hermeneutical issues may appear to be only the specialized interests of linguists or education theorists. But these issues, such as what form of the Arabic language should be taught in literacy classes or whether a learner should memorize the appearance of a word or read letters phonetically, shape ideas about secular and religious education and the kind of person who ought to be shaped through educative processes. When teachers and theorists attempt to privilege the eye over the ear in the act of reading, they weigh in on centuries of debates over how to encounter and process a text. These debates have been the touchstone of Islamic and education reformers in Egypt, as they have theorized and prescribed education and pedagogical methods for a modern and pious society. As I have shown, these debates are far from settled and are saturated with ideas about proper piety and social class.

Across various sites of Islamic literacy development, literacy is embedded in and further elaborates contemporary Muslim scripturalism—one grounded in autonomous reading and cognitive understanding of the Quran. When potential students asked if they would learn how to read the Quran in literacy class, they indicated a modern scriptural practice that forms a particular relationship between the reader and the text. Contemporary Muslim scripturalism is marked not only by this mode of reading—a particular kind of literacy—but also by how readers come to regard the Quran. Ebrahim

Moosa observes a modern turn to scripture across religious traditions: "It is peculiar as well as a luxury of modern literate and book-reading societies that people who are troubled by a moral or religious question can reach for their copies of the Qur'an, Bible, or Bhagwad Gita for solace. During earlier phases of each of these traditions questioners would have consulted living authorities. And there was no guarantee then that the answer would be found in some authoritative written book. Nowadays, most people find their answers in books!" (2006). Moosa points to modern autonomous reading as a phenomenon that disrupts traditional forms of religious authority. Holy books become texts to mine for "answers." This positioning of the subject to the text, made possible by autonomous reading, gives scripture a new role in the lives of believers and invests scriptures with new powers. Just as a modern reader may look to scripture for "answers," reading is itself offered as *the* answer.

I have depicted the ways that literacy sponsors directed and disciplined literacy to shape modern religious subjects. The chapters sketch distinct and at times overlapping religiously sponsored strategies in literacy activism. The campaigns and programs that I trace are not a comprehensive account of reformist efforts at literacy propagation but rather should be taken as an indication of the dense field of Islamic reformism through the propagation of literacy. The state programs I sketched in chapter 1 bear the mark of a late Islamic revival in literacy lessons that seek to cultivate a nonliberal reading subject. Basic literacy classes were occasions to learn religious fundamentals (*ta'sīs*) with special attention to how to perform basic religious rituals, such as ablutions before prayer. A different state-led literacy program, Read in the Name of Your Lord, made the Quran into a curriculum for basic literacy. The unpopular classes were intended as an explicit project to modernize Quran education while attracting rural women to literacy; however, relying on the short chapters of the Quran made it unclear to teachers whether students were reciting the verses or autonomously reading them. In contrast to Quran-centered basic literacy, the women of Batn al-Baqara demonstrated how nonliterate practices of Quran education can create opportunities to contemplate and affirm God's Word *without* the skill of autonomous reading. Their Quran lessons were not the mere product of their illiteracy but rather characteristic of dominant scripturalist trends in Egypt's late Islamic revival that rely on decentralizing religious authority and reliance on simplified texts to elaborate Quranic meaning in accessible language.

In yet another form of Islamic literacy development, KIP literacy classes in Batn al-Baqara revealed how secular education—with texts that promote civic and familial responsibility—is made virtuous not only through teachers' impromptu religious lessons but also in the very practice of autonomous reading itself. At the Arab Contractors shipyard, the virtues of literacy were associated with labor and productivity. Through KIP, autonomous reading was ingrained with the power of the Quranic call to *iqra*ʾ and, as such, was propagated as a pious activity, even an act of worship. KIP made literacy Islamic not through developing skills to help encounter the Quran but, rather, by making reading and writing skills for civil religion. Like Egyptian education more broadly, KIP provided civic-religious lessons that instructed an Egyptian Islam, one that made reading a practice to carry out one's religious and national duties.

Basic Literacy's Limits

When an Egyptian movement for literacy was rekindled in the embers of Hosni Mubarak's 2011 downfall, the literacy rate in Egypt was estimated to be 75 percent. KIP teachers saw their work as a continuation of the revolution, and many learners saw the political moment as one that could potentially open new possibilities for them. Literacy mobilized activists and pedagogues from long-standing national programs to grassroots groups developed out of neighborhood committees and revolutionary organizing. Such an undertaking was complex, with experienced teachers calling attention to the poor conditions of public education, while energized activists volunteered for the cause. New literacy campaigns were born, just as old state programs were relaunched.

Eighteen months after Mubarak's departure, the national agency for collecting data, the Central Agency for Public Mobilization and Statistics (CAPMAS), reported a slight increase in literacy in 2013, the highest rates the country had ever seen. However, the numbers declined immediately, and by 2017, the country recorded an illiteracy rate of 25.8 percent (30.8% of women and 21.1% of men). The rates were nearly identical to data from the late Mubarak era.[5] In Cairo, 16.2 percent of the population was non-literate (18.7% women and 12.9% men). In the same year, as part of Abdel Fattah el-Sisi's "New Republic" vision, the state pledged that by 2022, the Egyptian Authority of Adult Education (EAAE) would partner with civil society to reduce illiteracy to 17 percent.[6] In 2022, a CAPMAS press release led with the headline that illiteracy had declined to 17.2 percent (making it appear as though the EAAE had delivered on its promise). However, the statistic needed to be qualified. The rate applied only to people under the age of forty-five. Farther down in the press release, the usual measure used to document illiteracy, by reporting people aged ten and above (not ten to forty-five) reported a rate of 25.8 percent.[7] The seemingly positive gains are misleading—the literacy rates over the last fifteen years have fluctuated only slightly. The minor gains in the literacy rate recorded for 2013 may capture the brief window of the revolutionary push for literacy. Those documented as literate were among the few who wrote and passed the state test, students like Sayyid and Rifʿat at the Maʿsara Arab Contractors shipyard. But the vast majority of those in literacy classes does not pass the state exam, and many more never even have the opportunity to take it. These brief observations on the national literacy data are by no means a thorough statistical analysis. I consider Egypt's data on (il)literacy (as well as how it circulates) as part of an understanding of Egyptian literacy politics grounded in the ethnography of literacy campaigning.

One early evening in May 2013, as I reviewed my day's field notes, a power outage disrupted my stream of thought. While friends had been complaining of this inconvenience for several weeks, it was the first time my apartment succumbed to darkness. I was grateful for the light of my laptop, as I was not yet ready to be still. With the sound of generators churning from the street below, I reflected on my day. After nearly a year away, I had returned to Batn al-Baqara earlier that day. I visited Umm Rady's apartment, where she placed a warm baby in my lap, smiling broadly at the best piece of news I had missed while I was away. People from the neighborhood came by to share their news. Literacy classes were discontinued, and the community center canceled all of its activities. There had been a conflict among the center's leaders, but the women could not agree on what exactly caused the problem. Even the kindergarten classes were canceled, and the local teachers were left without work.

"Everything is broken (*kullu bāyza*)," Badriyya said to me. She seemed worn. My return was a reminder of her regret: she wished she had written the state literacy exam, but arrangements for her class to write it were never made. None of the other women in the neighborhood were keen to try to write it. Badriyya had been put off by the need to present her national identity card to write the exam, a card that she did not have. Few of the women in the neighborhood had one. Badriyya felt she could have passed the test at the time, but now, as she explained, she had forgotten most of what she had worked so hard to learn.

Two weeks after catching up with Badriyya in Batn al-Baqara, amid the rising pressures of the high cost of food and fuel, thousands took to the streets protesting President Morsi and the Muslim Brotherhood. A movement to bring down Morsi, *Tamarrud* (Rebel), described the protests as a continuation of the revolution, and the preservation of the same revolutionary aims that ousted Mubarak. The power outages ceased in the immediate aftermath of Morsi's ouster in early July 2013, only to resume in the spring of the following year. Nearly one thousand protesters, mostly Muslim Brotherhood supporters, were killed in the summer of 2013. On June 8, 2014, Abdel Fattah el-Sisi won the presidency in a two-candidate race against Socialist Hamdeen Sabahi, reportedly receiving almost 96 percent of the vote. El-Sisi projected himself (and his supporters described him) as a stabilizing leader who could guarantee the country's security. However, for many involved in the January 25 revolution, including the Muslim Brotherhood and other critics, his rise to power was evidence of the end of the revolution. Human rights groups recorded tens of thousands of prisoners under el-Sisi's supposed security arrests; nearly another thousand were sentenced to death under charges related to treason.

In the wake of Morsi's arrest, Amr Khaled dissolved his newly formed political party, the Future Party. Despite the strategic placement of a close Khaled ally, Khaled Abdel-Aziz, a member of Khaled's short-lived political party who was named minister of sports and youth in el-Sisi's first cabinet, Life Makers, like other NGOs associated with Islamic *khayr* work, fell under suspicion. Many Egyptians who once supported their work became wary of their motives and activities, casting them as Islamists during a backlash against the Muslim Brotherhood. In their day-to-day work, volunteers who previously donned Life Makers vests and spoke openly about the organization, began to downplay and even hide their association with it and Khaled (Mouftah 2017).

Less than four months later, KIP was canceled. Vodafone briefly continued the campaign under the new name Egyptians Are Learning (*Al-Masriyyūn Yataʿallimūn*). Volunteer teachers returned to their lives. Some teachers, like Omar, were ill at ease with what they had achieved through the campaign.

Some students, like Badriyya, were regretful looking back at the possibilities that literacy once held for them. A moment had passed.

Literacy's promises are expansive. Even as Egypt's literacy rate fell short of the national aims, planners continued to put faith in it. Islamically sponsored literacy efforts were about more than acquiring skills. When students failed to attain literacy, there were other, less measurable means of evaluation. The KIP teachers asked: *Are you optimistic? Do you have faith in the idea? Do you have faith in tomorrow?* Students expressed the intangible aspects of literacy another way, articulating literacy as a way toward dignity (as the workers insisted), and as a way toward negotiating power (as some of the women in Batn el-Baqara attempted).

Egyptian Literacy Politics in Process

Despite the trend of literacy breakthroughs seen in revolutionary contexts in other parts of the world, Egypt did not experience any major gains. The country's promotion of literacy was like the revolution itself. But to think of literacy only in terms of successes and failures is to miss what happens in the *process* of propagating and instructing basic literacy. As James Ferguson famously points out, the normative question of a project's success or failure yields less than examining what happens through these efforts (1994). In this vein, I have aimed to depict what happens *through* the push for universal literacy, the epistemological stakes and affective ramifications not accounted for in government tools that measure success and failure. To do this, I traced the methods and values of other forms of text processing and, more broadly, other ways of knowing that are not cultivated through autonomous reading.

Literacy development is fundamentally tied to the problem of recognition: the recognition of the dignity of nonliterate people, but also the recognition of other modes of text processing beyond autonomous reading. Illegibility is both a bureaucratic condition as well as the broader result of an inability to recognize the other in a more existential way.

The campaign's regular statistical reporting on the numbers of volunteers, learners, classes, and those who passed their exams was part of the accounting of "making life" and was necessary to the logic of productivity and accountability so central to literacy development. In Batn al-Baqara, the immeasurable mark of success became whether women came to desire literacy. This goal could not be captured in KIP's governmental enumeration that justified the campaign and gave urgency to its mandate. The worker-students' written passages do not represent some sort of culmination of the campaign with the legibility of workers. Instead, their writing should be seen as scripts, while consequential communication remained within the realm of face-to-face interaction. While workers sought dignity through recognition as people not roundly deemed ignorant, the ability to write was no guarantee to transcend this stigma.

The state project of literacy is one of legibility, and yet in practice makes apparent the erasure of those who are not literate. In the context of Egypt's "unregistered" (lam yusaggal)—those who have no official documentation like a national identification card—people like Badriyya cannot access government services like education, health care, or the ability to take the national literacy exam and earn the certificate. State officials claim that it is impossible to determine exactly how many people in Egypt are unregistered, but they estimate that roughly 10 percent of the population, some seven million people—mostly the rural and urban poor, orphans, and nonliterate—are unrecognized.

The residents of Batn al-Baqara wanted adequate sewage disposal but, instead, sat through lessons on basic hygiene. For these women, this conflict is a kind of "illegible subject," an issue that learners articulate but which literacy's champions are not attentive to. And in the shipyard, the workers described literacy as a way for them to gain dignity and be better fathers, two goals that fell beyond the purview of how KIP instructed literacy. Workers' illegible subjects were the complaints they aired in class discussions that were never put in writing. Illegible subjects are those complaints, demands, and topics that receive no response (and often cannot be heard). Similarly, illegible subjects are the nonliterate people who are continually reminded of their essential lack.

Beyond the challenges of instruction in basic Arabic literacy, educationists explained to me that the biggest problem they face is retention: while students can pass the state literacy exam (and be deemed legally literate), most of them forget what they have learned over time. Few neoliterates have the opportunity or desire to use their new skills. Teachers explained how these people require further exercises in reading and writing for them to be able to use their skills in real life. Literacy planners attempt to address this problem through what they call "post-literacy," (as briefly discussed in chap. 2). These classes introduce neoliterate learners to longer texts over an extended period so they can familiarize themselves with their newly formed skills. As one literacy advocate put it, "If we cannot make reading a part of their lives, then it is natural that they will forget what they learned." Post-literacy is the corrective to literacy in the same way that literacy is the corrective to the national education system. Post-literacy is a program that anticipates the failure of the program that precedes it.

In Paulo Freire's advocacy for the radical transformation of education in the English translation of *Pedagogy of the Oppressed* (1970), he brought world attention to his philosophy and methods that made literacy a tool of liberation. In a less cited work, *Pedagogy in Process* (1978), Freire writes letters to educators in Guinea-Bissau, at a moment when the country gained independence and was undertaking a major campaign for literacy. The format of the letters offered Freire the opportunity to reflect on what was unfolding in Guinea-Bissau as it was happening, rather than as a report or analysis at its conclusion. His writing bears the mark of an ongoing experiment. For Freire, process draws attention to the ways that literacy instruction must be nimble, reacting to and in partnership with learners. Process means working through the challenges of what language should be taught in individual classrooms and regularly asking students, What is literacy for? It may be for the Quran one day, and to compose a poem the next.

To think about literacy as a process means facing difficult and perhaps irresolvable problems. What would it look like to embrace all of the facets of *qirāʾa* in their fullness? It might mean humbly acknowledging that autonomous reading is not the exclusive way to encounter a text. What kind of pedagogies might enable all dimensions of *qirāʾa*? What are the possibilities for recognizing multiple literacies and their associated values and epistemologies? How might valuing different modes of text processing disrupt and help reimagine ideas of "progress"? What kinds of communities might be imagined from an expansive notion of "reading"?

Campaigning for literacy in post-Mubarak Egypt was caught between a long-standing method of nation-building and a yearning to carry out the revolution. Literacy activists revived a decades-long state project. The slogans and, in many cases, even the curricular strategies had been around for decades. But repetition is not mimesis. Teacher-student interactions became sites of cross-class experimentation that teachers took as edifying experiences and where students staged their own negotiations for material and symbolic gain. It was at these moments that literacy development mirrored the tensions and fissures that stymied political change in Egypt. The push for literacy, like the revolution itself, is incomplete. Rather than conceptualize this incompleteness as failure or surrender to a notion of development defined by megaprojects, it may be most stubborn and hopeful to witness this incompleteness as process.

Notes

1. I first came across the statistic in *Al Arabiya* "Arab Citizens Read Six Minutes a Year" (*Al-Muwātin al-ʿArabī Yaqra' Sitta Daqā'iq fī al-Sana*).

2. The Lebanese English news source *Al-Akhbar* ran the piece: "The Arab Reader and the Myth of Six Minutes," http://english.al-akhbar.com/node/3168. It investigated the source and traced the claim to an uncited footnote in a report issued by the Arab Thought Foundation (*Muʾassasat al-Fikr al-ʿArabī*). There was no explanation in the original source.

3. See World Bank (2016). The report noted that those recruits who wished to take on administrative roles or participate in suicide missions were the most educated of the group.

4. Such common tropes of militancy are challenged by Li (2019) and Devji (2008), who locate jihadism as the other side of the coin of universalist projects for justice and humanitarianism.

5. CAPMAS, "Census for Ages 10+ in Egypt 2018," https://www.capmas.gov.eg/Admin/News/PressRelease/2019112013343_666%20e.pdf.

6. On educational planning and reform under el-Sisi, see Herrera (2022) on the country's plan for a "New Education System," or "Education 2.0" (13). See especially, 193–200.

7. CAPMAS, "On the Occasion of International Literacy Day 2022," https://capmas.gov.eg/admin/news/PressRelease/2022911105815_%D8%A7%D9%84%D8%A8%D9%8A%D8%A7%D9%86%20%D8%A7%D9%84%D8%B5%D8%AD%D9%81%D9%89%20%D8%A7%D9%86%D8%AC%D9%84%D9%8A%D8%B2%D9%89%202022.pdf.

BIBLIOGRAPHY

Literacy Curricula

Al-Hasum, Jasim Mahmud. 1992. *Read in the Name of Your Lord: Teacher's Guide (Iqra' bi-smi Rabbika: Dalīl al-Muʿallim).* Tunis: al-Munazzama al-ʿArabiyya li-l-Tarbiyya wa-l-Thaqāfa wa-l-ʿUlūm, al-Jihāz al-ʿArabī li-Mahw al-Ummiyya wa-Taʿlīm al-Kibār.

———. 2010. *Read in the Name of Your Lord (Iqra' bi-smi Rabbika).* Cairo: al-Munazzama al-ʿArabiyya li-l-Tarbiyya wa-l-Thaqāfa wa-l-ʿUlūm, al-Jihāz al-ʿArabī li-Mahw al-Ummiyya wa-Taʿlīm al-Kibār.

Al-Lajna al-Maskuniyya li-Mukafahat al-Ummiyya. n.d. *Learn and Be Free (Itʿallam Itḥarrar).* Cairo: Sānt Mārī li-l-Tibāʿa wa-l-Kambyūtar.

The Bible Society of Egypt. 2009a. *The New Testament: Ten Selected Passages (Al-ʿAhd al-Jadīd: ʿAsharat Nusūs Mukhtāra).* Dār al-Kitāb al-Muqaddas: Matbaʿat al-Misriyyīn, 7th edition.

———. 2009b. *Read Your Book (Iqra' Kitābak).* Dār al-Kitāb al-Muqaddas: Matbaʿat AutoPrint, 7th edition.

Ibn Abd al-Hamid, Abu Nuran Hamid. 2011. *Baghdadi Primer (Qāʿida Baghdādiyya).* Cairo: al-Dārayn, 15th edition.

Mansur, al-Mutawalli Hasan, Fayiz Murad Mina, Ahmad Muhammad Mustafa, Muhammad Husni Yusuf al-Laythi, and Muhammad Hasan al-Rushdi. 2011. *Learn and Become Enlightened: Arabic Language (Itʿallam Itnawwar: Al-Lugha al-ʿArabiyya).* Cairo: Al-Hayʾa al-ʿĀmma li-Taʿlīm al-Kibār, Matābiʾ Dār al-Hilāl.

Bibliography

Abaza, Muhammad. 2023. "Hikāyat al-Asmarāt: Awwal Hayy Sakanī li-l-Qadāʾ ʿalā al-ʿAshwāʾiyyāt fī Misr (The Story of Al-Asmarat: The First Residential

Neighborhood to Eliminate Slums in Egypt)." *Al-Watan.* Accessed September 2023. https://www.elwatannews.com/news/details/6511628.

Abdel Haleem, M. A. S., trans. 2005. *The Quran.* New York: Oxford University Press.

Abu Hamid Muhammad bin Muhammad al-Ghazali. 1916. *Ihyāʾ ʿUlūm al-Dīn (The Revival of the Religious Sciences).* Cairo: Dār al-Kutub al-ʿArabiyya al-Kubra.

Abu-Lughod, Janet. 1971. *Cairo: 1001 Years of the City Victorious.* Princeton Studies on the Near East. Princeton, NJ: Princeton University Press.

Abu-Lughod, Lila. 1986. *Veiled Sentiments: Honor and Poetry in a Bedouin Society.* Berkeley: University of California Press.

———. 2005. *Dramas of Nationhood: The Politics of Television in Egypt.* Chicago: University of Chicago Press.

———. 2008. *Writing Women's Worlds: Bedouin Stories.* Berkeley: University of California Press.

Abu Zayd, Nasr Hamid. 1992. *Naqd Al-Khiṭāb Al-Dīnī.* Cairo: Sīnā li-l-Nashr.

———. 2006. *Reformation of Islamic Thought: A Critical Historical Analysis.* Amsterdam: Amsterdam University Press.

Adams, Charles Clarence. 1968. *Islam and Modernism in Egypt: A Study of the Modern Reform Movement Inaugurated by Muḥammad ʿAbduh.* New York: Russell & Russell.

Adely, Fida, and Gregory Starrett. 2011. "Schools, Skills, and Morals in the Contemporary Middle East." In *A Companion to the Anthropology of Education,* edited by Bradley Levinson and Mica Pollock, 349–367. New York: Blackwell.

Adely, Fida J. 2009. "Educating Women for Development: The Arab Human Development Report 2005 and the Problem with Women's Choices." *International Journal of Middle East Studies* 41 (1): 105–122.

———. 2012. *Gendered Paradoxes: Educating Jordanian Women in Nation, Faith, and Progress.* Chicago: University of Chicago Press.

Adly, Amr. 2014. "Mā Baʿd al-Nāṣiriyya (Post-Nasserism)." *Jadaliyya.* Accessed July 2015. http://www.jadaliyya.com/pages/index/16944/الناصرية-بعد-ما.

Afsaruddin, Asma. 2002. "The Excellences of the Qurʾān: Textual Sacrality and the Organization of Early Islamic Society." *Journal of the American Oriental Society* 122 (1): 1–24.

Agnaou, Fatima. 2004. *Gender, Literacy, and Empowerment in Morocco.* New York: Routledge.

Ahearn, Laura M. 2004. "Literacy, Power, and Agency: Love Letters and Development in Nepal." *Language and Education* 18 (4): 305–316.

Ahmed, Sara. 2004. *The Cultural Politics of Emotion.* New York: Routledge.

Ahmed, Shahab. 2015. *What Is Islam? The Importance of Being Islamic.* Princeton, NJ: Princeton University Press.

Ali, Khalid. 2012. "Precursors of the Egyptian Revolution." *IDS Bulletin* 43 (1): 16–25.

Ali, Said Ismail. 1974. *Al-Azhar ʿalā Masrah al-Siyāsa al-Misriyya: Dirāsa fī Tatawwur al-ʿAlāqa bayna al-Tarbiyya wa-l-Siyāsa (Al-Azhar in the Theater of Egyptian Politics: A Study of the Development of the Relationship between Education and Politics)*. Cairo: Dār al-Thaqāfa li-l-Tibāʿa wa-l-Nashr.

Alidou, Ousseina D. 2013. *Muslim Women in Postcolonial Kenya: Leadership, Representation, and Social Change*. Madison: University of Wisconsin Press.

Allan, Michael. 2016. *In the Shadow of World Literature: Sites of Reading in Colonial Egypt*. Princeton, NJ: Princeton University Press.

Al-Yacoub, Ikram. 2012. "Sum of All Fears: Arabs Read an Average of 6 Pages a Year." *Al Arabiya*. Accessed September 2023. https://english.alarabiya.net/arti cles/2012%2F07%2F14%2F226290.

Anderson, Benedict. 2006. *Imagined Communities: Reflections on the Origin and Spread of Nationalism*. New York: Verso.

Arkoun, Mohammed. 1984. *Pour une critique de la raison islamique*. France: Maisonneuve et Larose.

———. 1988. "The Notion of Revelation: From Ahl al-Kitāb to the Societies of the Book." *Die Welt Des Islams* 28 (1/4): 62–89.

Armanios, Febe, and Andrew Amstutz. 2013. "Emerging Christian Media in Egypt: Clerical Authority and the Visualization of Women in Coptic Video Films." *International Journal of Middle East Studies* 45 (3): 513–533.

Armbrust, Walter. 1996. *Mass Culture and Modernism in Egypt*. New York: Cambridge University Press.

———. 2019. *Martyrs and Tricksters: An Ethnography of the Egyptian Revolution*. Princeton, NJ: Princeton University Press.

Arnove, Robert F., and Harvey J. Graff, eds. 1987. *National Literacy Campaigns: Historical and Comparative Perspectives*. New York: Plenum.

Asad, Talal. 1986. "The Idea of an Anthropology of Islam." In *Occasional Papers Series*. Washington, DC: Georgetown University Center for Contemporary Arab Studies.

———. 1993. *Genealogies of Religion: Discipline and Reasons of Power in Christianity and Islam*. Baltimore: Johns Hopkins University Press.

———. 2003. *Formations of the Secular: Christianity, Islam, Modernity*. Stanford, CA: Stanford University Press.

———. 2018. *Secular Translations: Nation-State, Modern Self, and Calculative Reason*. New York: Columbia University Press.

Ashqar, Muhammad Sulayman al-. 2006. *Tafsir al-ʿUshr al-Akhīr min al-Qurʾān al-Karīm: Min zubdat al-tafsir*. Cairo: Al-Gazera International Press.

Assaad, Ragui. 2008. "Unemployment and Youth Insertion in the Labor Market in Egypt." In *The Egyptian Economy: Current Challenges and Future Prospects*. New York: American University in Cairo Press.

Associated Press in Cairo. 2011. "Cairo Institute Burned during Clashes." *Guardian*, December 19, 2011. Accessed March 13, 2024. https://www.theguardian.com/world/2011/dec/19/cairo-institute-burned-during-clashes.

Atia, Mona. 2013. *Building a House in Heaven: Pious Neoliberalism and Islamic Charity in Egypt*. Minneapolis: University of Minnesota Press.

Atiyeh, George, ed. 1995. *The Book in the Islamic World: The Written Word and Communication in the Middle East*. Washington, DC: Library of Congress.

Awad, Shaima Mostafa. 2017. "Global Citizenship Education and Civil Society in Egypt." In *Education during the Time of the Revolution in Egypt: Dialectics of Education in Conflict*, edited by Nagwa Megahed, 83–108. Rotterdam: Sense.

Babou, Cheikh Anta. 2016. "The Al-Azhar School Network: A Murid Experiment in Islamic Modernism." In *Islamic Education in Africa: Writing Boards and Blackboards*, edited by Robert Launay, 173–194. Bloomington: Indiana University Press.

Bahgat, Hossam. 2014. "The Mubarak Mansions." *Mada Masr*. Accessed April 2016. http://www.madamasr.com/content/mubarak-mansions.

Bano, Masooda. 2018. "At the Tipping Point? Al-Azhar's Growing Crisis of Moral Authority." *International Journal of Middle East Studies* 50 (4): 715–734.

Bano, Masooda, and Hanane Benadi. 2018. "Regulating Religious Authority for Political Gains: Al-Sisi's Manipulation of al-Azhar in Egypt." *Third World Quarterly* 39 (8): 1604–1621.

Baron, Beth. 1994. "Readers and the Women's Press in Egypt." *Poetics Today* 15 (2): 217–240.

———. 2005. *Egypt as a Woman: Nationalism, Gender, and Politics*. Berkeley: University of California Press.

———. 2014. *The Orphan Scandal: Christian Missionaries and the Rise of the Muslim Brotherhood*. Stanford, CA: Stanford University Press.

Bartlett, Lesley. 2007. "Literacy, Speech and Shame: The Cultural Politics of Literacy and Language in Brazil." *International Journal of Qualitative Studies in Education* 20 (5): 547–563.

———. 2010. *The Word and the World: The Cultural Politics of Literacy in Brazil*. Cresskill, NJ: Hampton.

Bassiouney, Reem. 2014. *Language and Identity in Modern Egypt*. Edinburgh: Edinburgh University Press.

———. 2020. *Arabic Sociolinguistics: Topics in Diglossia, Gender, Identity, and Politics*. Washington, DC: Georgetown University Press.

Bayat, Asef. 2007. *Islam and Democracy: What Is the Real Question?* Leiden: Amsterdam University Press.

———. 2017. *Revolution without Revolutionaries: Making Sense of the Arab Spring*. Stanford, CA: Stanford University Press.

———. 2021. *Revolutionary Life: The Everyday of the Arab Spring*. Cambridge, MA: Harvard University Press.

Beinin, Joel. 1987. *Workers on the Nile: Nationalism, Communism, Islam, and the Egyptian Working Class, 1882–1954.* Princeton, NJ: Princeton University Press.

———. 1994. "Writing Class: Workers and Modern Egyptian Colloquial Poetry (Zajal)." *Poetics Today* 15 (2): 191–215.

———. 2012. "The Rise of Egypt's Workers." Carnegie Endowment for International Peace. Accessed June 2016. https://carnegieendowment.org/2012/06/28/rise-of-egypt-s-workers-pub-48689.

———. 2015. *Workers and Thieves: Labor Movements and Popular Uprisings in Tunisia and Egypt.* Stanford, CA: Stanford University Press.

Beinin, Joel, and Frédéric Vairel. 2013. *Social Movements, Mobilization, and Contestation in the Middle East and North Africa.* Stanford, CA: Stanford University Press.

Bell, Richard, and W. Montgomery Watt. 1970. *Bell's Introduction to the Qur'ān.* Edinburgh: Edinburgh University Press.

Berlant, Lauren Gail. 2011. *Cruel Optimism.* Durham, NC: Duke University Press.

Bialecki, Jon, and Eric Hoenes del Pinal. 2011. "Introduction: Beyond Logos: Extensions of the Language Ideology Paradigm in the Study of Global Christianity(-ies)." *Anthropological Quarterly* 84 (3): 575–593.

Bielo, James S., ed. 2009a. *The Social Life of Scriptures: Cross-Cultural Perspectives on Biblicism.* New Brunswick, NJ: Rutgers University Press.

———. 2009b. *Words upon the Word: An Ethnography of Evangelical Group Bible Study.* New York: New York University Press.

Blecher, Joel. 2018. *Said the Prophet of God: Hadith Commentary across a Millennium.* Berkeley: University of California Press.

Bourdieu, Pierre, and Jean Claude Passeron. 1977. *Reproduction in Education, Society and Culture.* New Delhi: Sage.

Bowen, John Richard. 2012. *A New Anthropology of Islam.* New York: Cambridge University Press.

Boyarin, Jonathan, ed. 1993. *The Ethnography of Reading.* Berkeley: University of California Press.

Brand, Deborah. 1998. "Sponsors of Literacy." *College Composition and Communication* 49 (2): 165–185.

Brand, Laurie A., Rym Kaki, and Joshua Stacher. 2011. "First Ladies as Focal Points for Discontent." *Foreign Policy Blogs* (blog). February 2011. Accessed April 2014. http://mideastafrica.foreignpolicy.com/posts/2011/02/16/first_ladies_as_focal_points_for_discontent.

Brenner, Louis. 2001. *Controlling Knowledge: Religion, Power, and Schooling in a West African Muslim Society.* Bloomington: Indiana University Press.

Brinton, Jacquelene Gottlieb. 2015. *Preaching Islamic Renewal: Religious Authority and Media in Contemporary Egypt.* Berkeley: University of California Press.

Brown, Wendy. 1995. *States of Injury: Power and Freedom in Late Modernity.* Princeton, NJ: Princeton University Press.

"Bukra Ahlā" ("Tomorrow Is Better"). 2011. YouTube. Accessed June 2012. https://www.youtube.com/watch?v=dHUKnw2sU3E.

Calagione, John, Doris Francis, and Daniel Nugent. 1992. *Workers' Expressions beyond Accommodation and Resistance.* Albany: State University of New York Press.

Caldwell, Leah. n.d. "The Arab Reader and the Myth of Six Minutes." *Al-Akhbar.* Accessed November 2014. http://english.al-akhbar.com/node/3168.

CAPMAS. 2018. "Census for Ages 10+ in Egypt 2018." Accessed September 2023. https://www.capmas.gov.eg/Admin/News/PressRelease/2019112013343 _666%20e.pdf.

———. 2022. "On the Occasion of International Literacy Day." Accessed September 2023. https://www.capmas.gov.eg/Admin/News/PressRelease /201898102224_illiteracy.pdf.

Cardinal, Monique. 2005. "Islamic Legal Theory Curriculum: Are the Classics Taught Today?" *Islamic Law and Society* 12 (2): 224–272.

Caton, Steven Charles. 1990. *"Peaks of Yemen I Summon": Poetry as Cultural Practice in a North Yemeni Tribe.* Berkeley: University of California Press.

Cavallo, Guglielmo, and Roger Chartier, eds. 2003. *A History of Reading in the West.* Studies in Print Culture and the History of the Book. Amherst: University of Massachusetts Press.

Chejne, Anwar. 1968. *The Arabic Language: Its Role in History.* Minneapolis: University of Minnesota Press.

Chlebowska, Krystyna. 1990. *Literacy for Rural Women in the Third World.* Paris: UNESCO.

Clark, Charles E. 1995. "Literacy and Labour: The Russian Literacy Campaign within the Trade Unions, 1923–27." *Europe-Asia Studies* 47 (8): 1327–1341.

Cochran, Judith. 1986. *Education in Egypt.* Dover, NH: Croom Helm.

Cody, Francis. 2013. *The Light of Knowledge Literacy Activism and the Politics of Writing in South India.* Ithaca, NY: Cornell University Press.

Colla, Elliott. 2012. "The People Want." *Middle East Research and Information Project.* Accessed June 2022. http://www.merip.org/mer/mer263/people-want.

Collins, James. 1995. "Literacy and Literacies." *Annual Review of Anthropology* 24:75–93.

Collins, James, and Richard K. Blot. 2003. *Literacy and Literacies: Texts, Power, and Identity.* New York: Cambridge University Press.

Comerro, Viviane. 2012. *Les traditions sur la constitution du muṣḥaf de 'Uthmān.* Würzburg: Ergon-Verl. in Komm.

Committee to Protect Journalists. 2015. "China, Egypt Imprison Record Numbers of Journalists." Accessed November 2014. https://cpj.org/reports /2015/12/china-egypt-imprison-record-numbers-of-journalists-jail/.

Crapanzano, Vincent. 2000. *Serving the Word: Literalism in America from the Pulpit to the Bench.* New York: New Press.

Cromer, Evelyn Baring. 1908. *Modern Egypt*. London: Macmillan.

Cuno, Kenneth. 2015. *Modernizing Marriage: Family, Ideology, and Law in Nineteenth- and Early Twentieth-Century Egypt*. Syracuse, NY: Syracuse University Press.

Dabashi, Hamid. 2008. *Iran: A People Interrupted*. New York: New Press.

Debenport, Erin, and Anthony Webster. 2019. "From Literacy/Literacies to Graphic Pluralism and Inscriptive Practices." *Annual Review of Anthropology* 48 (1): 389–404.

Deeb, Lara, and Mona Harb. 2013. *Leisurely Islam: Negotiating Geography and Morality in Shi'ite South Beirut*. Princeton, NJ: Princeton University Press.

Denny, Frederick. 1988. "Quran Recitation Training in Indonesia: A Survey of Contexts and Handbooks." In *Approaches to the History of the Interpretation of the Qur'an*, edited by Andrew Rippin, 288–306. New York: Oxford University Press.

Devji, Faisal. 2008. *The Terrorist in Search of Humanity: Militant Islam and Global Politics*. New York: Columbia University Press.

Dodge, Bayard. 1961. *Al-Azhar: A Millennium of Muslim Learning*. Washington, DC: Middle East Institute.

Donadey, Anne, and Huma Ahmed-Ghosh. 2008. "Why Americans Love Azar Nafisi's Reading Lolita in Tehran." *Signs* 33 (3): 623–646.

Doorn-Harder, Pieternella van. 2006. *Women Shaping Islam: Indonesian Women Reading the Qur'an*. Urbana: University of Illinois Press.

Doumato, Eleanor Abdella, and Gregory Starrett, eds. 2006. *Teaching Islam: Textbooks and Religion in the Middle East*. Boulder, CO: Lynne Rienner Publishers.

Eccel, Chris. 1984. *Egypt, Islam and Social Change: Al-Azhar in Conflict and Accommodation*. Berlin: Verlag.

Egypt Independent. 2011. "Amid Street Clashes, Civilians Coordinate to Rescue Rare Documents." December 19, 2011. Accessed March 13, 2024. https://egyptindependent.com/amid-street-clashes-civilians-coordinate-rescue-rare-documents/.

Eickelman, Dale F. 1992. "Mass Higher Education and the Religious Imagination in Contemporary Arab Societies." *American Ethnologist* 19 (4): 643–655.

———. 1995. "Introduction: Print, Writing, and the Politics of Religious Identity in the Middle East." *Anthropological Quarterly* 68 (3): 133–138.

Eickelman, Dale F., and Jon W. Anderson. 1997. "Publishing in Muslim Countries: Less Censorship, New Audiences and Rise of the 'Islamic' Book." *Logos* 8 (4): 192–198.

———, eds. 2003. *New Media in the Muslim World: The Emerging Public Sphere*. Bloomington: Indiana University Press.

Eickelman, Dale F., and James P. Piscatori. 2004. *Muslim Politics*. Princeton Studies in Muslim Politics. 2nd ed. Princeton, NJ: Princeton University Press.

Eisenlohr, Patrick. 2009. "Technologies of the Spirit." *Anthropological Theory* 9 (3): 273–296.

El-Badawi, Emran, and Paula Sanders. 2019. *Communities of the Qur'an: Dialogue, Debate and Diversity in the 21st Century*. La Vergne, TN: Oneworld.

El Bernoussi, Zaynab. 2021. *Dignity in the Egyptian Revolution: Protest and Demand during the Arab Uprisings*. Cambridge: Cambridge University Press.

Elmouelhi, Hassan, Martin Meyer, Reham Reda, and Asmaa Abdelhalim. 2021. "Mediatizing Slum Relocation in Egypt: Between Legitimization and Stigmatization." *Media and Communication* 9 (4): 345–359.

El Shakry, Omnia S. 1998. "Schooled Mothers and Structured Play: Child-Rearing in Turn of the Century Egypt." In *Remaking Women: Feminism and Modernity in the Middle East*, edited by Lila Abu-Lughod, 126–170. Princeton Studies in Culture/Power/History. Princeton, NJ: Princeton University Press.

———. 2007. *The Great Social Laboratory: Subjects of Knowledge in Colonial and Postcolonial Egypt*. Stanford, CA: Stanford University Press.

El-Tom, A. Osman. 1987. "Berti Qur'anic Amulets." *Journal of Religion in Africa* 17 (3): 224–244.

Elyachar, Julia. 2005. *Markets of Dispossession: NGOs, Economic Development, and the State in Cairo*. Durham, NC: Duke University Press.

Engelke, Matthew Eric. 2007. *A Problem of Presence: Beyond Scripture in an African Church*. Berkeley: University of California Press.

———. 2013. *God's Agents: Biblical Publicity in Contemporary England*. Berkeley: University of California Press.

Engelke, Matthew Eric, and Matt Tomlinson, eds. 2006. *The Limits of Meaning: Case Studies in the Anthropology of Christianity*. New York: Berghahn Books.

Escobar, Arturo. 1995 (2011). *Encountering Development: The Making and Unmaking of the Third World*. Princeton, NJ: Princeton University Press.

Fadil, Nadia, and Mayanthi Fernando. 2015. "Rediscovering the 'Everyday' Muslim: Notes on an Anthropological Divide." *HAU: Journal of Ethnographic Theory* 5 (2): 59–88.

Fahmy, Khaled. 2013. "The Real Tragedy behind the Fire of Institut d'Egypte." *Cultural Anthropology*. Hot Spots, Fieldsights. Accessed May 2023. http:/culanth.org/fieldsights/the-real-tragedy-behind-the-fire-of-institut -degypte.

Fahmy, Ziad. 2011. *Ordinary Egyptians: Creating the Modern Nation through Popular Culture*. Stanford, CA: Stanford University Press.

Farid, Farid Y. 2017. "Egypt's War on Books." *Atlantic*. Accessed May 2023. https://www.theatlantic.com/international/archive/2017/12/egypt-sisi-books -freedom-of-speech/547259/.

Ferguson, Charles. 1959. "Diglossia." *Word* 15:325–340. Reprinted in *Language and Social Context*, edited by Pier Paolo Gligioli, 232–251. Harmondsworth: Penguin.

———. 1996. "Epilogue: Diglossia Revisited." In *Understanding Arabic: Essays in Contemporary Arabic Linguistics in Honor of El-Said Badawi*, edited by Alaa Elgibali, 49–67. Cairo: American University in Cairo Press.

Ferguson, James. 1994. *The Anti-Politics Machine: "Development," Depoliticization, and Bureaucratic Power in Lesotho*. Minneapolis: University of Minnesota Press.

Fortna, Benjamin. 2002. *Imperial Classroom: Islam, the State, and Education in the Late Ottoman Empire*. New York: Oxford University Press.

———. 2011. *Learning to Read in the Late Ottoman Empire and the Early Turkish Republic*. New York: Palgrave Macmillan.

Forum of Christian Leaders. 2018. "Opportunities and Challenges Facing Scripture Distribution in Egypt—Atallah Ramez." YouTube. Accessed June 2019. https://www.youtube.com/watch?v=E2feY2LvNqQ.

Foucault, Michel. 1983. "How We Behave." *Vanity Fair*, November 4, 1983.

Freire, Paulo. 1978. *Pedagogy in Process: The Letters to Guinea-Bissau*. London: Bloomsbury.

Frishkopf, Michael. 2009. "Mediated Qur'anic Recitation and the Contestation of Islam in Contemporary Egypt." In *Music and the Play of Power in the Middle East, North Africa and Central Asia*, edited by Laudan Nooshin, 75–114. Farnham: Ashgate.

Furet, François, and Jacques Ozouf. 1982. *Reading and Writing: Literacy in France from Calvin to Jules Ferry*. New York: Cambridge University Press.

Gade, Anna M. 2004. *Perfection Makes Practice: Learning, Emotion, and the Recited Qur'an in Indonesia*. Honolulu: University of Hawaiʻi Press.

Gasper, Michael. 2001. "'Abdallah al-Nadim, Islamic Reform, and 'Ignorant' Peasants: State Building in Egypt." In *Muslim Traditions and Modern Techniques of Power*, edited by Armando Salvatore, 75–92. Yearbook of the Sociology of Islam 3. Münster: LIT Verlag.

Geertz, Clifford. 1971. *Islam Observed: Religious Development in Morocco and Indonesia*. Chicago: University of Chicago Press.

Gershon, Ilana, and Dhooleka Sarhadi Raj. 2000. "Introduction: The Symbolic Capital of Ignorance." *Social Analysis: The International Journal of Social and Cultural Practice* 44 (2): 3–14.

Ghannam, Farha. 2013. *Live and Die Like a Man: Gender Dynamics in Urban Egypt*. Stanford, CA: Stanford University Press.

Gilmont, Jean-François. 2003. "Protestant Reformation and Reading." In *A History of Reading in the West*, edited by Guglielmo Cavallo, Roger Chartier, and Lydia G, 213–237. Cochrane. Studies in Print Culture and the History of the Book. Amherst: University of Massachusetts Press.

Goldberg, Ellis. 1986. *Tinker, Tailor, and Textile Worker: Class and Politics in Egypt, 1930–1952.* Berkeley: University of California Press.

———. 1991. "Smashing Idols and the State: The Protestant Ethic and Egyptian Sunni Radicalism." *Comparative Studies in Society and History* 33 (1): 3–35.

Goody, Jack, and Ian Watt. 1963. "The Consequences of Literacy." *Comparative Studies in Society and History* 5 (3): 304–345.

Graff, Harvey. 1979. *The Literacy Myth: Literacy and Social Structure in the Nineteenth-Century City.* New York: Academic Press.

———. 2010. *Literacy Myths, Legacies, & Lessons: New Studies on Literacy.* New Brunswick, NJ: Transaction.

Graham, William A. 1987. *Beyond the Written Word: Oral Aspects of Scripture in the History of Religion.* New York: Cambridge University Press.

Günther, Sebastian. 2002. "Illiteracy." In *Encyclopaedia of the Qur'an*, vol. 2, edited by Jane Dammen McAuliffe, 492–500. Leiden: Brill.

Haddad, Yvonne Yazbeck. 1994. "Muhammad Abduh: Pioneer of Islamic Reform." In *Pioneers of Islamic Revival*, edited by 'Alī Rāhnamā, 30–63. Studies in Islamic Society. London: Zed Books.

Haeri, Niloofar. 2003. *Sacred Language, Ordinary People: Dilemmas of Culture and Politics in Egypt.* New York: Palgrave Macmillan.

———. 2009. "The Elephant in the Room: Language and Literacy in the Arab World." In *The Cambridge Handbook of Literacy*, edited by David R. Olson and Nancy Torrance, 418–429. Cambridge: Cambridge University Press.

———. 2013. "The Private Performance of 'Salat' Prayers: Repetition, Time, and Meaning." *Anthropological Quarterly* 86 (1): 5–34.

———. 2017. "The Sincere Subject: Mediation and Interiority among a Group of Muslim Women in Iran." *HAU: Journal of Ethnographic Theory* 7 (1): 139–161.

———. 2020. *Say What Your Longing Heart Desires: Women, Prayer, and Poetry in Iran.* Stanford, CA: Stanford University Press.

Haj, Samira. 2009. *Reconfiguring Islamic Tradition: Reform, Rationality, and Modernity.* Stanford, CA: Stanford University Press.

Hallaq, Wael B. 2013. *The Impossible State: Islam, Politics, and Modernity's Moral Predicament.* New York: Columbia University Press.

Hamdy, Sherine. 2012. *Our Bodies Belong to God: Organ Transplants, Islam, and the Struggle for Human Dignity in Egypt.* Berkeley: University of California Press.

Handman, Courtney. 2015. *Critical Christianity: Translation and Denominational Conflict in Papua New Guinea.* Berkeley: University of California Press.

Hanna, Nelly. 2007. "Literacy and the 'Great Divide' in the Islamic World, 1300–1800." *Journal of Global History* 2 (2): 175–193.

Hasan, Sana. 2003. *Christians versus Muslims in Modern Egypt: The Century-Long Struggle for Coptic Equality.* New York: Oxford University Press.

Hefner, Robert W., and Muhammad Qasim Zaman, eds. 2007. *Schooling Islam: The Culture and Politics of Modern Education*. Princeton, NJ: Princeton University Press.

Heo, Angie. 2018. *The Political Lives of Saints: Christian-Muslim Mediation in Egypt*. Berkeley: University of California Press.

Hermez, Sami. 2011. "On Dignity and Clientelism: Lebanon in the Context of the 2011 Arab Revolutions." *Studies in Ethnicity and Nationalism* 11 (3): 527–537.

Herrera, Linda. 2022. *Educating Egypt: Civic Values and Ideological Struggles*. New York: American University in Cairo Press.

Herrera, Linda, and Carlos Alberto Torres, eds. 2006. *Cultures of Arab Schooling: Critical Ethnographies from Egypt*. Bristol: University Presses Marketing.

Heyworth-Dunne, James. 1968. *An Introduction to the History of Education in Modern Egypt*. London: Frank Cass.

Hirschkind, Charles. 2006. *The Ethical Soundscape: Cassette Sermons and Islamic Counterpublics*. New York: Columbia University Press.

———. 2011. "Is There a Secular Body?" *Cultural Anthropology* 26 (4): 633–647.

Hirschler, Konrad. 2011. *Written Word in the Medieval Arabic Lands: A Social and Cultural History of Reading Practices*. Edinburgh: Edinburgh University Press.

Hoffman, Valerie. 1985. "An Islamic Activist: Zaynab al-Ghazali." In *Women and the Family in the Middle East: New Voices of Change*, edited by Elizabeth Warnock Fernea, 233–254. Austin: University of Texas Press.

Hosny, Ola. 2017. "Young Rural Women's Perspectives on the Impact of Education Supported Development Projects." In *Education during the Time of the Revolution in Egypt: Dialectics of Education in Conflict*, edited by Nagwa Megahed, 109–134. *Comparative and International Education*. Rotterdam: Sense.

Hourani, Albert. 1962. *Arabic Thought in the Liberal Age, 1798–1939*. London: Oxford University Press.

Huebler, Friedrich, and Weixin Lu. 2012. *Adult and Youth Literacy, 1990–2015: Analysis of Data for 41 Selected Countries*. Montreal: UNESCO Institute for Statistics.

Human Rights Watch. 2019. "Egypt: New NGO Law Renews Draconian Restrictions." Accessed September 2020. https://www.hrw.org/news/2019/07/24/egypt-new-ngo-law-renews-draconian-restrictions.

Inan, Muhammad ʿAbd Allah. 1958. *Tārīkh al-Jāmiʿ al-Azhar*. 2nd ed. Cairo: Muʾassasat al-Khanji.

Ingram, Brannon. 2014. "The Portable Madrasa: Print, Publics, and the Authority of the Deobandi ʿUlama." *Modern Asian Studies* 48 (4): 845–871.

Jacob, Wilson Chacko. 2011. *Working Out Egypt: Effendi Masculinity and Subject Formation in Colonial Modernity, 1870–1940*. Durham, NC: Duke University Press.

Jay, Martin. 1988. "The Rise of Hermeneutics and the Crisis of Ocularcentrism." *Poetics Today* 9 (2): 307–326.

Jeffery, Arthur. 1924. "The Mystic Letters of the Koran." *Muslim World* 14 (3): 247–260.

Jirjis, Majdī, and Pieternella van Doorn-Harder. 2011. *The Emergence of the Modern Coptic Papacy: The Egyptian Church and Its Leadership from the Ottoman Period to the Present*. Vol. 3 of *The Popes of Egypt*. Cairo: American University in Cairo Press.

Joseph, Suad. 2013. "Anthropology of the Future: Arab Youth and the State of the State." In *Anthropology of the Middle East and North Africa: Into the New Millennium*, edited by Sherine Hafez and Susan Slyomovics, 105–124. Bloomington: Indiana University Press.

Jung, Dietrich, Marie Juul Petersen, Sara Lei Sparre, Dietrich Jung, Marie Juul Petersen, and Sara Lei Sparre. 2014. *Politics of Modern Muslim Subjectivities: Islam, Youth, and Social Activism in the Middle East*. New York: Palgrave Macmillan

Kalmbach, Hilary. 2020. *Islamic Knowledge and the Making of Modern Egypt*. Cambridge: University of Cambridge.

Kalmbach, Hilary E., and Masooda Bano, eds. 2011. *Women, Leadership, and Mosques*. Leiden: Brill.

Kaplan, Sam. 2006. *The Pedagogical State: Education and the Politics of National Culture in Post-1980 Turkey*. Stanford, CA: Stanford University Press.

Kashani, Maryam. 2023. *Medina by the Bay: Scenes of Muslim Study and Survival*. Durham, NC: Duke University Press.

Keane, Webb. 2007. "Language and Religion." In *A Companion to Linguistic Anthropology*, edited by Alessandro Duranti, 431–448. London: Blackwell.

Kenney, Jeffrey T. 2015. "Selling Success, Nurturing the Self: Self-Help Literature, Capitalist Values, and the Sacralization of Subjective Life in Egypt." *International Journal of Middle East Studies* 47:663–680.

Khalaf, Roseanne Saad, and Samir Khalaf. 2011. *Arab Youth: Social Mobilization in Times of Risk*. London: Saqi Books.

Khamis, Sahar. 2004. "Multiple Literacies, Multiple Identities: Egyptian Rural Women's Readings of Televised Literacy Campaigns." In *Women and Media in the Middle East: Power through Self-Expression*, edited by Naomi Sakr, 89–108. London: I. B. Tauris.

Kinberg, Leah. 2012. "*Muḥkamāt* and *Mutashābihāt* (Koran 3/7): Implication of a Koranic Pair of Terms in Medieval Exegesis." In *Tafsir: Interpreting the Qur'an*, vol. 2, edited by Mustafa Shah, 78–103. London: Routledge.

Kirkendall, Andrew. 2010. *Paulo Freire and the Cold War Politics of Literacy*. Chapel Hill: University of North Carolina Press.

Khoja-Moolji, Shenila. 2018. *Forging the Ideal Educated Girl: The Production of Desirable Subjects in Muslim South Asia*. Berkeley: University of California Press.

Lambek, Michael. 1990. "Certain Knowledge, Contestable Authority: Power and Practice on the Islamic Periphery." *American Ethnologist* 17 (1): 23–40.

———. 1993. *Knowledge and Practice in Mayotte.* Toronto: University of Toronto Press.

Lane, Edward William. 1978. *Lane's Arabic-English Lexicon.* Cambridge, MA: Islamic Texts Society, 1984.

Larkin, Brian. 2008. "Ahmed Deedat and the Form of Islamic Evangelism." *Social Text* 26 (3): 101–121.

Launay, Robert, and Rudolph T. Ware III. 2016. "How (Not) to Read the Qur'an? Logics of Islamic Education in Senegal and Côte d'Ivoire." In *Islamic Education in Africa: Writing Boards and Blackboards*, edited by Robert Launay, 344–362. Bloomington: Indiana University Press.

Lauzière, Henri. 2015. *The Making of Salafism: Islamic Reform in the Twentieth Century.* New York: Columbia University Press.

Levy, Reuben. 1957. *The Social Structure of Islam, Being the Second Edition of the Sociology of Islam.* Cambridge: Cambridge University Press.

Li, Darryl. 2019. *The Universal Enemy: Jihad, Empire, and the Challenge of Solidarity.* Stanford, CA: Stanford University Press.

Limage, Leslie. 1987. "Adult Literacy Policy in Industrialized Countries." In *National Literacy Campaigns: Historical and Comparative Perspectives*, edited by Robert F. Arnove and Harvey J. Graff, 293–314. New York: Plenum.

Limbert, Mandana. 2005. "Gender, Religious Knowledge and Education in an Omani Town." In *Monarchies and Nations: Globalization and Identity in the Arab States of the Gulf*, edited by James P. Piscatori and Paul Dresch, 182–202. London: I. B. Tauris.

Lockman, Zachary. 1994. *Workers and Working Classes in the Middle East: Struggles, Histories, Historiographies.* Albany: State University of New York Press.

Loimeier, Roman. 2016. *Islamic Reform in Twentieth-Century Africa.* Edinburgh: Edinburgh University Press.

Lutz, Catherine, and Lila Abu-Lughod, eds. 1990. *Language and the Politics of Emotion.* Paris: Editions de la Maison des Sciences de l'Homme.

Mada Masr. 2017. "New Minister of Education: Education is a 'Commodity.' And the State May Not Continue to Pay Its Bill." (*Wazir al-taʿlim al-jadid: Al-taʿlim ʿsilʿa.ʾ Wa-l-dawla qad la tastamir fi-dafʿ faturatha*). Mada Masr. Accessed July 2021. http://www.madamasr.com/ar/2017/02/16/news /وا.سياسة/وزير-التعليم-الجديد-التعليم-سلعة.

Madigan, Daniel. 2001. "Book." In *Encyclopaedia of the Qur'an*, vol. 1, edited by Jane Dammen McAuliffe, 242–251. Leiden: Brill.

Mahmood, Saba. 2004. *Politics of Piety: The Islamic Revival and the Feminist Subject.* Princeton, NJ: Princeton University Press.

———. 2006. "Secularism, Hermeneutics, and Empire: The Politics of Islamic Reformation." *Public Culture* 18 (2): 323.

———. 2008. "Feminism, Democracy, and Empire: Islam and the War of Terror." In *Women's Studies on the Edge*, edited by Joan Wallach Scott, 81–114. Durham, NC: Duke University Press.

———. 2016. *Religious Difference in a Secular Age: A Minority Report*. Princeton, NJ: Princeton University Press.

Makdisi, George. 1981. *The Rise of Colleges: Institutions of Learning in Islam and the West*. Edinburgh: Edinburgh University Press.

Makram-Ebeid, Dina. 2012. "Manufacturing Stability: Everyday Politics of Work in an Industrial Steel Town in Helwan, Egypt." PhD diss., London School of Economics and Political Science (University of London).

Manoukian, Setrag. 2011. *City of Knowledge in Twentieth Century Iran: Shiraz, History and Poetry*. Florence: Taylor & Francis.

Marlow, Louise. 1997. *Hierarchy and Egalitarianism in Islamic Thought*. Cambridge Studies in Islamic Civilization. New York: Cambridge University Press.

Massey, Keith. 1996. "A New Investigation into the 'Mystery Letters' of the Quran." *Arabica* 43 (3): 497–501.

Mattson, Ingrid. 2013. *The Story of the Qur'an: Its History and Place in Muslim Life*. Chichester: Wiley-Blackwell.

McAuliffe, Jane Dammen. 2012. "Text and Textuality: Q. 3:7 as a Point of Intersection." In *Tafsir: Interpreting the Qur'an*, vol. 2, edited by Mustafa Shah, 104–127. London: Routledge.

McLarney, Ellen. 2015. *Soft Force: Women in Egypt's Islamic Awakening*. Princeton, NJ: Princeton University Press.

Mehran, Golnar. 1992. "Social Implications of Literacy in Iran." *Comparative Education Review* 36 (2): 194–211.

Mervosh, Sarah. 2023. "'Kids Can't Read': The Revolt That Is Taking on the Education Establishment." *New York Times*. Accessed April 2023. https://www.nytimes.com/2023/04/16/us/science-of-reading-literacy-parents.html.

Messick, Brinkley. 1988. "Kissing Hands and Knees: Hegemony and Hierarchy in Shari'a Discourse." *Law & Society Review* 22 (4): 637–659.

———. 1993. *The Calligraphic State: Textual Domination and History in a Muslim Society*. Berkeley: University of California.

———. 1997. "Genealogies of Reading and the Scholarly Cultures of Islam." In *Cultures of Scholarship*, edited by Sarah Humphreys, 387–411. Ann Arbor: University of Michigan Press.

Meyer, Birgit. 1998. "'Make a Complete Break with the Past.' Memory and Post-Colonial Modernity in Ghanaian Pentecostalist Discourse." *Journal of Religion in Africa* 28 (3): 316–349.

Meyer, Birgit, and Annelies Moors, eds. 2006. *Religion, Media, and the Public Sphere*. Bloomington: Indiana University Press.

Mitchell, Timothy. 1988. *Colonising Egypt*. Berkeley: University of California Press.

———. 2002. *Rule of Experts: Egypt, Techno-Politics, Modernity*. Berkeley: University of California Press.

Mittermaier, Amira. 2019. *Giving to God: Islamic Charity in Revolutionary Times*. Berkeley: University of California Press.

Mohie, Mostafa. 2018. "Asmarat: The State's Model Housing for Former 'Slum' Residents." Translated by Salma Khalifa. *Mada Masr*. Accessed September 10, 2023. https://www.madamasr.com/en/2018/06/18/feature/politics/asmarat -the-states-model-housing-for-former-slum-residents/.

Moll, Yasmin. 2018. "Television Is Not Radio: Theologies of Mediation in the Egyptian Islamic Revival." *Cultural Anthropology* 33 (2): 233–265.

———. 2020. "The Idea of Islamic Media: The Qur'an and the Decolonization of Mass Communication." *International Journal of Middle East Studies* 52 (4): 623–642.

Moore, Clement Henry. 1980. *Images of Development: Egyptian Engineers in Search of Industry*. Cambridge, MA: MIT Press.

Moosa, Ebrahim. 2006. "Contrapuntal Readings in Muslim Thought: Translations and Transitions." *Journal of the American Academy of Religion* 74 (1): 107–118.

Mouftah, Nermeen. 2017. "Faith Development beyond Religion: The NGO as Site of Islamic Reform." In *Cultures of Doing Good: Anthropologists and NGOs*, edited by Amanda Lashaw, Steven Sampson, and Christian Vannier, 122–141. Tuscaloosa: University of Alabama Press.

Mouftah, Nermeen, and Abbas Barzegar. 2022. "Centering Muslims in Global Humanitarianism and Development." *Muslim World* 112 (1): 3–13.

Najmabadi, Afsaneh. 1998. "Crafting an Educated Housewife in Iran." In *Remaking Women: Feminism and Modernity in the Middle East*, edited by Lila Abu Lughod, 91–125. Princeton, NJ: Princeton University Press.

Nakissa, Aria. 2019. *The Anthropology of Islamic Law: Education, Ethics, and Legal Interpretation at Egypt's al-Azhar*. New York: Oxford University Press.

Nelson, Kristina. 1985. *The Art of Reciting the Qur'an*. Austin: University of Texas Press.

Nguyen, Martin. 2012. "Exegesis of the Ḥurūf Al-Muqaṭṭaʿa: Polyvalency in Sunnī Traditions of Qur'anic Interpretation." *Journal of Qur'anic Studies* 14 (2): 1–28.

———. 2016. "Modern Scripturalism and Emergent Theological Trajectories: Moving beyond the Qur'an as Text." *Journal of Islamic and Muslim Studies* 1 (2): 61–79.

Nöldeke, Theodor, Friedrich Schwally, Gotthelf Bergsträsser, Otto Pretzl, and Wolfgang H. Behn. 2013. *The History of the Qur'ān*. Leiden: Brill.

Ong, Walter J. 1982. *Orality and Literacy: The Technologizing of the Word*. New York: Methuen.

Osborne, Lauren E. 2014. "From Text to Sound to Perception: Modes and Relationships of Meaning in the Recited Qur'an." PhD diss., University of Chicago.

Peterson, Eugene H. 2006. *Eat This Book: A Conversation in the Art of Spiritual Reading*. Grand Rapids, MI: W. B. Eerdmans.

Pink, Johanna. 2010. "Tradition, Authority and Innovation in Contemporary Sunnī Tafsīr: Towards a Typology of Qur'an Commentaries from the Arab World, Indonesia and Turkey." *Journal of Qur'anic Studies* 12:56–82.

Pollard, Lisa. 2005. *Nurturing the Nation: The Family Politics of Modernizing, Colonizing and Liberating Egypt, 1805–1923*. Berkeley: University of California Press.

Posusney, Marsha Pripstein. 1997. *Labor and the State in Egypt: Workers, Unions, and Economic Restructuring*. New York: Columbia University Press.

Pregill, Michael. 2021. "The People of Scripture (*Ahl al-Kitāb*)." In *The Routledge Companion to the Qur'an*, edited by George Archer, Maria M. Dakake, and Daniel A. Madigan, 121–134. New York: Routledge.

Qutb, Sayyid. 1979. *In the Shade of the Qur'ān*. New Delhi: Mohammad Anas for Idara Ishaat e Diniyat.

Radscheit, Matthias. 2003. "Word of God." In *Encyclopaedia of the Qur'an*, vol. 10, edited by Jane Dammen McAuliffe, 541–549. Leiden: Brill.

Radwan, Raafat. 2008. *The National Report on Literacy and Adult Education*. Cairo: Egyptian Adult Education Authority.

Ramadan, Mustafa. 2012. "The Greatest Miracle." YouTube. Accessed August 2012. https://www.youtube.com/watch?v=Fqc7UdjyHwo&t=2s.

Ramzy C. M. 2017. "Singing Heaven on Earth: Coptic Counterpublics and Popular Song at Egyptian Mūlid Festivals." *International Journal of Middle East Studies* 49 (3): 375–394.

Rasmussen, Anne K. 2010. *Women, the Recited Qur'an, and Islamic Music in Indonesia*. Berkeley: University of California Press.

Reinhart, Kevin. 2010. "Fundamentalism and the Transparency of the Arabic Qur'an." In *Rethinking Islamic Studies: From Orientalism to Cosmopolitanism*, edited by Carl Ernst and Richard C. Martin, 97–113. Columbia: University of South Carolina Press.

Reynolds, Gabriel Said. 2009. *The Qur'an in Its Historical Context*. London: Routledge.

Robinson, Francis. 1993. "Technology and Religious Change: Islam and the Impact of Print." *Modern Asian Studies* 27 (1): 229–251.

Robinson, Neal. 2003. *Discovering the Qur'an: A Contemporary Approach to a Veiled Text*. Washington, DC: Georgetown University Press.

Robinson-Pant, Anna. 2004. *Women, Literacy, and Development: Alternative Perspectives*. New York: Routledge.

Rock-Singer, Aaron. 2019. *Practicing Islam in Egypt: Print Media and Islamic Revival*. Cambridge: Cambridge University Press.

———. 2022. *In the Shade of the Sunna: Salafi Piety in the Twentieth-Century Middle East*. Berkeley: University of California Press.

Rosenthal, Franz. 1970. *Knowledge Triumphant: The Concept of Knowledge in Medieval Islam*. Leiden: Brill.

Saad, Reem. 2012. "The Egyptian Revolution: A Triumph of Poetry." *American Ethnologist* 39 (1): 63–66.

Said, Atef Shahat. 2023. *Revolution Squared: Tahrir, Political Possibilities, and Counterrevolution in Egypt*. Durham, NC: Duke University Press.

Said, Edward W. 2003. *Orientalism*. New York: Vintage Books.

Saʿid, Labib as-, and Bernard Weiss. 1978. *The Recited Koran: A History of the First Recorded Version*. Princeton, NJ: Darwin.

Sajdi, Dana. 2013. *The Barber of Damascus: Nouveau Literacy in the Eighteenth-Century Ottoman Levant*. Stanford, CA: Stanford University Press.

Saleh, Walid. 2010. "Word." In *Key Themes for the Study of Islam*, edited by Jamal Elias, 356–376. Oxford: Oneworld.

———. 2020. "Contemporary Tafsir: The Rise of Scriptural Theology." In *The Oxford Handbook of Qur'anic Studies*, edited by Mustafa Shah and M. A. Abdel Haleem, 693–703. New York: Oxford University Press.

Sallam, H. 2011. "Striking Back at Egyptian Workers." *Middle East Report* 41 (259): 20–25.

Salvatore, Armando. 2001. *Muslim Traditions and Modern Techniques of Power*. Münster: LIT Verlag.

Schielke, Joska Samuli. 2012. *The Perils of Joy: Contesting Mulid Festivals in Contemporary Egypt*. Syracuse, NY: Syracuse University Press.

———. 2015. *Egypt in the Future Tense: Hope, Frustration, and Ambivalence before and after 2011*. Bloomington: Indiana University Press.

———. 2016. "Can Poetry Change the World? Reading Amal Dunqul in Egypt in 2011." In *Islam and Popular Culture*, edited by Mark LeVine, Karin van Nieuwkerk, and Martin Stokes, 122–148. Austin: University of Texas Press.

Schmidt, Leigh Eric. 2000. *Hearing Things: Religion, Illusion, and the American Enlightenment*. Cambridge, MA: Harvard University Press.

Sedra, Paul. 2011. *From Mission to Modernity: Evangelicals, Reformers and Education in Nineteenth Century Egypt*. New York: I. B. Tauris.

———. 2012. "Reconstituting the Coptic Community amidst Revolution." *Middle East Report* 42 (265): 34–38.

Sells, Michael A. 2001. *Approaching the Qur'an: The Early Revelations*. Ashland, OR: White Cloud.

Shah, Mustafa. 2012. "Introduction." In *Tafsir: Interpreting the Qur'an*, vol. I, edited by Mustafa Shah, 1–157. London: Routledge.

Sharkey, Heather J. 2008. *American Evangelicals in Egypt: Missionary Encounters in an Age of Empire*. Princeton, NJ: Princeton University Press.

Shehata, Samer S. 2009. *Shop Floor Culture and Politics in Egypt*. Albany: State University of New York Press.

Shepard, William E. 2003. "Sayyid Qutb's Doctrine of 'Jāhiliyya.'" *International Journal of Middle East Studies* 35 (4): 521–545.

Simon, Andrew G. 2022. *Media of the Masses: Cassette Culture in Modern Egypt.* Stanford, CA: Stanford University Press.

Sims, David. 2010. *Understanding Cairo: The Logic of a City Out of Control.* New York: American University in Cairo Press.

Singerman, Diane. 2013. "Youth, Gender, and Dignity in the Egyptian Uprising." *Journal of Middle East Women's Studies* 9 (3): 1–27.

Smith, Wilfred Cantwell. 1993. *What Is Scripture? A Comparative Approach.* Minneapolis, MN: Fortress.

Soares, Benjamin. 2006. *Muslim-Christian Encounters in Africa.* Leiden: Brill.

Spadola, Emilio. 2009. "Writing Cures: Religious and Communicative Authority in Late Modern Morocco." *Journal of North African Studies* 14 (2): 155–168.

———. 2013. *The Calls of Islam: Sufis, Islamists, and Mass Mediation in Urban Morocco.* Bloomington: Indiana University Press.

Starrett, Gregory. 1996. "The Margins of Print: Children's Religious Literature in Egypt." *Journal of the Royal Anthropological Institute* 2 (1): 117–139.

———. 1998. *Putting Islam to Work: Education, Politics, and Religious Transformation in Egypt.* Berkeley: University of California Press.

———. 2009. "Institutionalizing Charisma: Comparative Perspectives on the Promise of Higher Education." In *University Education in the Gulf States: Alternative Approaches to Building Economies, Societies and Nations,* edited by Christopher Davidson and Peter Mackenzie Smith, 73–91. London: Saqi Books.

Street, Brian V. 1993. *Cross-Cultural Approaches to Literacy.* New York: Cambridge University Press.

———, ed. 2001. *Literacy and Development: Ethnographic Perspectives.* New York: Routledge.

———. 2003. "The Limits of the Local: 'Autonomous' or 'Disembedding'?" *International Journal of Learning* 10:2825–2830.

Suit, Natalia K. 2020. *Qur'anic Matters: Material Mediations and Religious Practice in Egypt.* London: Bloomsbury.

Sukarieh, Mayssoun. 2012. "The Hope Crusades: Culturalism and Reform in the Arab World." *PoLAR: Political and Legal Anthropology Review* 35 (1): 115–134.

Sukarieh, Mayssoun, and Stuart Tannock. 2014. *Youth Rising? The Politics of Youth in the Global Economy.* New York: Routledge.

Tadros, Mariz. 2013. *Copts at the Crossroads: The Challenges of Building Inclusive Democracy in Contemporary Egypt.* New York: Oxford University Press.

Tawasil, Amina. 2019. "Reading as Practice: The Howzevi (Seminarian) Women in Iran and Clair de Lune." *Anthropology & Education Quarterly* 50 (1): 66–83.

Thompson, John Alexander. 1956. *The Major Arabic Bibles, Their Origin and Nature.* New York: American Bible Society.

Thurston, Alexander. 2018. *Boko Haram: The History of an African Jihadist Movement.* Princeton, NJ: Princeton University Press.

Vasalou, Sophia. 2009. "'Their Intention Was Shown by Their Bodily Movements': The Baṣran Muʿtazilites on the Institution of Language." *Journal of the History of Philosophy* 47 (2): 201–221.

Versteegh, Kees. 2014. *The Arabic Language.* Edinburgh: Edinburgh University Press.

Vicini, Fabio. 2020. *Reading Islam: Life and Politics of Brotherhood in Modern Turkey.* Leiden: Brill.

Ware, Rudolph T., III. 2014. *The Walking Qur'an: Islamic Education, Embodied Knowledge, and History in West Africa.* Chapel Hill: University of North Carolina Press.

Warner, Michael. 2004. "Uncritical Reading." In *Polemic: Critical or Uncritical,* edited by Jane Gallop, 13–38. New York: Routledge.

Warren, David. 2017. "Cleansing the Nation of the Dogs of Hell: ʾAli Jumʾa's Nationalist Legal Reasoning in Support of the 2013 Egyptian Coup and Its Bloody Aftermath." *International Journal of Middle East Studies* 49 (3): 457–477.

Weber, Max, and C. Wright Mills. 1947. *From Max Weber: Essays in Sociology.* New York: Oxford University Press.

Wehr, Hans. 1979. *A Dictionary of Modern Written Arabic.* 4th ed. New York: Spoken Language Services.

Winegar, Jessica. 2006. *Creative Reckonings: The Politics of Art and Culture in Contemporary Egypt.* Stanford, CA: Stanford University Press.

———. 2009. "Culture Is the Solution: The Civilizing Mission of Egypt's Culture Palaces." *Review of Middle East Studies* 43 (2): 189–197.

———. 2013. "Weighed Down: The Politics of Frustration in Egypt." *Middle East Research and Information Project.* Accessed January 2014. http://www.merip .org/weighed-down-politics-frustration-egypt.

Winter, Jessica. 2022. "The Rise and Fall of Vibes-Based Literacy." *New Yorker,* May 2023. https://www.newyorker.com/news/annals-of-education/the-rise -and-fall-of-vibes-based-literacy.

Wollenberg, Rebecca Scharbach. 2023. *The Closed Book: How the Rabbis Taught the Jews (Not) to Read the Bible.* Princeton, NJ: Princeton University Press.

Woolard, Kathryn A. 1998. "Introduction: Language Ideology as a Field of Inquiry." In *Language Ideologies: Practice and Theory,* edited by Bambi B. Schieffelin, Kathryn A. Woolard, and Paul V. Kroskrity, 3–47. New York: Oxford University Press.

World Bank. 2016. *Economic and Social Inclusion to Prevent Violent Extremism.* Accessed September 2023. https://documents1.worldbank.org/curated/en /409591474983005625/pdf/108525-REVISED-PUBLIC.pdf.

Yousef, Hoda. 2012. "Seeking the Educational Cure." *European Education* 44 (4): 51–66.

———. 2016. *Composing Egypt: Reading, Writing, and the Emergence of a Modern Nation, 1870–1930*. Stanford, CA: Stanford University Press.

Zadeh, Travis. 2009. "Touching and Ingesting: Early Debates over the Material Qur'an." *Journal of the American Oriental Society* 129 (3): 443–466.

Zeghal, Malika. 2007. "The 'Recentering' of Religious Knowledge and Discourse: The Case of al-Azhar in Twentieth Century Egypt." In *Schooling Islam: The Culture and Politics of Modern Education*, edited by Robert W. Hefner and Muhammad Qasim Zaman, 107–130. Princeton, NJ: Princeton University Press.

INDEX

Page numbers in *italic* indicate figures.

Abdel-Aziz, Khaled (member of Amr Khaled's short-lived Future Party, and Minister of Sports and Youth), 181

Abdel-Hady, Zein (head of National Library), 39, 61

Abduh, Muhammad, 13, 26, 43

Abir (Arab Contractors HR employee), 158

Abu-Lughod, Lila, 131, 150–51

activism, 9, 16, 26; literacy, 178. *See also* demonstrations; development; Egypt, uprising of 2011; literacy campaigns; protests; volunteer teachers

Adely, Fida J., 133

adult education programs, 14, 142. *See also* literacy campaigns; women's Quran lessons

affirmation, 98, 114–15. *See also* citation; recitation

agency, 95, 98, 117n3

Ali, Khalid, 156

alms, 163. *See also* charity; social services

Amal (volunteer teacher), 100, 124–25, 129–30, 131–32, 134–35, 142

Amin, Qasim, 134

Andeel (artist), 45, 46, 47

Anderson, Benedict, 23

Arab Contractors (AC), 154, 173n5

—Ma'sara shipyard: about, 154–55; author's experiences, 31; gender dynamics, 152–53; happiness (*sa'āda*), class on, 149–50, 159–60; and ignorance, 42–43; productivity, 151, 165–66, 172–73; students depicted, *153*; worker organization, 154, 157. *See also* workers

Arabic language: classical Arabic (*fushā*), 24–25, 37n20, 78; dialect, 24–25, 138–39; diglossia, 18, 24–25, 36–37n19; literacy, Arabic-language, 11, 18, 24–25, 68, 77, 79; Modern Standard Arabic (MSA), 37n20, 136, 138–39; Quranic, 68, 77, 101, 107–8, 118–19n17; sacredness of, 25, 36n18, 37n23, 68, 70, 78, 80, 81, 89–90; Van Dyck Bible translation, 87–88, 93n22

hybrid form, 95–96, 115; and
identity, 48–49; and ignorance,
43–44, 48; Islamic, 8, 22, 94–95;
modern, 7, 11, 12–13, 20–21, 41,
43–44, 48–49, 51; moral/civic
responsibility to develop, 7, 10, 11–
12, 53, 128; morality, education, 44,
48–49; reform, educational, 7, 10,
13, 26, 43–44, 95–96, 177; secular,
12, 23, 26, 36n18, 42, 45, 51, 60,
179; state-run literacy classes, 42,
56, 57–60, 72, 178; *ta'līm* (modern
education) vs. *tarbiyya* (cultivation),
44; uprising's impact on, 141–42;
in US, 69; and virtue, 10–11, 41,
51–52; Western, critiques of, 45,
62n5; women's, 133–34, 147n8. *See
also* ignorance (*jāhiliyya*); illiteracy;
literacy campaigns; teachers;
women's Quran lessons
Effat, Emad, 39, 40, 101–2
Egypt: civil society, 9–10;
Constitution of 1971, 13; education
crisis, 6–8; literacy politics,
11–12, 18, 31–32, 47, 180; literacy
statistics, 6, 13, 17, 35n13, 179–80;
industrialization, 154, 156; Islamic
revival (1970s), 34n4; labor rights
violations, 156; late Islamic revival,
9–10, 15–16, 27, 60, 178; unlettered
nation, 56, 61; "unregistered"
citizens (*lam yusaggal*), 183
—government: conflict with Life
Makers, 128–29; and education,
56; and literacy campaigns, 14, 29;
political cartoon on, 45, 46, 47;
state-run literacy classes, 42, 56,
57–60, 72, 178. *See also* el-Sisi,
Abdel Fattah
—uprising of 2011: al-Azhar, impact
on, 101; Batn al-Baqara, impact on,

125, 141; and counterrevolution, 9,
15, 19; and dignity, 151; education,
impact on, 141–42; Life Makers,
impact on, 128; and literacy, 5–8, 12,
14, 15, 16–17, 26, 72, 179, 184–85;
revolutionaries (*thuwwār*), 9; term
use, 9; Vodafone's suspension of
services during, 147n4; and workers,
155–58, 163, 167–69, 172
Egyptian Authority for Adult
Education (EAAE): about, 67;
author's experiences, 30; BLESS,
cooperation with, 85; creation of,
14; on eradication of illiteracy, 143–
44, 179–80; on literacy certificates,
161; on period of study for literacy,
125; religiously themed lessons, 58,
72–74. *See also* Read in the Name of
Your Lord (RITNOYL, *Iqra' bi-smi
Rabbika alladhī Khalaq*)
Egyptian Federation of Independent
Trade Unions (EFITU), 156
Egyptian Workers Federation (later
Egyptian Trade Union Federation,
ETUF), 156–57
Eickelman, Dale, 52
ElBaradei, Mohamed, 31
elections, 31–32, 47, 173n8
Elgindy, Shaykh Moustafa (Salafi
educationist), 70, 77–79, 89
emotions, 160–61; happiness (*sa'āda*),
149–50, 159–60
Engelke, Matthew, 83–84, 114
equality and inequality, 19, 25. *See also*
power; social class

factories, 19. *See also* Arab Contractors
(AC) Ma'sara shipyard; workers
Fahmy, Khaled, 40
Fahmy, Magdy (EAAE literacy
planner), 67–68, 72–75, 76, 84

79, 81, 86–87; in Islamic literacy
development, 23–24; *al-Kawthar*,
106–7; limitations of human
language to discuss, 98–99; material
form of (*mushaf*), 50, 52, 118n12;
al-Māʿūn, 109–11; nonliterate
engagements with, 18, 20, 22, 23–
24, 34–35n6, 97, 100, 176; reading
practices, 50; salvific powers, 50;
tajwīd (rules of proper elocution
of the Quran), 24, 99–100, 106–7;
and TBP, 79–81; transparency of,
71–72, 91n6. *See also* God's Word
(*kalām Allāh*); memorization (*hifz*);
recitation; scripturalism; women's
Quran lessons
—understanding meaning of: and
classical religious reading, 50; and
nonliterate engagement with Quran,
22, 100; particularity of Quranic
text, 86–87; RITNOYL's emphasis
on, 70, 74–77, 89; Salafis on, 26; and
textual authority, 13, 52, 62n11, 88,
108; women's Quran lessons, 94–95,
96–98, 104–5, 107–8, 110, 112–13,
114–16
Qutb, Sayyid, 44–45

Rabab (Quran student), 125
Ramadan, Mustafa, 51–52
rationality (ʿaql), 59
reading: corporeal experience, 71, 89–
90, 96, 100, 116; gendered uses of,
132; and modernization, 12; myth
of six minutes, 175–76; religious,
22, 23, 26, 41–42, 49–53, 176–77;
sacredness of, 50–52; scriptural,
176; silent/private, 20–21; and
virtue, 10–11, 41, 51–52, 126; visual
reading, 75–76, 89–90, 92n9. *See
also* auditory experience of text;

autonomous reading; *iqraʾ* ("read");
memorization (*hifz*); *qirāʾa* ("read,"
"recite," "proclaim"); recitation;
scripturalism; text processing
Reading for All (*Al-Qarāʾa li-l-Jamīʿ*)
literacy campaign, 29
"Read in the name of your Lord"
(Quranic command), 5, 19
Read in the Name of Your Lord
(RITNOYL, *Iqraʾ bi-smi
Rabbika alladhī Khalaq*): about,
72–74; autonomous reading, 70,
74–77, 89–90, 177–78; meaning-
centered approach, 70, 74–77, 89;
modernizing *kuttāb*, 82; Quran,
68, 70, 72–77, 178; visuality, 75–76,
89–90; word recognition (*al-tarīqa
al-kalima*), 75–76
Read Me a Book (Mubarak), 56–57,
63n17, 139
Read Your Book (RYB, *Iqraʾ Kitābak*),
69–70, 83, 85–89, 90
recitation: and affirmation, 98;
Bible Society of Egypt on, 87;
competitions, 100; al-Husari
tapes, 103; modernist critique
of, 22; *mujawwad*, 118n11; and
religious reading, 49–50; scholarly
discussions of, 34–35n6; women's
Quran lessons, 111–13, 115–16. *See
also* memorization (*hifz*)
reforms, educational, 7, 10, 13, 26,
43–44, 95–96, 177. *See also* Islamic
reformism
religion. *See* Bible; Christianity
and Christians; Islam; Quran;
sacredness
religious fundamentals (*taʾsīs*), 42, 44,
178
religious reading, 22, 23, 26, 41–42,
49–53, 176–77

repetition, 108–9. *See also* citation;
memorization (*hifz*); recitation
respect, dignity, honor, 150–51, 153,
155, 163, 166, 169, 172–73, 183
revelation, 54–55, 62–63nn13–15, 86
revivalism: Islamic revival (1970s),
34n4; late Islamic revival, 9–10, 15–
16, 27, 60, 178; and scripturalism,
70. *See also* Islamic reformism
revolution. *See* counterrevolution;
Egypt, uprising of 2011
revolutionaries (*thuwwār*), 9
Rida, Rashid, 43–44
Rif'at (worker/literacy student), 42,
153, 165–66, 169
Risala (*khayr* ("good works")
organization), 28
ritual performances, 50, 58–60

Saad, Noha (employee of Vodafone
Corporate Social Responsibility and
Vodafone Foundation Egypt), 130
Sabahi, Hamdeen, 173n8
sacredness: of Arabic language,
25, 36n18, 37n23, 68, 70, 78, 80,
81, 89–90; of reading, 50–52;
scripturalism's effect on secular
texts, 23, 26, 36n18; term use, 36n18
Sadat, Anwar, 154
Saeed, Khaled Mohamed, 16
Said, Edward, 40–41
Sa'id, Labib as-, 103
Salafis, 10, 16, 26, 78–80, 82, 92n10.
See also The Baghdadi Primer (TBP,
Al-Qā'idat al-Baghdādiyya)
Saleh, Walid, 29, 50, 104–5
Salih Fathi (worker/literacy student),
42–43, 61, 150, 159, 165
Salvatore, Armando, 41
Samiya (Quran/literacy student),
94, 96–97, 106, 111–12, 123–24,
129, 136

Sarah (KIP volunteer teacher),
142–43
Sayyid (worker/literacy student),
167–69, *170, 171*
schools: children's, 123–24; *kuttāb*
(institution of primary learning
centered on the Quran), 13, 35n7,
51, 68, 77, 82, 89, 90. *See also* literacy
campaigns; women's Quran lessons
scripturalism: about, 25–27, 70–71,
177–78; different kinds of, 71, 89;
making secular texts sacred, 23, 26,
36n18; and nationalism, 37n24;
women's Quran lessons, 95–97, 105,
115–16. *See also* God's Word (*kalām
Allāh*); Islamic outreach (*da'wa*);
Quran, understanding meaning of;
religious reading
scripture: defining literacy, 12, 13, 68;
distortion, scriptural (*tahrīf*), 88,
93n23; literacy campaigns' focus
on, 11–12, 67–70; and politics, 72;
term use, 91n3. *See also* Bible; God's
Word (*kalām Allāh*); Quran
The Secret (*Al-Sirr*), 53
secular education, 12, 42, 45, 51, 60,
179; made sacred, 23, 26, 36n18
self-edification (*tahdhīb*), 129
self-help books, 53, 160
semantic meaning, 33, 71, 94–95,
96–98, 103–5, 107–8, 110,
112–13, 114–16. *See also* Quran,
understanding meaning of
sensory experience, reading as, 71,
89–90, 96, 100, 116
sewage, 139, 140–42
sexual violence, 31
Shah, Mustafa, 92n7
shame ('*ār*), 151. *See also* stigma
Sharbouni, Mohammed al-, 39–40
sharia, 49
Shawqi, Tariq (Minister of Education), 7

INDEX 221

Nermeen Mouftah is Assistant Professor of Anthropology at the University of Illinois Chicago.

For Indiana University Press

Lesley Bolton, Project Manager/Editor

Anna Garnai, Editorial Assistant

Sophia Hebert, Assistant Acquisitions Editor

Samantha Heffner, Marketing and Publicity Manager

Brenna Hosman, Production Coordinator

Katie Huggins, Production Manager

Bethany Mowry, Acquisitions Editor

Dan Pyle, Online Publishing Manager

Pamela Rude, Senior Artist and Book Designer

www.ingramcontent.com/pod-product-compliance
Lightning Source LLC
Chambersburg PA
CBHW030408270326
41926CB00009B/1318